The Social Psychology of
Material Possessions

The Social Psychology of Material Possessions

To Have Is To Be

Helga Dittmar
Lecturer in Psychology
University of Sussex

HARVESTER WHEATSHEAF
ST. MARTIN'S PRESS

First published in the U.K. in 1992 by
Harvester Wheatsheaf
Campus 400, Maylands Avenue
Hemel Hempstead, Hertfordshire, HP2 7EZ
A division of
Simon & Schuster International Group

First published in the U.S.A. in 1992 by
St. Martin's Press
175 Fifth Avenue, New York, N.Y. 10010

Typeset in 10/12 pt Times
by Photoprint, Torquay, Devon

Printed and bound in Great Britain by
BPCC Wheatons Ltd, Exeter

Library of Congress Cataloging-in-Publication Data

Dittmar, Helga.
    The social psychology of material possessions : to have is to be /
Helga Dittmar.
        p.   cm.
    Includes bibliographical references (p.   ) and indexes.
    ISBN 0–312–08538–9
    1. Property–Social aspects.   2. Property–Psychological aspects.
3. Possessiveness.   4. Identity (Psychology)   I. Title.
HM211.D58   1992
302.5--dc20   92–13443
                                                                    CIP

British Library Cataloguing in Publication Data

Dittmar, Helga
    The social psychology of material possessions:
    To have is to be.
    I. Title
    302.5

    ISBN 0–7450–0955–7
    ISBN 0–7450–0956–5 pbk

1   2   3   4   5   96   95   94   93   92

To my parents, Margot and Heinrich Dittmar

Contents

Acknowledgements

Like all books, this one is a collaborative effort. Many people have been involved in its conception and execution, but I can name only those to whom I am particularly grateful.

The Landeswohlfahrtsverband Hessen in Germany provided financial help with the empirical research described in this book, and I would like to thank Rod Bond, Helen Petrie, David Hitchin, Colin Crook and Tony Stubbens for their assistance with various technical aspects.

I much appreciated the constructive comments, criticisms and support of many people, including Julie Dickinson, Monica Greco, Graham Hole, Sonia Livingstone, Pete Lunt, Lucia Mannetti, Kalliroi Papadopoulou, Eddie Piper, Floyd Rudmin, Pete Saunders, Peter Smith, Neil Stammers, Jo Tulloch, Mike Van Duuren and Jane Ussher. And I would like to express special and heartfelt gratitude to Gün Semin for the many hours he spared for discussing my work.

The final form of this book benefited greatly from the comments of Norman McLeod, who reminded me throughout the entire manuscript that 'Clarity of expression is paramount!', and from the encouragement and editorial skill of Farrell Burnett.

Last, but not at all least, very special thanks to Neil Stammers for his unflagging support, encouragement, confidence in me, and countless meals, without which I would have found it very hard either to begin or to finish this book.

1

To have is to be: is that the question?

(with apologies to William Shakespeare and Erich Fromm)

Individual ownership of material possessions is deeply rooted in Western culture. Material possessions surround us, we all have them. But what do they mean?

Many of the material objects we own are used as practical *tools* to make everyday survival easier, more comfortable and pleasurable. Cars, for example, are self-evidently functional possessions: we use them to travel from *A* to *B*. But even a brief look at some car advertisements quickly illustrates that they are not simply described as utilitarian means of transport:

> One look at the new Renault 21 hatchback tells you this car has a personality of its own. (*Mail on Sunday Magazine*, 24 September 1989)

or

> Consider for a moment why diplomats and company directors the world over choose to travel S-class. Perhaps it's because the Mercedes-Benz flagship conveys presence without courting ostentation. Its styling complements the demeanor of those who have nothing to prove . . . Something, once tried, you won't want to do without, whether you're a VIP or just a rather successful man in the street. (*Observer Magazine*, 17 September 1989)

These quite commonplace extracts suggest that car adverts are laden with *cultural meanings* and *images*, rather than merely emphasizing the practical and functional utility of the vehicle itself. When suggesting that the current era might well be dubbed the 'age of the automobile', Fromm (1978) refers to cars as status symbols and an 'extension of power' in a way that fits well with the advert texts just quoted: 'having acquired a car, the owner has actually acquired a new piece of ego'

Figure 1.1   The driver's ego

(p. 78). However, this observation may not always be displayed in quite as visible a form as in the number plate of the Porsche in Figure 1.1.

The notion that the symbolic meanings of material goods, which extend far beyond their immediate physical qualities, are stressed in adverts holds true for many, if not most, consumer products. For example, consider this headline describing a watch:

> Status on your wrist. (*Sunday Times Magazine Premier Supplement*, 24 September 1989)

Consumer goods have been described as *symbols for sale* because adverts are trying to convince potential owners that they can use these products for a variety of purposes: to project a desirable image to others, to express social status, and to make visible their personal characteristics. By buying goods, we magically acquire a different persona. If it is accepted that the symbolic significance of material possessions plays a crucial role in marketing strategies, what about that symbolic significance in everyday life? Does a good deal of the importance of material possessions lie in what they tell us and others about who we are? Do they help us to make sense of our social surroundings? Do they serve to locate us, as individual human beings, in the complex societal map of roles, groups, subcultures and social strata?

People often regard their photographs as a record of their personal history and as reminders of relationships with family members or friends. Tools give a sense of control over the environment, but they can also be at the core of the DIY person's feelings of practical ability and prowess. Earrings with a dangling women's symbol ♀ proclaim the wearer's commitment to feminism to others, but probably also to herself. Heavy leather wear and fast motorbike can bolster a macho image. Mascots and other sentimental nicknacks act as good luck charms and safety signals that all will go well. Rastafarians, punks or new romantics are distinguishable by the colours and type of their clothes and body adornment. We may well overhear a conversation in which one person says to another: 'I can't possibly wear this outfit, it's just not me!', or, 'You should have seen his house, he's the typical suburban yuppie!'. A Rolls Royce is still one of *the* declared status symbols in England, whereas a sporty Porsche with an elongated bonnet can be heard described facetiously as a *phallic* car, an outer manifestation of the driver's supposed masculinity and virility. Journalist Jaffé-Pearce observes caustically in the *Sunday Times Magazine*: 'Designer tags say more about you than conversation' (1989, p. 8). The dictum that modern consumers 'identify themselves by the formula: *I am = what I have and what I consume*' (Fromm, 1976, p. 36, emphasis in original) just seems another formulation of the recent (mal)adaptation of Descartes's *cogito ergo sum* into: *I shop, therefore I am*.

These examples would indeed suggest that material possessions have a profound symbolic significance for their owners, as well as for other people. They imply that possessions play an important role in everyday life: they influence the ways in which we think about ourselves and about others.

Moreover, the aspects of everyday reality touched upon in the anecdotal examples given above – self-conceptions, identity, values, group membership, stereotypes and perception of other people – are central concerns of social psychology. One would therefore expect to find that the theoretical perspectives within the discipline which deal with these topics have something to say about the meaning of material possessions. But they virtually ignore the material substratum of our existence. It is only recently that one can observe an emergence of contributions in various disciplines on the much broader subject of consumer processes, an 'upsurge of interest in the topic of consumption in both the social sciences and the humanities' (Campbell, 1991, p. 57). I suggest that an examination of the relationship between people and their material possessions from a social psychological perspective is of crucial importance for improving our understanding of everyday social reality in contemporary Western culture.

Erich Fromm describes two alternative basic modes of psychological functioning in our current Western industrialized world, and poses the question: *To Have or To Be?*. He concludes:

> In a culture in which the supreme goal is to have – and to have more and more – . . . how can there be an alternative between having and being? On the contrary, it would seem that the very essence of being is having; that if one *has* nothing, one *is* nothing. (1978, p. 25, emphases in original)

In a British television documentary, screened in the summer of 1989, anthropologist Nigel Barley embarks on a journey through our 'Native Land' in order to 'pin down some general idea of the contemporary English identity' (1989, p. 1). Among many interesting observations, one of the major themes in his journey of discovery is the argument that possessions are modern means of *acquiring and expressing identity*.

Private property and materialism

If psychology as a whole, and social psychology in particular, has tended to pay scant attention to material objects and property, this is certainly not the case for the social sciences as a whole. Even a few fleeting references to major and well-known fields of inquiry are sufficient to illustrate this point. The writings of Jeremy Bentham (1931/1894) or Adam Smith (1910/1890) tend towards analysing the *objective* functions of private property and possessions as utilitarian instruments which provide for human physical needs (cf. Ryan, 1982). Other philosophers – such as Kant or Hegel – go beyond this classical economic view and indicate that there are less *rational*, more *subjective* aspects of property (cf. Hollowell, 1982), as well as of property rights (cf. Carter, 1988). Despite many controversies, it is probably fair to say that the implications of private property and private ownership of the means of production for the nature and composition of society on the one hand, and individual well-being on the other, are among the major concerns of a Marxian perspective (e.g., Marx, 1973/1939; Marx and Engels, 1965).

Western culture has been criticized from many camps for its materialistic orientation and its emphasis on accumulating material goods (e.g., Belk, 1982, 1983, 1985; Tawney, 1922). For instance, Looft (1971) describes the detrimental effects of the contemporary *psychology of more* in the face of finite environmental resources and increasing pollution – issues which have become more pressing now than ever. Similarly, Fromm (1978) deplores the accelerating speed of consumption and the *throw-away* mentality that goes with it. He warns against the apparent social imperative to consume ever more and thus become a 'slave of one's possessions'.

It has been argued that another facet of Western materialism is that possession metaphors have become so incorporated into the way we think about the world that they have penetrated into how we construe ourselves and our relationships with others (e.g., Hirschon, 1984). MacPherson (1962) observes that '[t]he relation of ownership, having become for more and more men the critically important relation determining their actual freedom, . . . was read back into the nature of the individual (p. 3). Now, the *self* is viewed as our most exclusively owned object to do with as we see fit (e.g., Wikse, 1977). In the realm of psychological theory and practice, this theme is echoed in the emphasis on developing our *self*, such as striving towards self-actualization (e.g., Rogers, 1961), or in therapeutic language which describes psychological adjustment in terms of 'taking possession' of our lives and improving our ability to 'own our emotions' (e.g., Brashear and Willis, 1976). Derdeyn (1979) draws striking parallels between the legislation governing the adoption of children, and that on private property: children are construed legally as the *owned* assets of their biological parents, and they cannot be adopted without these ownership rights being relinquished. In a study on the relations between gender, power and property, Hirschon (1984) argues that the custom of fathers *giving away* brides is just one example of the ways in which women have been construed as property. And jealousy has been analysed repeatedly as the fear of losing *possession* of a loved one (e.g., Davis, 1949; Furby, 1978a).

All these kinds of analysis stress both the important part that is played by possessions and property in Western society, and the high value placed on them. But because of their focus on quite different property-related subject matters, they have little to offer in the way of insights about what material possessions mean to people and the role they play in our everyday dealings with others. With its emphasis on marketing strategies and purchase decisions, not even consumer research provides a systematic account of material goods as 'integral threads in the fabric of social life' (Solomon, 1983), although the symbolic meanings of consumer goods and the images associated with products are some of its most central concerns. However, the broader perspective on *symbolic consumption*, which has recently emerged, attempts to move closer to such an account (cf. Hirschman, 1981; McCracken, 1990).

The question of whether *to have is to be*, of whether the symbolic meanings of our belongings are an integral feature of expressing our own identity and perceiving the identity of others, has rarely been raised in this form in psychologically oriented contributions concerned with property-related human behaviour. Trasler's observation – made in

1982 – that the terms *possessions* or *property* are rarely found in the indexes of modern textbooks on psychology still holds true ten years later. Scholarly papers and books which have some bearing on the psychological aspects of the relationship between people and their possessions do, of course, appear in number in a literature search in the various fields of psychology and related social scientific disciplines, but few take material possessions as their exclusive focus. And those which do bear witness to the diverse and fragmentary nature of this field – in terms of theoretical concerns as well as research orientations. No doubt this is, at least in part, a reflection of the extremely complex relations between women and men and their material possessions. It goes without saying that many of their insights are perceptive, informative and invaluable. Yet rarely have they considered the intimate link between possessions and the owner's self by viewing them as *material symbols of identity*.

Material symbols

Human beings use *symbols* when they relate to each other and the world at large. Essentially, a symbol is an entity which represents and stands for another entity, such as a national flag, which can stand for a particular country or for patriotism and emotional identification with it. The most significant dimension of symbols is that they can have meaning only to the extent that individuals share the belief that they possess that meaning. Our most obvious system of symbols is language. For instance, the term *fridge* represents a particular, usually square household item used for cooling drinks and food *only* because we agree on the meaning of that word. A number of researchers and theorists seem convinced that material objects also constitute an intricate system of symbols which reflects the entire social fabric of our culture. Maybe not surprisingly, this notion has found more recognition in anthropology and consumer research than in other social scientific disciplines.

Diverse strands of investigations can be described under the umbrella heading of *material culture* studies, which use material objects themselves as primary data to examine the 'beliefs – values, ideas, attitudes, and assumptions – of a particular community or society at a given time . . . [they study] culture through artefacts' (Prown, 1982, p. 1). For instance, Hudson (1984) refers to the *projet du garbage*, carried out in the mid-1970s in France, as an example of how the systematic study of household refuse can serve as 'an unobtrusive measure of our conceptual models'. Kleppe (1989), who investigates material culture from an archaeological perspective, discusses the development of working iron in north African culture and focuses on iron objects as symbols of individuals' political and administrative authority, and as contributors to their group and ethnic identity. Even a graveyard can be interpreted as a 'cultural text' in which the location, design and epitaphs of gravestones chart the local community's historical development (Vidutis and Lowe, 1980).

From a somewhat different viewpoint, the French literary movement of *chosisme* in the mid-1960s was based on the portrayal of actors' characteristics, motivations and interactions with other people almost exclusively by reference to material objects (cf. Barbu, 1963; Perec, 1965). Material artefacts, including possessions, are thus seen as providing the reader with a perfectly understandable symbolic world, which exactly mirrors and communicates the interpersonal dynamics and social realities usually expounded in novels in a more straightforward manner.

Solomon (1983) argues from a marketing perspective that consumer behaviour constitutes a significant proportion of all social behaviour. Consumers employ product symbolism to define not only themselves, but also their relations to others and social reality generally. Some of the very recent developments under the umbrella of *symbolic consumption* attempt to address these issues more explicitly, often by viewing products as a quasi-language through which people can communicate with each other (cf. McCracken, 1990).

Douglas and Isherwood (1979) also advance a symbolic and communicational model of material goods, but from an anthropological perspective, which is broadly concerned with societal values, notions and behaviour, and their transmission from one generation to the next: 'Instead of supposing that goods are primarily needed for subsistence plus competitive display, let us assume that they are needed for making visible and stable the categories of culture' (p. 59). Material goods change culture: refrigerators have revolutionized shopping and eating habits, cars have created commuter suburbs and increased geographical mobility, television has changed how family members organize their time and interact with each other (e.g., Csikszentmihalyi and Rochberg-Halton, 1981). Consumption goods are used to 'notch off' temporal units in our social universe: they mark and remind us of anniversaries, birthdays or festive holidays. Material artefacts mark private and public space, as well as female and male space (e.g., Loyd, 1975). Douglas and Isherwood (1979) argue that people use consumption goods to make statements about themselves, their family and their friends. Subgroup cultures are marked by the way one dresses, where and how one lives, and how one consumes.

Goods that minister to physical needs are no less carriers of cultural meaning than literature or architecture – we have eating and drinking cultures which mark gender, race, class, religion and social position, rather than simply personal taste. The initiation, maintenance and dissolution of social relationships is accompanied by particular consumption patterns. Offering, accepting or refusing material goods reinforces or undermines social boundaries. What parts of our living space we make available for guests reflects the intimacy of the relationship we have with them. Social inequality can be meaningfully described in terms of characteristic patterns of consumption and use of goods (Douglas and Isherwood, 1979; see also Chapters 6 and 8).

The rapidly expanding literature concerned with postmodernism also evidences interest in the symbolic aspects of material culture, particularly fashion and style. The focus of this work is on the shifting, multiple identities we attempt to create, negotiate and maintain in an increasingly fragmented society, not least through the socially shared meanings of material objects and consumption, even if these meanings are struggled over and have to be recreated continuously (e.g., Connor, 1989; Featherstone, 1991; Wernick, 1991). Another, partly related, field of study has been concerned with analysing contemporary youth subcultures in terms of styles and consumption. Here the social and ethnic identities of underprivileged groups (such as working-class British adolescents or West Indian youths) find expression as well as cohesion in cultural practices of dress, hairstyle or surrounding oneself with particular types of popular music (e.g., Hebdige 1979, 1987; Willis, 1990). At the same time, these subcultural styles and consumption practices are also seen as partial protests, which go some way towards questioning class, gender and race distinctions. Willis (1990) emphasizes that, with the symbolic aspects of mass consumer culture, '. . . there is now a whole social and cultural medium of interwebbing common meaning and identity-making . . . élite or "official" culture has lost is dominance.' (p. 128).

Enumeration of examples could carry on endlessly, but I think the point can already be made: 'Take them [material goods] out of human intercourse and you have dismantled the whole thing' (Douglas and Isherwood, 1979, p. 72). In short, people use material goods and consumption patterns as a fundamental way of understanding, orienting themselves in, and interacting with their social environment. Such a perspective highlights the social dimension of material objects which – although self-evident – is often neglected and therefore deserves particular emphasis (see Chapter 2). Material objects can only be viewed as possessions because we share a system of rules and ideas about them. And, furthermore, the relationship between a person and her or his possessions always has reference to other people: s/he can lay exclusive claim to them only because other people do not.

These social aspects become clear when commonsense definitions of material possessions are considered. They also help to make it clear why the ownership of material artefacts makes them particularly suitable for signifying identity. Dürkheim (1957) and contemporary legal analyses of ownership (e.g., Cohen, 1954; Snare, 1972) single out an *exclusivity* criterion as a major feature of having possessions. This is echoed in interview responses to the question: 'What does it mean that something is yours, that it belongs to you?' (Furby, 1978a, b, 1980a). Furby's analysis of her respondents' explanations echoes the aforementioned exclusivity criterion, because they frequently referred to the use and control of objects, and the right to control use by others. A second prominent dimension of interview responses concerned positive feelings about possessions, including enjoyment and attachment. And, thirdly, their association with identity was emphasized, such as heightening individuality or making people feel important because possessions imply status and power.

Semantic studies of either verbs of possession (e.g., Miller and Johnson-Laird, 1976) or ownership criteria (Rudmin and Berry, 1987) also single out control and attachment as defining features of material possessions. Lukmani's (1979) conceptual analysis of the verb *to have* adds that possessions are linked to a self–other dichotomy of reality. A preliminary study on the definition of possessions also found these three characteristics: control, emotional value and association with self (Dittmar, 1986). These defining criteria not only highlight the *social* dimensions of material possessions, but they also fit well with the notion of possessions as *symbols of identity*. Exclusive association of objects with an individual is fundamental if material artefacts are to communicate something about that person, her or his social location and personal qualities. Their symbolic significance may partly explain people's attachment to their material possessions, and the fact that association with self was singled out is a further indication of the prominent role that possessions play as symbolic expressions of identity, among their range of symbolic functions.

Taken together, these contributions indicate that any understanding of what material possessions mean has to take account of *shared beliefs* and *values*, and has to investigate them within the *fundamental triadic unit of self, other and material object*.

Self, other and material symbols of identity

Psychological approaches in the late nineteenth and early twentieth centuries made some mention of the intimate link between *self-feeling* and possessions, but tended to conceptualize the notion of material possessions with respect to the *appropriative, possessive* or *acquisitive* behaviour individuals showed towards a variety of material objects. They thus located the significance of possessions in the dyadic relationship between owner and object, and were mostly concerned with the extent to which inherited and unlearned dispositions – particularly the *acquisitive instinct* – are the source of property-related behaviour. So they focus on biological, *intra-individual* dynamics as an explanation of people's relationship with their possessions. But available cross-cultural and ethological evidence suggests that exclusively biological accounts of possessions miss a good deal because they neglect the *social* nature of the meaning of 'things'.

In later decades, emphasis turned away from a nature–nurture controversy about the relative contributions of innate and social influences on how individuals relate to their possessions – which, incidentally, has had a recent resurgence in the debates surrounding human *sociobiology*. The work from a broadly psychological perspective since the 1950s can be characterized by its common concern with the *intra-individual* and *interpersonal functions* of material possessions. For example, they analyse material objects as instruments of control over the physical environment, as regulators of interpersonal relationships, or as symbolic expressions of values, attitudes and beliefs. But despite the pronounced diversity of this work, one of the recurring themes is the close association between people's possessions and their sense of identity. If one casts the net a bit more widely – which seems useful given the sparsity of social psychological research – relevant contributions can be found in diverse fields: abnormal and developmental psychology, consumer and marketing research, sociology, criminology, anthropology and gerontology. This book offers an overview of these perspectives, while attempting to select those aspects which can provide some insights into the complex link between *material possessions* and *identity*.

But having indicated the enormous range of symbolic features of material possessions, this book also addresses the question of whether the mainly *individual-centred* focus of much of the earlier work can be usefully supplemented by treating possessions as *symbols of identity*. It is this communicative aspect of material objects that must be investigated in order to understand why it is supremely important for people to convey the *right* messages about themselves to others through their possessions. Such an approach may also begin to explain how we *decipher* other people on the basis of their material circumstances.

It is argued here that possessions symbolize not only the personal qualities of individuals, but also the groups they belong to and their

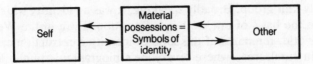

Figure 1.2   Material possessions as symbols of identity

social standing generally. This means that people express their personal and their social characteristics through material possessions, both to themselves and to others. It also means that we make inferences about the identity of others on the basis of their possessions. Schematically, the crux of this argument can be expressed as shown in Figure 1.2.

The notion that we express our identity through our material possessions, and make inferences about the identity of others, on the basis of what they possess, means that there must be socially shared beliefs about material objects as symbolic manifestations of identity. As Hirschman (1981) put it from a consumer research perspective:

> consumers (not necessarily all, but at least those in the reference group of interest) must have in common a shared conception of the product's symbolic meaning. For example, driving a 'prestige' automobile will not serve as an effective symbol of one's social status unless others in the relevant social groups share the driver's belief that the automobile is, indeed, prestigious. (p. 5)

This role of material possessions as symbolic *mediators* between self and other has only come to play such a prominent role in our society in the relatively recent past. Just to give a historical backdrop, the increasing significance of this mediating role can be located within the wider context of social, economic and political changes during the industrial revolution and the rise of mass consumer society.

The rise of mass consumer society: we are what we have

Taking a broad sweep, it can be argued that writers from various social scientific disciplines describe Western society before the industrial revolution as one in which a sense of self was mainly derived from kinship ties with family or clan. Life was public with respect to these kinship groups, rather than private, and '[f]ear of publicly incurred shame function[ed] in the place of an inner-directed conscience' (Weintraub, 1978, p. 5). Conduct was governed by the normative models accepted within the group, and a person was seen as an inextricable part of the whole. Identity was therefore conferred on individuals through their closely-knit group. Broadly speaking, it was an identity which was *ascribed* on the basis of one's inherited position. Even in the Western industrial world, remnants of this kind of identity construction can still be found in rural areas where 'everyone's biography is public knowledge, where who you are and what you are are woven into the texture of your whole life . . . [and] community . . . People are the way they are because of *who* they are' (Barley, 1989, pp. 33, 39, emphasis in original).

The accelerating development of the industrial revolution from the mid-eighteenth century onwards meant a complete reorganization not only of the economy, but also of society in general. Part of these changes was the increasing consciousness that *who somebody is* and their social position are not necessarily fixed and inherited any longer. The rise of an individualistic awareness is particularly pronounced during the early decades of the industrial revolution (see also Chapter 8). Identity is no longer group-based but *achieved* by the individual herself or himself. An important element of such *achieved* identity appears to be the acquisition of material possessions and wealth (e.g., Barley, 1989; Belk, 1984b; Bellah *et al.*, 1985; Fromm, 1978). This characterization is one that would probably fit any Western industrialized country, but it was made particularly visible in the recent British Thatcherite ethos of individual responsibility for material betterment.

The aspects of this change from *ascribed* to *achieved* identity which are of particular interest for the present argument are intimately linked to the rise of mass consumer society. The growth of consumption and *commodity fetishism* are integral features of the *capitalist mode of production* (e.g., Marx, 1930/1878). However, they have received little attention in their own right, compared to the massive literature concerned with the *forces of production* (see also McKendrick *et al.*, 1982). Recently, various contributions discuss the roots and development of Western mass consumer society, focusing on England (McCracken, 1985, 1990; McKendrick *et al.*, 1982; Mukerji, 1983) and France (Williams, 1982). The following basic thumbnail sketch can be gleaned from these contributions, despite their differences in emphasis and argument. Concomitant with the beginning of colonial imports of new goods, the late sixteenth-century and early seventeenth-century nobility started to engage in a 'riot of consumption' with vast expenditure on housing, clothing, furnishings and food. This competitive, status-conscious extravagance drew the 'noble man' away from his traditional obligations to his extended family. Instead, '[h]e now engaged in consumption behaviour controlled by new concerns for fashion and devoted to the aggrandizement of self rather than the material and symbolic needs of the family and locality' (McCracken, 1985, p. 151). In the eighteenth century consumption exploded a second time, but on a greatly enlarged scale, with the additional participation of 'bourgeois', middle-class consumers. From then on, the consumer revolution unfolded steadily, and consumption increasingly served the symbolic needs of the individual, over and above the practical, utilitarian requirements of the family or local community:

> Both marketers and consumers began to explore the expressive potential of goods. This exploration meant . . . the development of new 'consumer lifestyles', through which social groups communicated their values and relationship to the larger society through the increasingly sophisticated deployment of the symbolic properties of consumer goods. The multiple realities of modern society were now under construction as consumer goods were used by all classes and sectors as means of self- and group-definition. (McCracken, 1985, p. 152)

It appears that *who we are* has been defined more and more through *what we have* as individuals: material possessions have become symbols of personal and social identity.

Identity through possessions

In his anthropological study of contemporary Britain, Barley (1989) describes what he terms the 'objectivization of identity' through material possessions as a pervasive basis for our lay psychology about people. Among others, he interviewed Denis Lewis, the art director of a major advertising agency in London, who concludes:

> I think all things say something about you. It might be 'I don't care' or it might be 'I think I'm wonderful – take a good look at me', but I think everyone finds their balance by buying the things that reflect them best. (as quoted in Barley, 1989, p. 45)

The conclusions Barley draws about material possessions from talking to the advertising industry as well as to people on the street deserve quoting at some length:

> one can express an identity through exercising choice in the things one buys. The notion of brand is an interesting one, seemingly an imposition on the world of objects of the notion of personality. It is, significantly, in the life of the city that identities are created and maintained in this way. In the fluid conditions of city life, with a gulf between work and private life and the anonymity of the street, a person can attempt to pass in as many identities as he can successfully perform . . . Moreover, although people may claim that they are striving for individuality, they all end up looking more or less predictably the same. Individuality is therefore a

sham. Only group identity remains . . . We need material objects to confirm our social identity. In the West poverty is expressible not simply in terms of not having enough to eat, but also as being unable to sustain a proper identity through possessions . . . [Ours is an] 'identity through possessions' model of the world. (pp. 43-4).

Some indication of just how ingrained and taken for granted this *identity through possessions* notion is can be inferred – paradoxically – from a feature article in the *Sunday Times Magazine*, entitled: 'No mod cons'. The boldly printed headlines greet us with:

They don't give a hoot for hoovers. Fridge freezers leave them cold. Michelle Jaffé-Pearce meets five individuals who prefer ideas to objects. (Jaffé-Pearce, 1989, p. 8)

The mention of 'five individuals' already indicates that they must be somewhat unusual to say the least, and the text blows up their curiosity value by portraying them as definite, though maybe admirable, eccentrics:

Shari Peacock, a talented and prolific painter/illustrator, has few signs in her home that the year is 1989. The two-room flat that she has owned for five years has basic conveniences, but very little else. She has a cooker, but no kettle . . . To make tea, she boils up water in a saucepan. That same saucepan (her only one) is used for cooking . . . Style in such ascetic circles is defined by lack of material possessions . . . [These] consumer refuseniks stand out from the crowd. (pp. 8-10)

Even this single brief example can serve to illustrate just how taken for granted the construction of *identity through possessions* has become in the mass media, but probably also in everyday understanding: rather than noting the presence of this view of identity, we are more likely to be struck by its absence.

This book attempts to examine in some detail this *identity through possessions model*, by drawing on a variety of social scientific disciplines, by applying social psychological theories to possessions and by introducing my own research in this area. When talking about material possessions, it is probably useful to contrast them with non-material possessions, such as a person's right to free speech. However, the definitional problem of just what constitutes a material possession is unlikely to be solved by compiling yet another typology (see also Belk, 1988). But if people are asked *themselves* which possessions are important to them, they typically refer to a range of personally owned objects that are relatively durable, i.e. possessions which surround them for some time after they are first acquired. These *sets* of belongings, which are most likely to become invested with social and psychological significance, are the concern of this book – rather than single posses-sions or special types of object. This relatively broad approach taken towards *material possessions* is repeated with respect to *identity*, which is employed in a wide social psychological sense to refer to the personal qualities and social locations of individuals, as seen by both themselves and others.

Essentially, two different kinds of strategy present themselves for embarking on an exploration of a topic as elusive and complex as the link between possessions and identity: *narrow focus* or *broad collage*. On the one hand, a particular theme could be selected from an extensive range of issues, such as the role of material possessions in the expression and maintenance of gender identity. The main advantage of such a strategy is that it can focus on a specific question in some depth. However, there is a danger that the narrow focus strategy could be akin in some respects to the proverbial blind men, who explore different body parts of an elephant and arrive at rather disparate conclusions about its nature. Although one may gain a clear perspective of a particular aspect, such a narrow focus can obscure, rather than reveal, the overall 'nature of the beast'. This would be particularly true if the 'beast' were of a fairly unknown kind.

That certainly appears to be the case for material possessions which, to date, have been virtually ignored by social psychology. In fact, it is only during the last decade that social psychologists have taken a *systematic* interest in topics related to economic issues. Only a few years ago, Michael Argyle commented in his foreword to *The Economic Mind* (Furnham and Lewis, 1986): 'Psychologists and economists until quite recently have had very little to do with each other . . . For psychologists there is a new field here – 'economic psychology' (p. xi). And the following observation, although addressed to the social sciences as a whole, still continues to ring particularly true with respect to social psychology:

> Social scientists tend to look for the understanding of human life in the internal psychic processes of the individual or in the patterns of relationships between people; rarely do they consider the role of material objects. (Csikszentmihalyi and Rochberg-Halton, 1981, p. 1)

Even as recently as 1990, McCracken still avows:

> Our culture, with a thoroughness and enthusiasm unheralded in the ethnographic record, has subjected its beliefs and practices to detailed study. It has with the same thoroughness and enthusiasm also made material possessions one of its most compelling preoccupations. It is therefore doubly odd and unfortunate that study of the use of goods in the construction of self and world should have suffered such prolonged and profound neglect. (p. 89)

Therefore – to return to the metaphor just used – likening the subject of material possessions and identity to an elephant and social psychologists to blind people may not be such a bad analogy after all, given that the topic is wide-ranging and multi-faceted, yet hardly explored. So a case can be made for a rather different strategy – one that takes a less circumscribed approach and investigates different aspects of the link between identity and possessions from diverse angles. Such a broad collage may have a better chance of succeeding in meeting the twofold aims of this book: to give an *overview* of psychologically oriented perspectives on the relationship between people and their possessions, and to explore the potential of a *social constructionist approach* for providing an initial, yet I hope provocative, account of their implications for identity.

This introductory chapter highlights the prominent role played by material possessions in contemporary society, and hints at their social and psychological significance for identity. Even the most cursory consideration of the mass media, everyday communication, and arguments from a variety of sources suggests that the preliminary answer to the question *To Have is to Be?* has to be a decided 'yes'. But what have psychology and related disciplines to offer by way of research and theoretical analysis, going beyond such anecdotal and rather general evidence? If possessions and identity are intimately related, what is the nature of this link? How do people *themselves* construe this link? And what does it imply for the ways in which we – and psychological theory – think about what it means to be a person?

The next chapter addresses the question of whether our relationship with our possessions can be explained as the consequence of an *acquisitive instinct*, and assesses the merits and demerits of biological approaches to material possessions from a social psychological perspective. The evidence which suggests that material possessions are, in fact, regarded by people themselves as integral parts of the self leads to a discussion of *individual-centred* approaches to the meanings and functions of possessions for adults. Their neglect of the symbolic, socially shared meanings of material possessions sets the stage for the *social constructionist* perspective which forms the foundation of the entire book: material possessions are conceptualized as *material symbols for identity*. This perspective finds support in anthropological, sociological and consumer research, which deals with material objects as symbols. But its viability can be illustrated more directly by a series of studies which applies established theoretical frameworks in social psychology to the issue of material possessions, including gender identity, stereotyping, social identity theory and person perception. Finally, it becomes necessary to consider the potentially paradoxical tension between the *identity through possessions* model developed throughout the book and the contemporary dominant Western view of identity as a decontextualized, abstract and wealth-free set of enduring personality traits: a *materialism–idealism paradox* with possibly ideological dimensions.

In conclusion, rather than pretending to be able to offer a comprehensive, definitive assessment of the social psychology of material possessions, this book hopes much more humbly to make a contribution towards a just opening field of inquiry that is not only interesting, but imperative for a more complete understanding of the consequences of our Western materialist, consumption-dominated societies for everyday social reality, and particularly for our identity. Finally, a note to allay any ideological suspicions readers may have: the argument that a thorough investigation of the social psychological aspects of material possessions is both overdue and worthwhile is *not* tantamount to an endorsement of the Western consumption-driven free market system.

2

Biological accounts of possessions and property:
The 'acquisitive instinct' past and present

The assertion that people's *desire to own possessions* has an instinctual, biological basis is not a recent claim. At the turn of this century we find statements proposing that

> [p]sychologically, the acquisition impulse (or instinct) . . . is very deeply rooted. The existence of this instinct is a refutation of the opinion which considers the rights of property as something conventional and artificial. (Baldwin, 1908, as quoted in Litwinski, 1943, p. 36)

But this claim that possessiveness is instinctual, and hence natural, is by no means dated. The former British Prime Minister, Margaret Thatcher, boldly assures us that 'the desire to have and to hold something of one's own is basic to the spirit of man' (as cited in Pahl and Wallace, 1988, p. 145). In a more academic context, a recent socio-logical treatise on home ownership in Britain argues for the possibility of an innate basis for wanting one's own home in the form of an instinct for possessiveness: 'as regards possession, there do seem to be strong grounds for arguing the plausibility of a genetic basis to our behaviour' (Saunders, 1990, p. 83).

But before asking just what these grounds consist of, and how strong they are, another question needs to be raised. Why should a book on the link between material possessions and identity concern itself with arguments surrounding the supposed existence of an *instinct to possess*?

As the introductory chapter emphasized, work which focuses on possessions and property from what can broadly be termed a psycho-logical perspective is fragmented and lacks theoretical integration (cf. Furby, 1980a; Loewental, 1976; Rudmin, 1986; Trasler, 1982). Within this literature, early work up until the 1950s is dominated by *instinct-*

oriented investigations. For the most part, they are concerned with the question of the extent to which human possessive behaviour can be attributed to a universal 'acquisitive' instinct and the extent to which it is a product of social and cultural factors. They thus address property-related behaviour from a nature–nurture perspective, often referring to observations of different human and non-human societies, or invest-igations of young children's 'hoarding' activities, as circumstantial evidence for a biological basis of possession. More recently, it has been argued that such nature–nurture debates can rarely be resolved on either theoretical or empirical grounds. This consideration appears to have been the driving force towards changing the angle of investigations on possessions to a focus on the *functions* possessions may fulfil – both as utilitarian instruments and as expressive symbols. Moreover, given that the 'acquisitive instinct' as an early explanatory model has been seen as superseded by different theoretical approaches (e.g., Furby, 1978a, 1980a; Loewental, 1982; Trasler, 1982), it could be argued that this topic has become irrelevant and need not be addressed in a contemporary book on material possessions.

This chapter nevertheless addresses, albeit briefly, the usefulness of an instinctual approach to explain the link between self and possessions. The reasons are fourfold. First of all, this approach clearly has not gone out of fashion altogether, as the opening quotations show. Furthermore, it remains as an aspect of everyday 'folk psychology'. Wrightsman's (1974) investigations illustrate that the belief in the desire to accumulate wealth as a ubiquitous aspect of 'human nature' is a widely held commonsense notion.

Secondly, biological explanations of social phenomena have had a fairly recent, much publicized resurgence in the form of sociobiology, which argues that customs and structures in both animal *ahd* human societies have a genetic basis. Well known beyond academic circles, and hotly debated within them, are biological models of *human* social behaviour, such as that proposed by Wilson in his earlier writings (cf. Wilson, 1975, 1976). One of the core assertions of this 'pop' sociobiolo-gical school (cf. Kitcher, 1985, 1987) is that any organism acts to maximize the likelihood that it (or rather, its gene pool) will survive. In terms of property, this means that any organism will strive to control as many resources as it can and will thus display an *urge to possess*. At least at this very general level, both the early instinctual and modern sociobiological conceptions view the accumulation of possessions and property as a function of innate, biological factors. The 'acquisitive instinct' can be regarded as a precursor to sociobiological approaches to possessions in various ways (see also Sharp, 1986).

A third good reason for evaluating biological accounts of possessions and property is that, whether intended or not, the acceptance or rejection of such accounts has clear and important political implications. The significance of the argument that an acquisitive instinct, or the urge to possess, is an integral and inevitable part of human nature lies in its ramifications for social organization and social change (Tawney, 1922). For example, Friedman (1962) argues that capitalism is the most appropriate economic system because it is best suited to the universal desire for private gain, whereas proponents of alternative economic systems typically reject the notion of innate motives as the basis for possessions and property (e.g., Schmitt, 1973; see also Furby, 1978a). Similarly, much of the heated critique of popular sociobiology has revolved around the fact that it makes social inequalities appear at least *natural*, if not downright acceptable, because their foundations lie in our genes. Frequently, biological arguments have simply been treated as 'self-evidently absurd' and relegated to the status of right-wing ideologies (cf. Saunders, 1990). To dismiss a particular approach on the grounds that it is politically suspect is not a forceful strategy – there is after all the possibility that more left-wing circles just do not like to hear the unpalatable truth. However, the political implications of an innate *urge to possess* are real enough, and therefore any 'grand claims about human nature and human social institutions . . . [become] wild speculation precisely where they [sociobiologists] should be most cautious' (Kitcher, 1985, pp. 15, 9).

As a final reason, a critical appraisal of viewing human possessive behaviour through a purely biological lens leads to the consideration of vital social aspects of material possessions. These are not necessarily obvious or generally acknowledged, but they inform the basic theoretical perspective taken in this book.

The evidence that can be used to assess claims about the genetic basis for people's relationship with their possessions falls into three broad categories. Studies under the heading of comparative anthropology offer insights into whether similar forms and degrees of possessive behaviour exist in different cultures and societies. Developmental investigations address the question of possessiveness in infants and young children, and the possible relationship between childhood and adult behaviour with respect to possessions. Ethological and sociobiological research looks for parallels between human and animal behaviour, particularly with respect to animals which are close to us in evolutionary history and share a good deal of our genetic make-up (i.e., primates).

But before launching into this material, a few brief comments about the notion of 'instinct' are in order. Despite the ease with which we use this concept in everyday parlance, it is one best 'handled with care' (Reber, 1985, p. 361). Reber identifies four main meanings of instinct in the psychological and biological literature:

1. An unlearned response characteristic of the members of a given species.
2. A tendency or disposition to respond in a particular manner that is characteristic of a particular species, i.e., a tendency presumed to underlie 1.
3. A complex, coordinated set of acts found universally (or nearly so) within a given species that emerges under specific stimulus, drive and developmental conditions.
4. Any of a number of unlearned, inherited tendencies that are hypothesized to function as the motivational forces behind complex human behaviours (e.g., classic psychoanalytic perspective). (extracted from Reber, 1985, pp. 360-1)

Instinct in sense 3 means a sequence of behaviours which, given specific conditions, occur in fixed order and invariably in every individual (of a species). An example is *fixed action patterns* (FAPs), such as the begging response of herring-gull chicks where the parent's yellow beak acts as a releaser for the chick to peck it which, in turn, induces the parent to regurgitate food for the chick (cf. Tinbergen and Perdeck, 1950). No such tightly defined and orchestrated behaviours have been postulated with respect to an 'acquisitive instinct', nor has it been claimed that there is an 'acquisitive' gene as such which is directly, causally linked to specific possessive behaviours. In other words, no one-to-one correspondence is proposed between genes and acquisitive behaviour. Rather, instinct has been used in senses 1, 2 and 4, generally referring to an inherited and unlearned disposition to behave possessively. In addition, this disposition has been viewed as a product of natural selection in the sense that the control of valued material resources would clearly confer an evolutionary advantage in terms of survival.

Critics have argued that the available evidence only allows, at best, for a rather general, biological substratum to property-related behaviour which dilutes the link between instinct and actual behaviour to such an extent that it becomes meaningless as an explanatory construct. If one wanted to be facetious, an (admittedly rather exaggerated) analogy could be drawn with the biological need to eat as a possible, underlying explanatory construct for food-related customs, ranging from macrobiotics to cannibalism to the 'breaking of the bread' in Roman Catholic religious rituals.

This chapter presents a brief discussion of biological approaches to material possessions and relevant research, including early investigations on the 'acquisitive instinct' as well as more recent contributions from a sociobiological angle. The basic theoretical approach of this book is *social constructionist*, i.e., based on the assumption that people act in their environment in terms of meaning systems they have learned and share with others. So, this chapter attempts a critical appraisal of an instinctual approach from such a viewpoint, not because a biological framework for investigating property-related behaviour is thought to be inherently untenable or misguided, but because it can only postulate an underlying potential at a very abstract level. For this reason, explanations derived from an exclusively biological viewpoint for how individuals relate to their possessions tend to be both individualistic and reductionist.

The 'acquisitive instinct'

Proponents of instinct theories in the late nineteenth and early twentieth centuries paid some attention to human possessive and property-related behaviour. The lists of human instincts which featured in prominent psychological textbooks of this time include the instinct of acquisitiveness, alongside instincts for sex, parental affection, gregariousness or pugnacity (e.g., Wallas, 1932/1925; McDougall, 1923/1908). Advocates of the early instinctual approach focused on a biological basis for acquiring and retaining possessions and implied that people's relation to their material possessions can be explained as the consequence of an acquisitive disposition which has biological survival value (e.g., Bernard, 1924; Drever, 1917; Kline and France, 1899; McDougall, 1923/1908; Wallas, 1932/1925; Ward, 1923). This work made reference to the collecting and hoarding activities of various animal species, including insects, birds and rodents, and regarded these as circumstantial evidence for the existence of one or more instincts, common to animals and humans, which were seen as the source of much property-related behaviour. Similarly, investigations which examined human collecting behaviour were regarded as evidence that there are prominent and fairly universal forms of possessive behaviour in child development. This perspective is illustrated in the following quotation:

> Even with animals one finds the recognition of *meum* and *tuum* . . . The bird claims the nest and the whole tree as its own, and the dog defends its kennel with its life . . . Certain birds like magpies even appropriate useless objects and consider them as their own. With children this impulse develops very early. It must be considered as an innate tendency.
> (Baldwin, as quoted in Litwinski, 1942, p. 36)

A similar argument can also be found in McDougall's influential *Social Psychology*:

> The impulse to collect and hoard various objects is displayed in one way or another by almost all human beings, and seems to be due to a true instinct; it is manifested by many animals . . . it ripens naturally and comes into play independently of all training. Statistical inquiry among large numbers of children has shown that very few attain adult life without having made a collection of objects . . . such collecting is no doubt primarily due to the ripening of an *instinct of acquisition*. (McDougall, 1923/1908, p. 75, emphasis in original)

McDougall, like other instinct theorists, describes an inherited and unlearned disposition which underlies possessive behaviour, maintaining that the desire for 'mere possession of goods' is probably the 'most fundamental' motive in human economic activities. But he did not assert that a 'sentiment' of property is the sole consequence of a single, specific instinct of acquisition. Broadly speaking, he viewed instincts as comprising cognitive, behavioural and emotional elements, some of which are subject to social and cultural influences. Moreover, any sentiment for possessions is psychologically complex, likely to derive from several instincts. As Trasler noted about McDougall's analysis:

> a sentiment such as pride in one's home (or some other possession) is a complex cognitive-emotional system which may have its 'conative-affective roots' in more than one instinct: in this example, the instincts of food-seeking, construction, acquisition and self-assertion together form the instinctual roots of the sentiment which causes the individual to purchase, furnish and defend his house. (1982, p. 34)

Thus, on closer inspection, these early accounts tend to present us with a conceptual model of a distant, complex and essentially tenuous relationship between a hypothesized acquisitive instinct and the actual meaning of possessions to women and men.

A further problematic area for the notion of selfish acquisitiveness is such common practices as gift-giving – which would run counter to an urge to possess. Such concerns are echoed in the anthropological writings of that time. In order to account for gift-giving and, more generally, for the cultural variety in possession-related customs, various anthropologists proposed a refined concept of the 'acquisitive instinct' (e.g., Malinowski, 1922; Rivers, 1920). These refinements go a long way in acknowledging limitations of the 'acquisitive instinct' as an explanation for the relationship between people and their possessions. They saw acquisitiveness either as interacting with other, opposing instincts (such as gregariousness) or as subject to suppression by societal factors:

> Both Melanesian and bird show that an instinct of acquisition can be so greatly modified in response to gregarious needs that it practically

disappears . . . Such modification can [also] take place through the agency of social tradition and example. (Malinowski, 1922, p. 272)

Again, we find a rather qualified proposal of an instinctual basis to property-related behaviour with different instincts as contributory, but rather tenuous, causal factors.

Sociobiology: the 'acquisitive instinct' in modern disguise?

A thesis of genetic determinism has been attributed to sociobiology, which proposes that complex human social behaviour and institutions can be understood as the product of naturally selected genetic make-up. Sociobiology's core evolutionary assumption is that those genes survive which make behaviour adaptive and fitness-maximizing. Critics see human social conduct being reduced to an inevitable competitive scramble for dominance and survival, in which possessive and property-related behaviour becomes a function of the evolutionary advantage stemming from securing valued material resources.

Kitcher (1985, 1987), who gives a detailed yet readable description and critical assessment of sociobiology from a philosophy of science point of view, warns against a glib dismissal of sociobiology as mindless 'genetic reductionism' on two important counts. Firstly, a wholesale rejection of biological approaches to animal and human behaviour, which starts from the unqualified accusation of simplistic genetic determinism, is in danger of burning a straw opponent who acknowledged the interaction between biological heritage and environment all along. And, secondly, a necessary distinction has to be drawn between approaches concerned with non-human animals and the study of human social behaviour. Sociobiology is not a monolithic theory, but comprises different developments and theoretical strands, only one of which has been the main centre of the so-called 'sociobiology debate' which has raged over a decade (cf. Caplan, 1978; Montagu, 1980). This is an approach he terms 'pop sociobiology', most well known in the form of Wilson's early writings on human sociobiology in the mid-1970s, which received much media coverage (Wilson, 1975, 1976). Put crudely, this form of sociobiology conceptualizes human beings as the outer manifestation of genes – 'survival machines' for genes, which actively *compete* to maintain and increase their position in the gene pool. A person simply becomes the genes' way to manufacture more copies of themselves. Dawkins's (1976) contribution entitled *The Selfish Gene* graphically captures the essential notion that virtually any form of behaviour is thought to serve the preservation of one's genetic material.

This neo-Darwinian model of natural selection has also been applied to the explanation of human behaviour and customs concerning possessions and property (e.g., Camras, 1984; Ellis, 1985; Weigel, 1984, 1985). For example, Charlesworth and Le Frenière (1983) illustrated that a child's dominance rank in her or his peer group is significantly and positively related to her or his use of desired material resources. Ellis (1985) argues that the rudiments of possessions and property clearly have a (socio)biological origin. Human 'pop' sociobiology interprets behaviour as if specific genes for it existed, which shows clear parallels with the earlier use of 'instinct' in psychology (Sharp, 1986). A further point where the early 'acquisitive instinct' perspective and that of modern sociobiology closely resemble each other is in their emphasis on the evolutionary significance of the drive towards possession:

> The importance of the instinct of acquisition . . . is due to the fact that it must have greatly favoured that accumulation of wealth which was necessary for the progress of civilisation beyond its earliest stages. (McDougall, 1923/1908, p. 322)

> The present perspective of possessive behaviour and property as having evolved due to natural selection . . . [means] . . . that, both within and between societies, those primates who own the most would typically have a reproductive edge over those who own the least. (Ellis, 1985, p. 130)

A commonly raised objection to sociobiology's basic tenet of the 'selfish gene' is that human beings show selfless, altruistic behaviour which benefits others. For example, with respect to possessions, the common practice of gift-giving clearly runs counter to the supposed urge to possess. Sociobiology's answer to this 'central theoretical problem' (Wilson, 1975, p. 3) is twofold. Firstly, the principle of group or kin selection maintains that by benefiting relatives who share a certain proportion of genetic material with the altruist, her or his genes are preserved even if s/he is not the one to perpetuate them. For example, providing resources to make possible the survival of more than two siblings (each with 50 per cent genetic overlap) would mean an actual increase in one's own genetic future representation, even if one were to die as a consequence. Secondly, altruistic acts towards non-relatives are explained by reference to 'reciprocal altruism' (Trivers, 1971), whereby beneficial behaviours act as a kind of insurance policy for receiving support in the future, thus enhancing survival chances.

The concept of 'reciprocal altruism' would have to be rather stretched to account for various possession-related and exchange rituals in non-Western cultures (to be discussed in the next section). It does not seem to fit well with children's explanations for sharing behaviour either. For example, a study in Israeli kindergartens showed that among the variety of reasons children gave for why they shared their sweets with a playmate, purely altruistic reasons were used more prominently (27 per cent) than reasons which referred to reciprocity in any form (6 per cent) (Dreman and Greenbaum, 1973). Furthermore, there is suggestive evidence that being altruistic, in this case delivering somebody from suffering, is intrinsically rewarding for people. Such altruistic acts were used successfully as instrumental reinforcers in traditional, behaviourist conditioning experiments, which suggests the existence of an 'altruistic drive' (Weiss *et al.*, 1973).

Having already touched upon some areas which are difficult to reconcile with any straightforward version of an acquisitive instinct, it seems appropriate to turn to the kinds of evidence which supposedly support the existence of instinctual possessiveness.

The early instinct theorists referred not only to adults' possessiveness, but also to children's excessive collections and animals' hoardings. Ellis (1985) argues in a similar vein that

> ownership and related phenomena are neither uniquely human nor dependent upon linguistic learning for expression and recognition . . . processes that humans share with other primates . . . must cause us to claim property and generally honor the claims of other social group members . . . The present perspective [views] possessive behavior and property as having evolved due to natural selection. (Ellis, 1985, pp. 129-30)

These arguments suggest that both early and contemporary biological approaches carry broadly similar implications. Although somewhat oversimplified, the common claims they make can be summarized in terms of two main statements. The stronger an innate, biological basis for possession-related behaviour, the more these two statements would have to apply:

1. That human possessive behaviour and the general forms it takes should be universal.
2. That there should be a continuity between human and animal possessive behaviour.

The first implication means that a strong biological basis should reveal itself in broadly similar forms of possession-related behaviour which should be found in a great variety of human societies, including contemporary as well as traditional, pre-capitalist ones. Differences between societies should be a matter of degree, rather than kind. It also suggests that possessive behaviour should be a universal characteristic of child development. The second refers to similarities between animals and humans in the ways in which they relate to their possessions (see also Loewental, 1976). Empirical evidence which can be used to assess these implications falls into three groups: cross-cultural comparisons (anthropology), generational analyses (developmental psychology) and cross-species comparisons (ethology and sociobiology).

Possession-related behaviour in different cultures

Early work in comparative anthropology has a bearing on the question of whether universal forms of human behaviour exist among different cultures with respect to possessions and ownership, although these contributions were often presented in the form of general reviews of economic systems in different cultures (e.g., Ellwood, 1927; Herskovits, 1940; Hoebel, 1968; Lowie, 1920; Malinowski, 1922; Rivers, 1920). Differences of opinion abound. For instance, Hobhouse *et al.* (1915) surveyed records from almost three hundred traditional societies and concluded that some rudimentary form of private property existed in virtually all of them. But this was only true with respect to a limited range of objects: mostly weapons, dress or ornaments. In contrast, Karl Marx's son-in-law, Paul LaFargue (1975/1890), asserted, on the basis of an extensive study of pre-capitalist societies, that contemporary forms of property as a universal human institution are an unwarranted projection of current economic representations on to different societies. His survey indicates that communal, rather than individual, forms of ownership are prevalent in traditional societies (see also LeTourneau, 1892). Rather more recently, Rudmin (1990) compared two data bases on different cultures with the aim of finding distinctive customs and practices which occur when objects and land are owned individually and privately. He found that private property correlated with the 'social ecology of agriculture' (e.g., permanent residence, domesticated animals), with 'social and material stratification' and with 'social security'. This leads to the tentative conclusions that the institution of private property arose alongside agricultural socio-economic systems and that private property serves the individual's physical and social security as well as supporting an institutionalized social order.

Recent reviews of this kind of anthropological material arrive at the conclusion that the cultural variety of contemporary societies and historical differences is so great that they offer little corroboration for any universal manifestations of human behaviour with respect to possessions (e.g., Beaglehole, 1931, 1968; Belk, 1982; Furby, 1978a, c, 1979, 1980a, b; Klineberg, 1940; Litwinski, 1942; Loewental, 1976; Trasler, 1982). For example, biological explanations would be hard pushed to account for the lack of possessiveness among the Ihalmiut

Eskimos in Canada, where need dictates who uses an object, rather than ownership (see Belk, 1982). Malinowski's (1922) well-known account of the Kula exchange among the Trobriand Islanders of Melanesian New Guinea describes a custom involving possessions which is unusual and does not serve any obvious survival functions. They exchange non-utilitarian objects like coloured necklaces or shells. Possessions involved in the Kula exchange do not have permanent owners; they circulate continually among individuals and villages. It is the giving and receiving of highly valued possessions, the actual *act of exchange*, which increases owners' honour and social standing, rather than having possession of these objects (see also Belk, 1984b).

Recently, Wallendorf and Arnould (1988) carried out comparative research on American city dwellers and peasant villagers in Niger to investigate the meanings and origins of people's 'favourite things'. In Third World cultures, the amount of consumer goods and the opportunity to acquire, exchange and display them have been more limited than in the Western industrial world (cf. Appadurai, 1986). Measuring possessiveness (general attachment to one's material objects), Wallendorf and Arnould found that Americans are substantially more materialistic and possessive than Nigeriens, for whom nutritional self-sufficiency remains the main consumption goal. In terms of favourite objects, the US sample expressed stronger attachment on average to their most treasured things than the Nigerien participants. Southwest American women and men chose both mass-produced and handmade goods, with functional items such as chairs or clocks as the most prominent category (24 per cent), followed by objects which provide entertainment, such as a stereo or TV (21 per cent). In the Nigerien group, favourite objects were virtually gender-segregated: women referred to marriage or household goods, such as jewellery or hangings (85 per cent), whereas almost half of the men chose religious or magical items like the Koran or charms (46 per cent). The reasons given as to why these things were treasured and their symbolic significance are even more culturally diverse than the objects named (see Chapter 5). Moreover, possessiveness and strength of attachment to a favourite object were unrelated in both cultures. This finding indirectly challenges the explanatory value of 'possessiveness' as a general motivation which underlies different possession-related behaviours and customs. The authors conclude that personal possessions may have similar functions cross-culturally, but on a rather general level. They make cultural norms and categories visible and stable, and thus sustain people's sense of self in both societies, although in rather diverse, specific ways.

The giving of presents and gifts seems to be a characteristic of virtually any society (cf. Belk, 1979), evidently contrary to an instinctual

disposition to possess, and it seems difficult to explain such a phenomenon away as a *cultural overlay* of possessiveness. Moreover, Schudson
(1986) emphasizes that giving gifts is a basic human way of establishing
and strengthening social relationships. Another much-quoted custom
relating to possessions is that of the American Northwest Coast peoples'
'potlach' feasts, the giving of large quantities of material goods and
foods to guests. The sociobiological concept of 'reciprocal altruism' may
just about be able to account for the custom of potlach feasts, or maybe
gift-giving. But it is hard to see how it would explain the fact that these
feasts involve not only the ostentatious display and consumption of
goods, but also the deliberate *destruction* of great masses of food and
material objects in front of guests in order to impress them.

> This practice consists of ceremonious feasts given by a chief or other
> important person in which the main apparent goal is to humiliate rival
> guests by presenting them with food and presents that cannot later be
> reciprocated at a similar feast given by the guest . . . prestige is won by
> such materially contemptuous acts as destroying possessions, burning one's
> house. (Belk, 1984b, p. 294)

Even these brief examples give an inkling of the complexity of
property-related behaviour, in which biological components may play a
role, but not an overriding one. What these examples highlight instead
is that possessions regulate and reflect social relations between people
and that they can contribute to the perceived attributes of the owner,
such as prestige. In fact, anthropology now encompasses a distinctive
subfield specifically concerned with the analysis of 'material culture' as a
reflection of social relations and customs (e.g., Hudson, 1984; Prown,
1982).

Possessive behaviour and childhood

Early instinct theorists referred to studies which examined human
collecting behaviour as evidence that there are universal, historically
invariant forms of possessive behaviour in child development. Hall and
Wiltse (1891) and Burk (1900) studied over one thousand children and
adolescents, ranging from 6 to 17 years of age, and provided empirical
evidence that 80–90 per cent of their subjects had extensive and
systematic collections. One 10-year-old boy boasted as many as sixty-six
different collections. Burk (1900) saw these findings as a clear indication
that the 'collecting instinct' is 'wonderfully universal' and 'wonderfully
intense' among children and adolescents. But a series of investigations
with similar samples carried out some thirty years later (Lehman and
Witty, 1927; Whitley, 1929) found that only 10 per cent of children were

engaged in collecting activities. Beaglehole (1931) concludes: 'if an instinct of acquisition were part of the innate make-up of the child . . . then one should expect to find a close correspondence between the incidence of collecting at one decade as compared with another' (p. 258).

More recently, Newson and Newson (1968, 1976) have carried out a longitudinal study in Britain, interviewing about seven hundred mothers from different social class backgrounds about their children's behaviour. At 4 years of age, 80 per cent of boys and 66 per cent of girls had specific collections, often coming into conflict with parents who wanted to reduce the bulk of their youngsters' possessions by discarding broken and worn-out toys. Collections were significantly more prevalent in middle-class homes than in working-class homes. This fact is particularly interesting when considered in conjunction with the stronger belief in working-class mothers that toys should be owned communally (17 per cent) than in middle-class mothers (9 per cent), which suggests social influences on children's collecting activities. Not only does collecting seem subject to social factors and possibly economic climate, it is also a highly specific activity which constitutes, at best, a particular segment of possessive and property-related activities. It is therefore difficult to see a theoretical justification for deducing a general acquisitive instinct from children's gatherings of birds' eggs or stamps. Rather than viewing their findings as supporting the existence of an acquisitive instinct, Newson and Newson emphasize the importance of having one's own possessions as a child for developing a sense of self:

> A child's personal possessions, including first of all his name and his memories, but extending to the material objects that he can touch and hold and know to be his, establish him in his own identity and confirm him as a person in his own right. (Newson and Newson, 1976, p. 128)

The role of possessions for self-development is explored further in the next chapter.

It has also been argued that most infants have a favourite possession, a *cuddly*, during their first year or two. The apparent universality of the cuddly has been viewed as another indication of the instinctual basis of possessiveness. In contrast to such a claim, more recent studies show that about 60 per cent to 80 per cent of Western children have a favourite possession, compared to a much lower incidence or even absence of cuddlies in rural areas of Turkey, Italy, India and Gabon, as well as in Japan and Israel (cf. Gulerce, 1991; Stanjek, 1980). These findings would suggest that the cuddly may be more of a Western cultural phenomenon than a universal manifestation of possessive behaviour. Furby's (e.g., 1980b) cross-cultural interview study with

American, Israeli city and Israeli kibbutz children showed that kibbutz children reported more instances of collective possessions outside the family than non-kibbutz and American children, although all three groups had similar notions of what personal possessions mean and why people have them.

From a very different developmental perspective, Freud's classic work on anal eroticism (1908, 1917, 1933; see also Beloff, 1957; Jones, 1919) includes the claim that adults' relation to material possessions stems from early experiences, particularly toilet-training. On the basis of clinical observations, Freud argued that individuals who displayed 'parsimoniousness' and strong attachment to possessions had childhood histories characterized by difficulties in toilet-training and a strong interest in their own faeces, which they were reluctant to give up to others. Acquisitiveness and hoarding in adulthood were conceptualized as the result of restrictive toilet-training through which the high value of bodily productions, and the associated physical pleasure, becomes attached to symbolic 'faeces' in the form of material possessions and money. These symbolic faeces can be controlled, withheld or given, and – put simply – acquisitive people hoard possessions to compensate for being forced to give up real faeces in infancy. Thus, possessive behaviour is produced by the transformation of infant instincts through socialization practices. Kline (1981) reports research findings on anal eroticism which support the existence of an *anal character* (i.e., a triad of parsimoniousness, obstinacy and orderliness). However, the hypothesized link between possessive behaviour and infant-rearing patterns has not been demonstrated empirically. This classic psychoanalytic approach has also been criticized theoretically from a neo-psycho-analytic point of view for its disregard of the fact that possessions have socially defined meanings and dimensions (cf. Bloom, 1991; Suttie *et al.*, 1935). To conclude, children's possessive behaviour does not seem to exhibit the kind of historical and socio-cultural universality which would constitute convincing circumstantial evidence for an acquisitive instinct.

Humans and other animals

If there were a genetic basis to property-related behaviour, we would expect that animals which are particularly close to us in evolutionary history and genetic make-up would behave similarly to us. Primates are the obvious choice. The genetic differences (in nucleic acid and sequence) between humans and chimpanzees amount to a surprisingly small 1.1 per cent (cf. Gribbin and Gribbin, 1988). Ellis's (1985) ethological and sociobiological approach to the 'rudiments of possessions and property' summarizes a sizeable number of studies on the possessive behaviour of primates. He argues that the 'fundamental driving forces behind human tendencies to make and defend property claims' are biological, a claim bolstered by three kinds of argument: firstly, that 'possessive behaviour is essentially universal in human societies'; secondly, that possessive activities have clear reproductive advantages and that even 'mutual "respect" for the possessions of others' (i.e. recognition of ownership) would be 'favoured by natural selection'; and finally, that non-human primates 'possess things' in ways comparable to humans.

The studies he reviews he argues not only demonstrate the frequent occurrence of possessive behaviour in primates, but also provide evidence for a true ownership phenomenon in animals. They engage in exchanging objects, and a primate's exclusive access to an object is 'recognized and honored by fellow social group members' (Ellis, 1985, p. 119). This recognition, however, is dependent on the primate's dominance rank in the group and proximity to the object in question. In other words, ownership claims depend on an animal's direct access to an object and the capability to defend that claim at the same time, reflected by its position in the group's hierarchy. So-called ownership amounts to little more than *temporary physical custody*. No shared and generally recognized system of conventions and rules exists, which defines an object as somebody's property – on a relatively permanent basis, and regardless of the owner's physical presence or absence. Kummer (1991) also gives an account of the evolutionary roots of having possessions, but he stresses their uniquely human aspects.

Still a very comprehensive study of possessive behaviour of non-humans, Beaglehole's (1931) *Property: A study in social psychology* examines in great detail the activities of insects, birds, rodents, carni-vores and apes. He concludes that acquisition among animals is restricted to the realm of food storage, and constitutes an instinctive reaction to scarcity of resources. The few exceptional cases of storing objects other than food and of defence of territory can be viewed as part of the larger configuration of sexual and parental instincts. Therefore he argues that although acquisitive behaviour is often found in the animal world it is purely a function of satisfying basic organismic needs, whereas humans accumulate possessions as an end in itself. There are further grounds on which it is not advisable to be too impressed with surface similarities between human and non-human 'possessions'. The problem of inferring genetic origins of complex human social behaviours on the basis on similar observations in animals has long been acknow-ledged, for example, in the dictum that 'analogy does not imply homology'. Hallowell's analysis of property as a social institution underscores this point:

Neither the *de facto* control exercised by animals over certain objects, nor the aggressive defence of them, is itself evidence that property as an institution exists among them . . . All we observe is the utilization of possession in the sense of physical custody of certain objects which bear a relation to the biological needs of the organism. (1943, p. 248)

To express the point in more psychological terms: people in any society can interact with respect to possessions and property only in so far as they share the same underlying rules, ideas and conceptions, and they require symbolic, self-reflective thought to do so – which any form of human societal organization presupposes as its context (cf. Hallowell, 1955; Heelas and Lock, 1981). Humans are a highly social, self-reflective and self-conscious species. Moreover, human action is unique in the sense that symbolic communication frees people from stimulus-response chains because they can preview 'in imagination the consequences of different courses of behaviour' and choose between them (Lea, 1984, p. 112). The crux in controversies about the extent to which ethological studies of property-related behaviour can illuminate how humans relate to their possessions has, perhaps, to be this question: what is meant by possession and property? Although an oversimplification, the answer to this question roughly divides those who uphold that similar observable behaviours in human and animal societies have similar causes and meanings from those who see a radical discontinuity between them because human beings are culture-bearing, symbolizing and historical creatures, who act and interact in terms of socially transmitted and socially shared meaning systems (see also Chapter 4). In that sense, a radical disjunction exists between animal and human relationships to 'possessions' which must question any claims of essential similarities between the possessive behaviours of human and non-human species. This criticism leads to a consideration of important social aspects of material possessions, which are not always recognized and acknowledged. The purpose of the following section is not to provide an actual definition of possessions, but rather to draw attention to the social dimension of material objects. This social dimension constitutes a uniquely human aspect, but is often neglected and therefore deserves particular emphasis.

Social aspects of material possessions

In fact, detailed consideration of property behaviour suggests that the nature–nurture debate has resulted in misleading over-simplification. More informative than enquiring whether an act is learnt or unlearnt is to enquire what is the *social meaning or intention of a given act in a given social context*. (Loewental, 1976, p. 345, emphasis added)

The notion of material possessions as used by humans entails fundamental social aspects. Possession and property are not as such located in the 'things' they refer to, i.e., the objects one possesses or owns. Neither do they reside in the dyadic relationship between owners and their things, given that a person cannot have an exclusive relationship to anything without recognition of this fact by other people. In his sociological analysis of the nature of possession and property, Hollowell (1982) encapsulates this social dimension as follows:

> any object or custom viewed as property can only be considered as an upper layer supported by an invisible composite social substructure . . . Inasmuch as property is conditional upon the existence of certain types of social relations between people, it is essentially a social phenomenon. (pp. 1-2)

At first sight, possession of material objects seems a straightforward notion – people know what they mean when they talk about their possessions and property. But on closer inspection, there are aspects which are often overlooked. Moreover, it is exactly those aspects which place possessions firmly in the field of social psychology. The following shorthand definition taken from a philosophical dictionary is one most people would probably agree with: 'property denotes the exclusive relationship of a person or a group of persons to an object or complex of objects of . . . value' (Friedmann, 1973, p. 650). But this definition is at best incomplete and at worst misleading. Although it may implicitly acknowledge social aspects of possessions, it neglects to make these vital aspects explicit. Its omissions are twofold. Firstly, objects can only be viewed as possessions because we share a system of rules and ideas about them. And, secondly, the relationship between a person and her or his possessions is always one which has reference to other people.

People can conceive of and interact with respect to material possessions only because they share the same underlying conceptions about them. This notion is neatly encapsulated in Mead's *Mind, Self and Society* (1934):

> If we say 'This is my property, I shall control it', that affirmation calls out a certain set of responses which must be the same in any community in which property exists. It involves an organised attitude . . . which is common to all the members of the community . . . The man is appealing to his rights because he is able to take the attitude which everybody else in the group has with reference to property, thus arousing in himself the attitude of others. (pp. 161–2)

This necessity of commonly shared attitudes and rule systems about possessions also means that a person cannot possess an object unless this fact is recognized by others: '"the property relation is triadic: A owns B against C", where C represents all other individuals' (Hallowell, 1943, p. 120). From a less sociological and more psychological viewpoint, Isaacs (1967) also stresses the role of material possessions in the relations between self and others:

> I do not believe that the relation between a person and a physical object
> . . . is ever a simple affair between a person and a thing; it is always a
> triangular relation between at least *two* people and the thing in question.
> The object is a pawn in the game, an instrument for controlling and
> defining the relation between two or more persons. (pp. 255-6, emphasis
> in original)

Taken together, these contributions indicate that any understanding of what material possessions mean has to take account of *shared beliefs and values* on the one hand, and has to investigate them within the *fundamental triadic unit of self, other and material object* on the other.

Instinct revisited

So what can be concluded with respect to a claim such as the following?

> The peasant farmers tilling their personal plots in the Soviet Union, the
> three-year-olds squabbling over the bucket and spade in the sandpit, the
> home owners spending every weekend improving their homes, and the
> proto-hominids clutching their rudimentary weapons as they roamed
> across the African plains all speak to the generic quality of human
> possessiveness. (Saunders, 1990, p. 83)[1]

Considering the last few sections in combination, it seems to be somewhat of an ironic paradox that the evidence the earlier-mentioned sociobiologists and instinct theorists *themselves* refer to is problematic for at least some of their basic tenets. Even this brief and rather cursory examination of ethological, sociobiological, anthropological and developmental material provides evidence which challenges both the notions of universality of human possessive behaviour and its continuity with animal behaviour, which form the backbone of an innatist account. In contrast, the discussion so far would seem to suggest that social and cultural, i.e., acquired, factors significantly influence how people relate to their material possessions.

No link is forged between hypothetical genes for specific forms of human behaviour and the resulting behavioural dispositions. Empirically, the existence of physiological, genetic or neurological mechanisms which underlie possessive behaviour is assumed, rather than acknowledged as being in need of supporting evidence. Such evidence is not available (cf. Trasler, 1982). Theoretically, an obvious objection to a general 'acquisitive disposition' which can manifest itself in a variety of ways is that it does not explain very much. To call possessive behaviour innate is more a description, rather than an explanation: 'To say that some behaviour takes places without conscious calculation, or even without individual learning, [i.e. is *innate*], is in no way to explain it, it is simply to label it as being, so far, unexplained' (Lea, 1984, p. 19). Evidential holes in the more dated acquisitive instinct argument, as well as in more modern genetic approaches, are complemented by general theoretical criticisms of biological explanations of human social phenomena (e.g., Caplan, 1978; Montagu, 1980; Sahlins, 1977). In other words, *exclusively* biologically based accounts of possessive behaviour have to be seen as reductionist and individualistic (e.g., Ginsberg, 1935; Loewental, 1976), if it is recognized that the ownership and meanings of possessions constitute social phenomena which cannot be explained as the consequence of individual acquisitive motivations (see also Hallowell, 1943).

The problem with the whole question of an innate basis for people's relationships to their possessions is that hardly anybody would disagree with the broad commonplace that this relationship may well have biological as well as social elements (see also Gould, 1978). As Kitcher (1985) points out, the alleged proponents of the 'iron hand of genes' (genetic determinism) are probably as much a myth as assumed theorists who argue for 'infinite malleability' or a 'blank mind' (socio-cultural determinism). Early Wilsonian sociobiology did not pay much more than lip-service to non-genetic influences on human behaviour, but in his later writings genes and culture act as joint forces, where genetic make-up constrains social behaviour: 'genes hold culture on a leash'.[2] Hardly anybody would dispute the general claim that biology has some influence on social behaviour, but what is debatable is the *extent* to which human possessive behaviour can be attributed to an innate urge to possess. In other words, the crux of the debate is just how long that leash is. Coming back to the evidence reviewed, even the early instinct theorists, notably McDougall, pointed to the flexibility of the postulated instinctual basis of property-related behaviour. Such behaviour was seen as based on various instincts and, conversely, the acquisitive instinct was described as giving rise to a number of different behaviours. In a similar vein, Trasler (1982) concludes that any connections that may exist between women's and men's relationships to their material possessions and, for example, the hoarding behaviour of hibernating rodents are both complex and tenuous. No single, innate acquisitive instinct can satisfactorily account for both and provide a convincing theoretical bridge between them:

such characterisations . . . seem to imply such distant and complex connections between the hypothetical instinct of property (or acquisition) and the ways in which men and women feel about, and behave in relation to, their possessions that they amount to little more than saying that these aspects of behaviour are motivated. The notion of an instinct as an inherited disposition to behave in particular ways in certain circumstances, which convincingly describes the complex, apparently unlearned activities of the squirrel or the mason wasp, must necessarily be so diluted and qualified before it can be made to fit human social behaviour that it loses its explanatory value. (Trasler, 1982, p. 35)

It would seem a rather removed theoretical perspective to ask for *ultimate* explanations for human property-related behaviour in terms of evolutionary principles. People's relationships with their possessions are the product of many factors: maybe some basic predispositions, but certainly our representations and reasoning, and the societies we interact with and live in:

Human beings never experience 'raw' instincts: Even hunger and sexual drives always appear in consciousness *transformed* and *interpreted* through the *network of signs* one has learned in one's *culture*. To assume that only the biological source of the experience is real while its symbolic interpretation in consciousness is just an epiphenomenon is certainly possible, as long as . . . one realizes that it ignores precisely what makes human experience *human*. (Csikszentmihalyi and Rochberg-Halton, 1981, p. 5, emphases added)

For example, wearing clothes almost certainly has evolutionary aspects and aids biological survival, but this knowledge tells us rather little about fashion. Fashion is an intricate socio-cultural system (e.g., Barthes, 1983) which may bear little relationship to the needs and choices of individuals, but which forms a prefabricated code for the meanings and images material objects convey and thus influences what will be bought.

As a further and related example, naturally selected 'mate preferences' have been conceptualized as a 'central evolutionary force' (Buss *et al.*, 1990). If the choice of long-term sexual partners in humans is governed by their having characteristics which maximize the chances that offspring will survive, rather than by cultural tastes and conventions, one would expect the following findings in a cross-cultural research project:

1. That species-typical preferences exist which transcend cultures and the sexes.
2. That, by comparison, women should value characteristics which signal 'resource acquisition potential' in a male partner, whereas men should focus on cues to the woman's 'reproductive capacity'.

Buss and collaborators carried out such a project with over nine thousand adults from thirty-seven different cultures in order to examine which characteristics are valued in 'mates'. Buss (1989) reports, with much flourish, relative sex differences across cultures which support the second expectation on the previous page. But in a more extensive and complete report on the *International Mate Selection Project* (Buss *et al.*, 1990) a somewhat different picture emerges. We are told that culture 'appears to exert *substantial* effects on mate preferences' (Buss *et al.*, 1990, p. 42, emphasis added), in the sense that culture accounted for an average of 14 per cent of the variance in valued mate characteristics. Findings thus point to cultural diversity rather than to a pattern of universal preferences. Moreover, 'the effects of sex on mate preferences were small compared to those of culture' (*ibid.*, p. 44), given that only 2.4 per cent of the total variance in preferences is explained by biological sex. In Buss's own words, what this means is 'that there may be more similarity between men and women from the same culture than between men and men or women and women from different cultures' (*ibid.*, p. 17). By implication, preferences for long-term sexual partners appear as a cultural rather than a biological phenomenon – similar to possession-related behaviour.

Conclusion

The argument put forward in this chapter certainly questions any glib statements that acquisitiveness is natural, or that the association between self and possessions has a clear instinctual basis. It is by no means intended to dismiss altogether the possible role of residual biological and instinctual factors in people's acquisition and use of property, particularly such items as shelter or clothing (cf. Saunders, 1990). But even if it were accepted that possessive and property-related behaviour has a limited biological component in terms of survival, this knowledge tells us very little about the questions a psychological, and especially a *social* psychological, investigation on possessions would want to address and investigate (see also Furby, 1978a; Hirschon, 1984; Trasler, 1982). To argue for a biological substratum to possessions seems rather uninformative when asking questions such as: What is the meaning of material possessions? What is their role in the perception and evaluation of self and others? Do they serve as means for symbolically communicating identity? Or, as Ginsberg (1935) put it: 'acquisitiveness as such, if it exists at all in man as a specific instinct, plays a comparatively unimportant role in fashioning the institutions and behaviour connected with property' (p. 65).

Early self-theorists refer to the close connection between material possessions and self or personality (e.g., Cooley, 1902, 1908; James 1981/1890). Rather than considering possible *causes* of property-related behaviour, it may be more informative to consider the *functions* possessions may play as self-extensions. The next chapter therefore introduces an array of more recent, diverse areas of empirical work. A good number of them are not directly concerned with psychological and social psychological dimensions of material possessions, although they have a bearing on this topic. For this reason they will be reviewed selectively, with an eye to those aspects which are particularly relevant for an exploration of the link between possessions and self. The chapter also offers an initial review of the rather disjointed approaches which characterize the mainly descriptive or exploratory orientation of these contributions. These analytical frameworks differ in emphasis, but can be discussed jointly because they focus on the *functions* possessions fulfil, as instruments of control, signifiers of interpersonal relationships, and symbolic expressions of beliefs, values and attitudes.

Notes

1. In the parts of his book concerned with the 'desire to own', Saunders argues for a qualified and 'open' instinctual basis to home ownership in the sense that he views the *expression* of any possessive instinct as socially and culturally bound. In contemporary Britain, one important way in which a possessive instinct would reveal itself is in 'the desire for security, privacy and personal identity which owners articulate when they talk about . . . their housing' (1990, p. 118). Gurney (1989) refers to housing and 'onto-logical security' from a similar perspective.

2. Wilson's writings with Lumsden (Lumsden and Wilson, 1981, 1983) offer a highly technical theory of evolution in which genetic make-up produces constraints on the kinds of social custom and institution that are developed and transmitted over time. But critics still maintain that their conception of culture remains on an atomistic level, and that the highly integrated nature of social systems is not acknowledged (e.g., Dupré, 1987).

3

The individual-centred approach:
Material possessions as parts of the extended self

It is quite likely that you have overheard conversation snippets similar to this one, and probably more than once:

> A (looking at a shop window): I think that yellow jumper with the pattern would suit you really well!
> B: I could never wear something like that – it's just *not me*!

Clothes are seen as the outer skin of our personality and identity. For the fashion industry, the pervasiveness of this notion is a financial gold mine. Important changes in outlook and one's personal life often find expression in new outfits. In everyday social life, people are adept judges of what the social and personal layers of this outer skin tell you about the wearer. Clothing provides information about social and occupational standing, sex-role identification, political orientation, ethnicity, and personal qualities and preferences (e.g., Cassell, 1974; Solomon, 1986). Clothes clearly form part of an *extended* sense of self (e.g., Stone, 1962), and are the focus of growing, self-contained areas of research in media studies or consumer research, for example[1]. The question this chapter addresses is whether material possessions other than clothing are viewed as parts of the self. Given that a majority of adult respondents in a questionnaire survey in South England agreed with the statement that 'If I lost all my possessions, I would feel stripped of a sense of self' (Dittmar, 1988), the preliminary answer seems to be yes.[2]

As already pointed out in the introductory chapter, research on possessions is fragmented, but it is nevertheless possible to distinguish three different, broad theoretical frameworks:

1. *Biological*: The 'acquisitive instinct'.
2. *Individual-centred*: The functions possessions fulfil for individuals.
3. *Social constructionist*: Possessions as material symbols of identity.

The previous chapter considered the usefulness of conceptualizing the relationship between people and possessions as the consequence of a biologically based, acquisitive disposition. It ended with the conclusion that, rather than asking the ultimately unsolvable question '*Why* do people possess?' in a nature–nurture framework, it may be more informative and interesting to consider the psychological meanings and functions material possessions have. This concern describes what I have called the individual-centred approach, which is discussed in this chapter. Individual-centred is used here as a convenient umbrella term for a variety of research efforts either examining very specific meanings of possessions or touching on their psychological functions without necessarily investigating possessions as such. Despite this diversity, this perspective shares with the third, social constructionist, framework the assumption that possessions are regarded as a part of the self. In contrast to this third approach, however, it focuses on the meaning and functions of material possessions at an intra-individual or interpersonal level. Without a doubt, the individual-centred approach is valuable in its own right, but it tends to miss out on the more explicitly social and symbolic features of possessions. It is exactly those aspects of material objects which are given most attention by the social constructionist framework.

This chapter gives an overview of research which illustrates that possessions are regarded as integral parts of the self and can therefore be considered self-extensions. Relevant work can be found in fields as diverse as anthropology, market research, criminology and abnormal and developmental psychology. The chapter also explores diverse research areas in developmental psychology, with respect to what they tell us about the processes through which possessions may come to be incorporated into the extended self. Although relatively few of these empirical studies are directly concerned with material objects as self-extensions, they touch upon important psychological aspects of possessions. An exhaustive overview of this material is beyond the scope and purpose of this chapter, but research will be discussed selectively with respect to the insights or implications it offers for the relationship between possessions and the self. The discussion then turns to individual-centred formulations of the functions possessions fulfil for adults. A discussion of research which is more directly concerned with material objects as social symbols of identity is postponed until Chapter 5, after a social constructionist perspective is introduced in Chapter 4 as a third theoretical framework – the approach which informs the remainder of the book.

Possessions as parts of the self

The notion that, knowingly or unknowingly, people regard possessions as an integral part of the self is not a recent one. Beaglehole's (1931) analysis of anthropological studies with respect to property argues that material objects fulfil more than just utilitarian needs, such as providing shelter or sustenance. He describes what he termed the 'magico-animistic' practices of traditional peoples, which indicate that a person's possessions (e.g., eating utensils, canoe, weapons) were seen as infused with the owner's 'life-spirit'. In order to avoid being 'contaminated' by the other's 'personality', possessions were not touched by others and were eventually buried with their owner (see also Belk, 1988). Weapons, clothing and other everyday implements were viewed as incorporated into the owner's self: 'Property is . . . the periphery of [the] person extended to things' (Jhering, as quoted by Beaglehole, 1931, p. 302).

This close link between possessions and *who somebody is* was also described by early self-theorists, although they still adhered to the notion of innate motivations (Cooley, 1902, 1908; James, 1981/1890). It is epitomized by the well-known and often-quoted passage on the *Material Self* in William James's *Principles of Psychology* (1981/1890):

> The Empirical Self of each of us is all that he is tempted to call . . . *me*. But it is clear that between what a man calls *me* and what he simply calls *mine* the line is difficult to draw. We feel and act about certain things that are ours very much as we feel and act about ourselves . . . *In its widest possible sense, however, a man's Self is the sum total of what he CAN call his*, not only his body and his psychic powers, but his clothes and his house, . . . his reputation and works, his lands and horses, and yacht and bank account . . . If they wax and prosper, he feels triumphant; if they dwindle and die away, he feels cast down. (pp. 279-80, emphases in original)

Although James presents theoretical speculations rather than empirical work, the above quote includes both the *descriptive* statement that possessions are viewed as part of the self and the argument that possessions have, at the same time, implications for how people *evaluate* themselves. These points have been examined empirically in more recent studies. Three areas of work are relevant in this context. The first consists of contributions which investigate the role of material objects in self-description and self-perception. Secondly, a few studies investigate the implications of possessions, or lack of them, for self-esteem and a feeling of well-being. And, finally, research concerned with property crimes or accidental loss of possessions includes references to the implications of such experiences for the owners' sense of self.

Prelinger (1959) argued that an individual's self is represented by different self-regions, or 'conceptual spaces'. In order to test this hypothesis, he asked adults to rate 160 items in terms of the extent to which they were 'definitely a part of your own self' on a scale ranging from 0 to 3. These items were diverse and included intra-organismic processes, body parts, objects in the physical environment, abstract ideas and other people, as well as possessions. It was found that 'possessions and productions' ranked fourth among the eight conceptual categories of items he used, with a mean score of 1.6. Not surprisingly, body parts were seen as closest to self ($X = 3.0$), followed by body-internal processes ($X = 2.5$) and personally identifying characteristics, such as name or age ($X = 2.2$). Prelinger therefore concluded that material possessions constitute important self-extensions. Gordon (1968), who employed the Twenty Statements Test in which respondents repeatedly answer the question 'Who are you?', showed that people spontaneously name material objects as elements of their self – even when possessions are not directly mentioned. Both studies were conducted with adults, but similar findings were obtained for children and adolescents by Dixon and Street (1975) and by Keller *et al.* (1978), who found that only body parts and actions are seen as more prominent parts of the self than possessions. This is also corroborated by Montemayor and Eisen (1977), although they describe a relative decline in possessions being described as parts of one's self with increasing age. This is echoed in an extensive British interview study which documented an increase in the importance toddlers and young children attach to their possessions and toys until about the age of 4 or 5, because they confirm that the child is 'a person in [her or his] own right' (Newson and Newson, 1976). In a study of schizophrenic patients, Lierz (1957) demonstrates that this link between self and possessions is maintained even during psychotic breakdown, when other aspects of self and self-awareness may be severely disturbed.

Studies directly concerned with the relation between self-evaluation and material possessions are sparse, but an investigation by Ertel *et al.* (1971) indirectly shows that material possessions are used as a source of self-esteem. Their findings indicate that participants used valued objects to bolster their momentarily low self-esteem, which had been induced experimentally. More recently, Beggan (1991a) applied findings from attributional research, that people tend to self-enhance in order to counteract the negative implications of failure, to the domain of personal property. Respondents' tendency to evaluate objects they owned more favourably than the same objects when not owned was more pronounced when they had experienced (experimentally induced) failure, rather than success. Jackson (1979) demonstrates a direct correlation between self-esteem and 'material goods need fulfilment', which means the ratio between possessions wanted and those actually owned. This last finding indicates that greater quantity or quality of possessions does not simply equal higher self-esteem, but that self-evaluation on the basis of material goods is mediated by a complex array of factors, such as expectations and comparisons with relevant others. In fact, it could be argued that a consensus about what constitutes an adequate standard of living rests on lay theories of necessities and luxuries (cf. Lunt and Livingstone, 1991).

This theme is discussed at some length in Crosby's (1976, 1982) model of egotistical relative deprivation, which proposes that 'objective and subjective well-being are not isomorphically related, so that sometimes the better-off one is, the worse-off one feels subjectively' (p. 85). In an attempt to integrate several theoretical approaches on the basis of an extensive literature review, Crosby (1982) includes among the essential preconditions for *felt* deprivation[3] comparisons with relevant others which make one's own material standing appear below what one deserves. Her study on relative deprivation in working women implies that low pay is not directly linked to resentment, but that economically disadvantaged groups may have accepted the unequal distribution of financial rewards to a greater extent than people on average or fairly high incomes. The importance of comparisons with others as far as material possessions as such are concerned is documented anecdotally by the theme of the considerable financial strain people accept just to 'keep up with the Joneses', and is illustrated empirically in a question-naire study on attitudes towards possessions (Dittmar, 1988). Within a more extensive questionnaire, respondents were given statements to agree or disagree with on seven-point scales which form a *social comparison* measure, including items such as 'People tend to buy the same or a better car than their friends or neighbours even if they cannot afford it', 'Possessions give one a sense of belonging to a certain group of people', or 'If people had the choice they would rather buy a car that impresses others than a functional one'. Although responses tended to be neutral overall, in the sense that there was neither agreement nor disagreement with these statements ($X = 3.8$), working-class people gave significantly less emphasis to using possessions as comparative standards than middle-class respondents (working-class: $X = 3.6$;

middle-class: $X = 3.9$). Although tapping into general commonsense beliefs rather than directly self-relevant ones, this result is compatible with Crosby's findings of fewer feelings of relative deprivation in women with low pay.

If material possessions are constitutive parts of self, it follows that their unintentional loss should be experienced as a lessening of self. Studies on people who lost their possessions through a natural disaster (e.g., McLeod, 1984), and particularly research on burglary victims, suggest strongly that the ordeal people feel they are going through is related not so much to the value of property lost as to the violation and loss of self (cf. Paap, 1981; Van den Bogaard and Wiegman, 1991). Interesting in this context is the fact that *The British Crime Survey* found that, rather than crimes which involve physical injury, burglary is *the* crime people feel most anxious about: a national average of 44 per cent of the British adult population expressed their fear of being burgled when asked 'What sorts of crime do you worry about most?' (Hough and Mayhew, 1983). Brown and Harris (1989) interviewed women in the USA who had been burgled, and found that those whose houses had been ransacked and who had lost personally meaningful items suffered greatest emotional upset and found it hardest to recover a long-term sense of security. A study comparing property crimes with physical assaults shows that the psychological distress and sense of violation experienced by victims of theft and burglary seems comparable in kind with the trauma of rape or domestic violence, although it is less severe in degree (Wirtz and Harrell, 1987). This sense of personal violation is echoed by female respondents in Maguire's (1980) study on burglary victims, who 'used words such as "pollution", "violation" . . . Many made an explicit analogy with a sexual assault, expressing revulsion at the idea of a "dirty" stranger touching their private possessions' (p. 265). Donner (1981) reports a student's imagined response to his bicycle being stolen, which clearly highlights the self-related meanings of personal possessions (see also Belk, 1988):

> It hurts to think that someone else is selling something that for me is more precious than money . . . Personal achievements are not the only memories bequeathed to me by my bike. I fell in love for the first time on that bike . . . And you ripped it off. You stole a piece of my life. You didn't just steal a chunk of metal to sell . . . You walked off with my memories, my transportation and my fun. (p. 31)

In a study carried out in the USA on police response to burglary, Stenross (1984) found that, quite regardless of how much financial loss people suffered, the police employed more elaborate criminal inquiry techniques (e.g., fingerprinting) when particular kinds of possession had been stolen, typically jewellery and sentimental items. She interprets this finding as the police's enactment of a *negative rite*, in the sense that they acknowledge in this way the greater distress people experience over the loss of possessions 'typically regarded as markers of the self' (Stenross, 1984, p. 389). The acute discomfort and anxiety of victims described in this literature is one of losing a part of themselves when possessions are stolen or destroyed against their will. This holds true only for the unintended loss of possessions. Although this is supported only by anecdotal evidence, it appears that people rid themselves of possessions if they feel they are no longer compatible with their sense of self – 'It's just not me any more!'.

However, despite the interesting insights into people's relationships with their personal possessions offered by this kind of criminological material, it does not (and is not intended to) offer a detailed analysis of the link between loss of possessions and loss of self. In the attitude survey mentioned already (Dittmar, 1988), respondents generally expressed agreement with a loss scale which consisted of items such as 'If I lost all my possessions I would feel stripped of a sense of self', 'Without my things, I would feel out of touch with my past', or 'Not all of one's possessions are replaceable' ($X = 4.5$). Women expressed a greater sense of losing part of their selves through loss of their personal possessions than men (X women $= 4.7$; X men $= 4.3$). This finding may be partly due to the fact that women tend towards viewing their personally meaningful things as concrete manifestations of their relationships with others, which contribute significantly towards their sense of self (see Chapter 6).

In summary, sufficient empirical evidence exists to demonstrate that material possessions are regarded as a part of the self, by children as well as by adults. Possessions are spontaneously *described* as being part of one's self, they are related in a complex fashion to *evaluative* aspects of self (e.g., self-esteem and subjective well-being), and the unintended loss of personal possessions transcends financial set-backs because it is experienced as a violation and lessening of self. Furthermore, the evidence sketched in this section indicates the usefulness of a concept of *extended* self, a self which stretches beyond the boundaries of the physical body to include material objects. However, although the research discussed so far vividly demonstrates that material possessions constitute extensions of the self, it tells us very little in itself about the *nature* of the link between them. If such an intimate bond exists between who a person is and what they have, it seems reasonable to ask whether this bond develops during childhood. Therefore several areas of developmental research are introduced next, which may offer some insights into the processes through which material objects are incorporated into the self.

A developmental perspective on possessions and self

Developmental investigations which are broadly concerned with aspects of possessions and possessive behaviour are somewhat more numerous than those in other psychological areas, but they are just as varied. They cover such diverse topics as the first treasured possession, language development, neo-psychoanalytical work on power and independence through possessions, quarrels over toys, control and effectance motivation, acquisition of concepts related to property and possessions and, finally, economic and political socialization. This section is not intended to offer an exhaustive presentation of this material, but research fields are discussed selectively with respect to the insights or implications they offer for processes through which possessions may become self-extensions.

The first treasured possession

Social psychologist Gordon Allport (1949) argues that the process of gaining identity progresses from infancy to adulthood by extending self through an expanding set of things regarded as one's own. These 'things' can include memories, skills and relationships with other people, but, by implication, subsume material possessions. Hall (1898) discusses the role of clothes in children's early sense of self as important extensions of their awareness of their physical self. But infants appear to establish a special relationship with just one or two material objects during the first two years of their lives, usually a *cuddly* which is used for comfort and reassurance (e.g., Passman, 1976; Stevenson, 1954; Winnicott, 1953). Winnicott (1953), in particular, focuses on the peculiar status of this treasured object as the first 'not-me possession', for which he coins the term *transitional object*. He isolates two main processes which account for the immense importance of this object. Firstly, children establish an affective relationship with their cuddly because it symbolizes the nurturing person in the sense that it provides comfort and security. And, secondly, transitional objects play a significant role in the beginning development of a self–other distinction: the cuddly is perceived partly as self and partly as belonging to the environment. More recent contributions on transitional phenomena propose explicitly that early possessions play a significant and quasi-universal role in the successful individuation and construction of a sense of self-identity in very young children (e.g., Eggers, 1983, 1984; Mitscherlich, 1984). Essentially, because children learn to treat their transitional objects as a substitute for the absent nurturing person, they gradually come to discover themselves as entities separate from their nurturers, and as persons who interact with an external physical environment.

However, even this very early development of a self–other distinction and the meaning of treasured possessions are subject to social influences. For example, Furby and Wilke (1982) found that the type of preferred object and the way infants interact with it reflect gender stereotypes. As early as the end of their first year of life, girls tended to prefer soft, arousal-reducing objects and boys solid, arousal-stimulating possessions. Moreover, Stanjek's (1980) cross-cultural investigation on transitional possessions in (West) Germany, rural India and East Gabon indicates that the special importance of the first treasured possession for self-development may well be a Western cultural phenomenon. He found that neither Indian nor Gabonese children had any special objects at all, but had almost continuous body contact with the nurturer. In contrast, over 70 per cent of (West) German children needed at least one such object to be able to go to sleep. In an overview of a series of studies, Gulerce (1991) questions the supposed universality of trans- itional objects by contrasting figures of between 54 per cent and 77 per cent of American middle-class children having cuddlies with the much lower figures of 4 per cent for Turkish children from lower socio- economic strata. This finding implies that transitional objects may serve culture-specific functions for self-development:

> The evident cross-cultural variations in the prevalence rates of transitional object attachment also add to the discussion by intensifying the importance of social structure . . . and the importance of the transitional objects as the means of socialization. (Gulerce, 1991, p. 203)

Language acquisition and possessive behaviour

Recent contributions concerned with children's verbal expressions of possessive relationships tend to focus on the acquisition of linguistic rules and investigate possession-related language only for illustrative purposes. However, some of their findings complement the notion of a developing self–other distinction touched upon above. Several authors point out that the comprehension and verbal expression of possessive relationships is one of the very first stages in children's language development (before 2 years of age). This becomes an even more astonishing feat when it is considered that the correct (i.e., adult) use of possessive pronouns varies with the 'distribution of communicative roles' (Cooley, 1902, 1908), i.e. 'my' or 'your' means something different according to which person uses it, and correct pronominal usage does not appear until 3–4 years of age (e.g., Leveille and Suppes, 1976). Authors who explicitly relate language use to possessive behaviour (e.g., Cooley, 1902, 1908; Rudmin, 1985a, b) argue that the common content of 'my' as used by self and by others can be found in its simultaneous expression of appropriation and assertion of self over others. But drawing on a variety of recent sources, it appears that children's increasing use of 'my' and 'mine' as a motivational statement of self-assertion and self-feeling is accompanied by spontaneous productions of two-word phrases – such as 'Mommy sock' – which function as descriptive statements of ownership (e.g., Charney, 1980; Chiat, 1981; Deutsch, 1984; Deutsch and Budwig, 1983; Eisenberg-Berg *et al.*, 1981; Golinkoff and Markessini, 1980; Rodgon and Rashman, 1976; Staub and Noerenberg, 1981; Wilkins, 1981). Moreover, these contributions suggest that an understanding of ownership is accompanied not only by self-assertion via possessions ('mine'), but by the emergence of the pronouns 'mine' and 'your' as a dichotomous pair. What this implies is that both expression and assertion of self are part and parcel of establishing a *self–other distinction* through the objects people own (e.g., Cooley, 1902, 1908; Ruke-Dravina, 1979). In other words, the use of possessive pronouns and other possession-related language is not only aimed at appropriation and self-assertion, but may also serve as a means of self-definition.

Possession disputes and early self-definition

This particular aspect of the role of early possessions in self-development becomes even clearer when the patterns of children's interactions with respect to objects are scrutinized. Numerous investigations document the frequency and predominance of quarrels over toys during play activities up until the age of about 4 or 5 years (e.g., Bakeman and Brownlee, 1982; Bronson, 1975; Dawe, 1934; Ramsey, 1986, 1987). Lewis (1963) explains possessiveness in pre-school children as an expression of 'individuality and self-awareness', rather than as a manifestation of acquisitiveness. Levine (1983) carried out an observational study of 2-year-olds and concludes in a similar vein that their claims on toys are a 'progressive developmental step rather than a sign of selfishness' (p. 544). This 'progressive developmental step' means children's concern with defining the boundary of self as distinct from others, which is expressed by claiming possessions as 'mine' and by commenting on the possessions of others: 'your'. The notion of a developmental phase finds support in investigations which discovered that the use of possessions as a predominant category of self-definition declines somewhat after about 4–5 years of age (e.g. Keller *et al.*, 1978; Montemayor and Eisen, 1977; Newson and Newson, 1976).

Different strands of developmental work are more directly concerned with possessions, namely with their role as instruments of control and social power. These contributions shed some further light on the role of material objects for self-definition, although their main conceptual focus is not on the possessions–self link.

Instruments of control and power

Two very different approaches deal with the role that possessions play for infants and children by focusing on the exercise of control and power. Psychoanalytically informed approaches build on Freud's work on possessions as 'symbolic faeces', but change from an instinctual to an interactional focus (Isaacs, 1935, 1967; Suttie, 1935; Ginsberg, 1935; Marshall, 1935; see also Bloom, 1991). They thus retain an emphasis on the *symbolic* aspects of material objects, whereas a different approach, advocated by Furby, is mainly concerned with their *instrumental* functions as quasi-physical extensions of the self, which aid the child in controlling the environment (1976, 1978a, b, 1980a, 1991).

Neo-psychoanalytic contributions (Suttie, 1935; Ginsberg, 1935; Isaacs 1935; Marshall, 1935) continue to subscribe to the notion that possessions are symbolically related to bodily products in infancy, but emphatically discard the 'picture of the infant on his pot experiencing erotic sensations which he is destined to recall, in disguised form, at his office desk, when calling his stockbroker, or poring over his stamp collection' (Trasler, 1982, p. 37). Instead, they tend to focus on the interpersonal dynamics in toilet-training, for instance, where infants might take advantage of fights over having to use their potty for trying to exert their own will and defying adult instruction. Interactions surrounding toilet-training can thus become a first battle-ground on which infants are able to explore power and status as aspects of human relationships, as well as attachment. The development of attitudes towards possessions is thus placed in a more interactional framework, which moves beyond the predominantly intra-individual focus of the classic psychoanalytic anal personality. Similarities between bodily products and possessions arise in the sense that both can be withheld, given or struggled over, thus shaping and coming to signify aspects of relationships with others.

Suttie (1935) criticizes Freud's central thesis of the 'excretory significance' of possessions and argues that the initial instrumental function of possessions, in the sense of making enjoyable activities possible, becomes bound up with an early comprehension that possessions serve interpersonal needs, such as securing the attention of others. Children's possessions are 'means of increasing the social significance of the owner and commanding on his behalf the attention of his social environment' (Suttie, 1935, p. 59). He also argues that anxious feelings, produced by a distrust of the mother's continued affection, are at the root of the importance attached to possessions because they provide compensatory relief through 'social integration'. In agreement with both Isaacs (1935) and Marshall (1935), he thus provides a particular version of the thesis that materialism can serve as a substitute for meaningful personal relationships (see Chapter 5 for further details). Isaacs (1967) claims in this context that 'The material objects embody and substitute relations with people. They are in the main a substitute for love, and counter the fear of loss of love' (pp. 264–5).

Both Marshall (1935) and Ginsberg (1935) agree with Suttie that possessive behaviour is motivated by the desire for security, but both authors also emphasize the role of possessions as markers of power and indicators of belonging to different social groups. Susan Isaacs (1935, 1967) was particularly concerned with the ways in which children use material objects to control and define their interactions and relations with peers. Possessions almost literally *embody* social relationships, in the sense that children's positions in the group's hierarchy and their friendships are reflected in their decisions about who is allowed to use their possessions and who is not. She also recognized the emotional significance of possessions in social relations, given that gifts are symbols not only of the affection and generosity of the giver, but also of the love-worthiness of the recipient. By the same token, the giving of presents contains important control and power dimensions:

> For if one has the wherewithal to give, one is indeed both safe and good.
> One is no longer the helpless puling infant, dependent upon the gifts of others, and driven by helpless anxieties to rage and jealousy . . . It is more blessed to give than to receive, because to be able to give is *not to need*. (Isaacs, 1935, p. 73, emphasis in original)

Taken together, these formulations succinctly suggest that, because of their symbolic aspects, possessions are viewed as signs of relationships, but also as 'pawns in the game' which serve to regulate, undermine or cement connections with others. In this literature, power and control are conceptualized in an interpersonal sense, made possible by the meanings of possessions which symbolize owners' qualities or express their desires and intentions.

A rather different approach to control forms part of a recent extensive cross-cultural project on the meaning of, and motivation for, human possession (Furby, 1976, 1978a, b, c, 1979, 1980a, b; see Furby 1991 for a brief summary). This set of open-ended interview studies with children, adolescents and adults from America, Israeli kibbutzim and Israeli cities constitutes one of the most comprehensive attempts to analyse various aspects of possessions and property. A more detailed overview of Lita Furby's work is postponed to a later part of this chapter. Only her analysis of the developmental origins of the possessions–self link is discussed here.

Myers (1915) argues that the newborn's automatic grasping reflex is a rudimentary possessive act which becomes gradually transformed into purposive reaching for and handling of objects. Furby (1978a, 1980a) proposes that such activities are due to effectance motivation or the need for control. People's intrinsic interest in producing intended results in the environment or the desire for contingency between a person's actions and outcomes (e.g., Seligman, 1975) are described as variations on the central theme that 'human beings are motivated to affect and control their environment' (Furby, 1978b, p. 60). Because of this 'major motivational force' underlying human behaviour, infants' investigations and manipulations of physical objects around them are viewed as a potentially universal feature of human development. But such explorations of objects are bound to come into conflict with the social environment of the infant, particularly from the age of about 1 year onwards when physical mobility increases rapidly. Adults and older siblings have to prevent the child from touching and handling many objects in order to avoid damage. The result of these interactions is that children will gradually learn to identify with those objects which they can explore and control and come to view them as theirs, whereas objects which occasion restriction and interference will become defined as belonging to somebody else. In this way, possessions are used to draw a boundary between what is self and what is other. The distinction between self and not-self is thus viewed as closely linked to the infant's behavioural control over certain objects. In other words, the developmental significance of possessions resides in their instrumental function as quasi-physical extensions of the self, which aid the child in controlling the environment. This means that Furby's explanation of this process emphasizes *intra-individual* rather than *social* determinants:

> an object might be considered a part of the self to the degree to which the state of the object depends on the individual's actions: that is, the degree to which there is a correlation between the child's actions and intended consequences to the object. Possessions become integrated with the child's developing concept of self because they offer a very high degree of contingent control, almost as great as the control one experiences over one's body. (1980a, p. 35)

The implication of this assertion is that the link between material possessions and self resides in the control they afford as quasi-physical extensions of the person, at least during child development. Furby's formulation undoubtedly pinpoints an important function of material objects, but tends to neglect symbolic dimensions of possessions, such as increasing the owner's 'social significance' or embodying friendships, as highlighted in the psychoanalytically informed approach discussed earlier. It also underplays the influence of socio-cultural belief systems on the construction of meanings of possessions and knowledge relevant to possessions. Indirect evidence for such social influences can be gleaned from research on children's acquisition of specific possession-related concepts and from work on political and economic socialization, although none of these contributions is concerned directly with the implications of material possessions for identity.

Acquisition of specific possession-related concepts

Most studies concerned with how children come to know about property and ownership describe in some detail the developmental sequences of children's ideas about certain aspects of possessions and economic relations, with a view to confirming or questioning Piaget's cognitive maturational approach to the development of knowledge about the physical and social world (e.g., Berti *et al.*, 1982; Burris, 1983; Danziger, 1958; Dickinson, 1986; Furby, 1976; Furnham, 1986; Furnham and Jones, 1987; Jahoda, 1979; Moessinger, 1975; Ng, 1983, 1985). Essentially, Piaget describes children's thinking as passing through a sequence of stages: sensorimotor, pre-operational, concrete operational and formal operational. At the beginning of their cognitive development, children interpret the world unsystematically and exclusively from their own position (pre-operational), a stage which is followed by the mastery of more abstract and logical notions (concrete operational). But only from about 11 years onwards do children become increasingly capable of coping with complex hypothetical ideas, integrating their thoughts systematically and viewing a problem from various perspectives simultaneously (formal operational). Studies concerned with the development of both micro-economic concepts (e.g., specific institutions, possessions) and macro-economic concepts (e.g., poverty, wealth, justice) generally reach the conclusion that the *form* of children's knowledge progresses from concrete to more complex and abstract notions, consistent with Piaget's stage model of cognitive maturation (e.g., Ginsburg and Opper, 1988). For example, Furby (1978a, 1980a) outlines a general developmental sequence in children's concepts of personal possessions. Initially, possessions are viewed in terms of physical proximity and custodianship of objects, and only later do children understand that somebody not present at the time may be the owner of an object, that possessions entail responsibility and care, and that property has complex legal underpinnings. Similar developmental sequences of increasing breadth and complexity of explanations were also demonstrated with respect to such economic notions as realizing profit from selling goods (e.g., Burris, 1983; Furth, 1980; Jahoda, 1979; Stacey, 1978), social inequality (e.g., Dickinson, 1986; Leahy, 1983b), fair division of property (e.g., Moessinger, 1975), or ownership of the means of production (Berti *et al.*, 1982).

But it nevertheless appears that the *contents* of that knowledge is structured, at least in part, by the beliefs and information available in the child's socio-cultural environment (e.g., Berti *et al.*, 1982; Furnham, 1986; Jahoda, 1979; Leahy, 1981, 1983a, b; Oerter, 1984; Stacey, 1982). For example, Dickinson (1986, 1990) investigated explanations and justifications for the unequal distribution of wealth given by working-class and middle-class children and adolescents, and found substantial differences in both form and content. She explained these by reference to the different social representations (cf. Moscovici, 1984, 1988) and beliefs prevalent in the respective class backgrounds of the children, which act as a 'thinking environment'. Several researchers have studied knowledge development in a cross-cultural context (e.g., Jahoda, 1983; Ng, 1983, 1985; Furnham, 1986) and found, for example, that African and Hong Kong children's understanding of profit and banking emerged earlier than that of European children. In a review of this material, Furnham (1986) concludes that it may therefore 'not be valid to assume similar developmental trends across industrial countries' (p. 227).

Political and economic socialization

More direct evidence that the meaning of possession-related phenomena is socially constructed comes from studies concerned more generally with socialization. They tend to document the growing alignment of children's conceptualizations of political, economic and consumer aspects of possessions with belief systems dominant in the society in question, which are transmitted though parents, schools, peers and the mass media (e.g., Connell, 1971, 1977, 1983; Moschis and Smith, 1985; Stacey, 1983; Ward, 1974; Ward *et al.*, 1977). For example, Cummings and Taebel (1978) demonstrate that economic socialization in American schools progressively orients children towards a favourable view of private property and social inequality.

Cross-cultural developmental studies support the argument that children's general normative attitudes towards possessions are closely related to the respective socio-cultural norms they grow up with (e.g., Faigin, 1958; Furby, 1976; Henderson *et al.*, 1982). Children brought up in Israeli kibbutzim – which are characterized by a more communal, socialist approach to property than individualist Western culture – were found to develop norm systems with respect to possessions which revolve around sharing and social interaction, whereas American children expressed rules relating to personal, exclusive use and ownership of objects (Faigin, 1958). Furby's (1976) more recent finding, that kibbutz children's attitudes become more closely aligned with Western norms as they become older, may be related to the progressive restructuring of kibbutz social life according to Western notions, a development which was much less pronounced at the time Faigin's (1958) study was carried out.

Taking this and the previous subsection together, the literature on children's acquisition of possession-related concepts suggests that, although cognitive and linguistic abilities clearly affect the complexity of information children can comprehend and communicate, knowledge about material possessions is gained during interaction with the respective socio-cultural environments and particularly with the socially shared meaning systems within them.

Summary

It can be concluded that – at least in Western cultures – material possessions play a profound role in the self-development of children. One of the processes through which children come to draw a clear distinction between self and other involves controlling material objects which belong to them and learning to identify different objects as belonging to others. Owning material possessions has significant consequences for social interaction, as they afford direct power over others, but also offer recognition and social prestige. There are several suggestive hints that the meaning of possessions has important aspects which are socially defined and constructed. This implies that their meaning as parts of the extended self is of a social rather than a purely instrumental nature. Western culture is characterized by its materialistic orientation and the assessment of identity through 'what one has' (e.g., Belk, 1982, 1983, 1984a, b; Bellah *et al.*, 1985; Fromm, 1976; Looft, 1971; Tawney, 1922), and there are some indications in the work discussed that the integral role of possessions in self-development may be a phenomenon which is particularly prominent in our part of the world (see also Engel, 1985). The research literature reviewed so far offers little in terms of explicit theoretical formulations concerning the link between possessions and self. A variety of sources *describe* the close association between the two, but they do not *analyse* systematically the nature of the material self. The developmental work discussed is, for the most part, peripheral to this question. It was considered selectively in order to draw on those areas which have implications for the processes through which possessions may become incorporated into children's forming sense of self. There appear to be only two noticeable exceptions. Firstly, there is the neo-psychoanalytical work – particularly Isaacs's (1935, 1967) – on possessions as direct and symbolic interpersonal regulators which can signify various aspects of relationships with others. Secondly, we find Furby's model, concerned with the origins of the possessions–self link in the control material objects afford the owner over the environment. In that sense, they are contributions which not only are explicitly concerned with personal possessions, but which also present theoretical frameworks that distinctly conceptualize material objects in terms of the *intra-individual* and *interpersonal functions* they fulfil for infants and children. They move beyond a descriptive orientation and thus fit explicitly into the classification of *individual-centred* approaches to material self-extensions introduced at the beginning of this chapter. The emerging notion that material possessions fulfil both instrumental and symbolic functions as self-extensions is echoed in the sparse literature on adults.

Instrumental and symbolic extensions of the adult self

Overall, psychological conceptualizations of the role possessions play for adults fall into two broad camps. On the one hand, their instrumental functions are emphasized, particularly with respect to exerting control over the environment. On the other hand, their symbolic aspects are highlighted: the fact that material objects can represent aspects of interpersonal relationships or aspects of people's values, attitudes and beliefs. All the contributions considered in this section acknowledge, implicitly or explicitly, that an important link exists between material possessions and people's sense of self. But this link is conceptualized predominantly at an *individual* rather than an explicitly *social symbolic* level of analysis. A detailed discussion of the literature specifically concerned with possessions as social symbols of identity is postponed to a later chapter, after a social constructionist approach has been introduced as a third, general theoretical perspective on possessions.

Furby's control model

Furby's (1978a, b, 1980a) developmental theory postulates that the relationship between people and their possessions may largely be a function of effectance motivation, the fundamental human drive to produce desired outcomes in the environment. The rather complex functions material objects fulfil for adolescents and adults are clearly and explicitly acknowledged in her cross-cultural interview study. For instance, Furby refers to possessions as enhancers of social power and status, or as means of self-expression, individuation and individuality. Moreover, she offers rich, descriptive accounts of a variety of property-related commonsense notions, such as explanations for having possessions (1978a, b, 1980a) and beliefs about sharing possessions (1978c), collective ownership (1980b) and unequal distribution of property (1979). However, when analysing the 'motivation for possession', she nevertheless appears to extrapolate from her developmental theory by arguing that the instrumental aspects of possessions for exerting control are also a major feature of the relationship between adults and their possessions:

> Possessions have an instrumental function – they make possible certain activities and pleasures. In other words, they enable one to effect desired outcomes in one's environment . . . The importance of this instrumental factor *at all ages* (and *for all three cultural groups*) is provocative . . . The results here suggest possession may be one manifestation of effectance motivation in that a central feature of possession is the ability to affect and control the object in whatever way one wishes. (1978b, p. 60, emphases added)

Drawing on McClelland's (1951) proposition that material objects are regarded as parts of the self when we can exercise control over them, Furby argues that possessions constitute self-extensions primarily because they express a person's ability to exert direct control over her or his social and physical environment. McClelland (1951) suggested that external objects are regarded as a part of the self when an individual controls them, in a fashion similar to the control over arms or legs. Tools, instruments, clothes and weapons are clear illustrations of such physical self-extensions. It follows that the greater the control a person can exert over objects the more closely they should be linked with self. This hypothesis was partially tested and confirmed in the second part of

Prelinger's (1959) study (described earlier in this chapter). Several judges sorted the items respondents had rated in terms of whether or not they are parts of their selves into three categories: those that are *controlled by* people, those that *control* or affect people, and *neutral* ones. Whereas the neutral items had been classed by respondents as clearly not self ($X = 0.2$ on a scale ranging from 0 to 3), *controlled* items were seen as definite parts of the self ($X = 2.0$), slightly more so than the items which *affect* people ($X = 1.8$). But given that a broad range of items had been used and that specific results for material possessions are not reported, this finding cannot offer conclusive support for Furby's control model.

Furby's analysis of responses to open-ended interviews with children and adults from three cultural backgrounds closely echoes McClelland's (1951) standpoint. She, too, singles out the following two related themes. Firstly, she argues that possessions are important because they afford not only direct control over the physical environment, but also social control of other people through regulating their use of, or access to, possessions. And, secondly, she concludes that they are closely linked to self for this reason:

> I propose that the *central* feature of possession – its principal defining characteristic . . . seems to lie in the very high degree of control it entails. The magnitude of control I exert over my possessions is of the same order as the control I exert over my body. Thus, possessions are included in one's concept of self . . . That over which I exercise . . . control becomes a part of my sense of self. (1978a, pp. 322-3, emphasis added)

Although she does not deny the influence of social and cultural factors (e.g., 1976, 1978b), she nevertheless singles out this instrumental function of possessions as quasi-physical self-extensions. Furby's assertion that a major basis of the link between material possessions and self resides in the control they afford owners de-emphasizes their symbolic meanings and social dimensions. It also underplays the influence of social and cultural belief systems on the meanings of material objects (see Chapter 5). Indirect evidence for such social influences can be gleaned from research on children's acquisition of specific possession-related concepts and from work on political and economic socialization, already described.

Moreover, Furby's functional-instrumental emphasis does not appear to be warranted by the interview responses she describes. Adolescents and adults repeatedly stated that their possessions help them to define identity and individuality, that they enhance self-image and function as symbols of status and achievement. Her description of these obviously symbolic features of possessions at best sits uneasily with her intra-individual focus on control – despite her assertion that possession-related phenomena are of a 'multidimensional nature'.

Consumer products as expressions of personality

Consumer goods have been described as *symbols for sale* (Levy, 1959). They have self-referent meanings which serve as symbols for the consumer's personal qualities, attitudes and values on the one hand, and as markers for social affiliation and position on the other. While this approach describes the more recent market research literature, earlier studies tended to conceptualize product use and product preference as a direct reflection of the individual consumer's underlying personality traits. For example, Evans's (1959) much-debated work on cars investigated whether the typical Ford owner and the typical Chevrolet owner possessed distinct personalities, but failed to uncover any systematic differences between them. Other research which attempted to relate frequency of product use to personality (e.g., Rosenfeld and Plax, 1977; Sparks and Tucker, 1971; Tucker and Painter, 1961) also suffered from obtaining weak relationships, in the sense that 'some two percent of the variance in the use of mouthwash may be accounted for by cautiousness' (Sparks and Tucker, 1971, p. 69). Slightly more substantial correlations were found by Martin (1973) who, instead of focusing on single items, related personality profiles to product profiles.

Evans's (1959) car personality study sparked a series of investigations which contended that products and product use function as *symbolic* extensions of self, rather than being a consequence of ('objectively' existing) personality traits. Birdwell (1968) postulated that personality is not directly reflected in product use or preference, but is mediated by *image*, i.e., subjective representations of self. He was thus one of the first consumption investigators to argue that self-concept measures are a more fruitful starting point than 'objective' personality inventories for empirical research on product symbolism. In support of this contention, a set of studies found that both semantic differentials and Q-sorting of products could be used as valid measures of self-concept as long as the products in question were actually owned (e.g., Belch and Landon, 1977; Hamm and Cundiff, 1969). Using adjective checklists, Birdwell (1968) himself demonstrated that owners' self-image was closer to the image of the car they used than to the image they associated with other car brands.

This basic notion that characteristics of self-image are *congruous* with characteristics of brand-image was confirmed for products actually owned in a good number of studies (e.g., Dolich, 1969; Green *et al.*,

1969; Landon, 1974; Ross, 1971; Sirgy, 1982; Snyder and DeBono, 1985), although various authors point to a variety of possible further theoretical refinements concerning, for example, ideal self-image as compared to actual self-image, or publicly conspicuous versus private consumption. Although interesting, this earlier market research is of limited relevance for a social psychological analysis of material possessions for two reasons. Firstly, it focuses on the similarities between self-image and product-image for *individual* consumers, which neglects the socially defined meanings of consumer goods. And, secondly, its emphasis on implications for purchase behaviour and marketing strategies severely curbs its analytical scope for understanding the role of possessions people actually own and treasure in everyday social life (see also Solomon, 1983).

The instrumental–symbolic dichotomy

The social psychological model put forward by Abelson and Prentice (Abelson, 1986; Abelson and Prentice, 1989; Prentice, 1987) argues for a major functional dichotomy with respect to material possessions. They fulfil *instrumental* purposes, such as providing control, entertainment or activities, but they also serve as *symbolic* expressions of aspects of self, such as personal and social identity. The authors describe a series of studies of which the first dealt with the meaning dimensions of favourite possessions. Respondents were asked to list their most treasured possessions, and results indicate a fundamental distinction between expressive and instrumental objects. These symbolic, expressive possessions can be subdivided further into those which symbolize the historical continuity of self (e.g., photographs), those which express artistic or intellectual interests (e.g., book collections) and those which signify status and wealth (e.g., sailing boats). Typical instrumental possessions include tools or means of transport. For the second of these studies, subjects were divided into 'symbolic' possessors and 'instrumental' possessors on the basis of the possessions they had listed. They then rated how favourable they felt towards sets of arguments (concerning different social issues) which were presented in either a symbolic or an instrumental version:

> One set of materials advocated a symbolically toned resolution, with arguments expressing the social ideals and symbolic values that this resolution would support. The other set of materials proposed an instrumentally toned course of action, with arguments expressing outcomes . . . that could be directly and instrumentally beneficial. (Prentice, 1987, p. 997)

The main findings showed a correspondence between possessions, attitudes and values in the sense that individuals were shown to have a general outlook which was dominated by either a symbolic or an instrumental orientation. But rather than focusing on the possible social aspects of a link between possessions and attitudes, the authors conclude that such a general symbolic or instrumental outlook has to be seen as a reflection of intra-individual motivational concerns. In other words, possessions are subsumed under the more general umbrella of attitudinal objects towards which individuals show a consistent motivational-cognitive perspective. But the issue of why some people may be 'symbolic' possessors and others 'instrumental' possessors is left untouched. Studies which illustrate that these different 'modes' of possessing are systematically related to social category dimensions, such as gender, age and social class, are discussed in Chapters 5 and 6. It is interesting to note that, although not reported in Prentice (1987), the great majority of symbolic possessors in this study were women, and the majority of instrumental possessors men (Prentice, 1991, personal communication).

Conclusion

Starting from the well-documented proposition that clothing can be viewed as an outer, material manifestation of personality and identity, this chapter has discussed evidence from a variety of psychological disciplines, as well as criminological and consumer research, which demonstrates that material possessions, too, are regarded as parts of an *extended* self. Both children and adults spontaneously describe possessions as aspects of self, their loss is experienced as personal violation and a lessening of self, and they have complex implications for self-esteem and self-evaluation. The intimate link between material objects and self develops early in childhood – at least in the Western world. The literature on transitional objects, aspects of language acquisition and conflicts over toys and possessions illustrates that possessions can symbolize early attachments to others and that they play a profound role for children by being instrumental to their drawing a distinction between self and other. They also serve as direct and symbolic interpersonal regulators of relationships – direct in the sense that control and power over others can be exerted through decisions about who can and cannot use one's possessions, and symbolic in the sense that possessions can increase the owner's social significance and that toys and gifts can maintain, undermine or deepen personal relationships. In this work, the functions of possessions are thus conceptualized as being either *intra-*

individual or *interpersonal* instruments of self-definition, control and power.

The distinction between *symbolic* and direct *instrumental* functions of material objects which emerges in the developmental literature is echoed in studies on adults. Furby puts forward a model in which possessions attain psychological significance mainly because of the environmental control they afford owners as quasi-physical self-extensions. In contrast, consumer research concentrates on the match between products' symbolic meanings and consumers' sense of self. Abelson and Prentice propose a model which integrates both instrumental and symbolic dimensions of possessions.

The main conclusions to be drawn from an analysis and overview of this disparate material are twofold. Firstly, it seems clear that the psychological significance of possessions transcends their instrumental and utilitarian functions: they also serve as symbols for personal interests, qualities, attachments and regulators of interpersonal relationships. Many contributions referred to draw attention to these symbolic dimensions of material objects, but they nevertheless tend to share a common perspective with those models which emphasize instrumental aspects of objects. Secondly, then, the sources reviewed in this chapter conceptualize the meanings and functions of possessions at an *individual* level of analysis. This *individual-centred* perspective subsumes work which concentrates on intra-individual dimensions of possessions, such as Furby's control model. It also encompasses contributions which focus on the role material objects play at an interpersonal level as definers and regulators of relationships.

This work offers important descriptive as well as analytical insights into the psychological role of possessions as self-extensions. However, conceptualizing the meanings of material self-extensions at a predominantly individual level underplays the influence of social and cultural belief systems on the construction of the meanings of possessions and knowledge about them. Although implicitly acknowledged in several contributions, this work neglects to pay sufficient attention to the fact that symbolic meanings must be shared within a social group or within a society in order for material objects to be used as means for communicating who someone is (or would like to be) to others and to oneself.

The proposition that the meanings of possessions are socially constructed within socio-cultural 'thinking environments', at least in part, is supported by the developmental literature concerned with the acquisition of specific possession-related concepts and economic socialization. Children's cognitive and linguistic capabilities act as obvious constraints on the breadth and complexity of information they can comprehend and communicate. Nevertheless, not only gender and cross-cultural differences in favourite cuddlies, but also culturally or class-specific development of notions about the socio-economic world make plausible, if perhaps not providing direct support for, the proposition that the meanings of material possessions as self-extensions are socially shared and constituted. The next chapter addresses the question of whether a focus on the social, symbolic dimensions of material objects may further elucidate the possessions-identity link by formulating a social constructionist approach and attempting to develop a symbolic-communicational model of material possessions.

Notes

1. The literature on clothing is not reviewed in this book, but some studies are touched on where their findings have more general implications for appearance and possessions.
2. This exploratory study examined a broad range of attitudes towards and beliefs about possessions. Respondents were 176 Open University students, roughly half women and half men, who are more representative of the general adult population than a usual undergraduate student sample, at least in terms of age (range 21–64), although the majority of them were in middle-class (83 per cent) rather than working-class (17 per cent) occupations.
3. An extensive, self-contained body of literature is concerned with relative material deprivation generally, rather than with material possessions *per se* (e.g., Runciman, 1966; Crosby, 1982), which is not reviewed here.

4
A social constructionist perspective:
Possessions as material symbols of identity

One way of summarizing what has been argued so far is to say that we are not only *homo sapiens*, sentient beings, we are also *homo faber*, the makers and users of material objects (cf. Avineri, 1968; Csikszentmihalyi and Rochberg-Halton, 1981). The relationship between people and their 'things' is exceedingly complex and involves a lot more than functional usage or commercial value, contrary to the view of classic utilitarian economics (for a spirited critique see Douglas and Isherwood, 1979). Beyond its economic and practical features, our material environment plays an important role in shaping our consciousness, our self-awareness and our perception of the world.

The social sciences have taken time to recognize the significance of material objects and have been even slower in starting to examine the relationship between people and their things. Beyond their functional and market value, the significance of material goods stems largely from the symbolic meanings they carry and communicate. Acquiring or exchanging these meanings are important factors in motivating us to lavish money, time and attention on our possessions. Symbolic meanings may often weigh more heavily when people buy 'new things' than rational decision-making in terms of costs and resources. Yet rational choice theory remains the predominant explanatory framework in economic theory, and has started to spill into other social scientific disciplines, such as politics (cf. Belk, 1991; Hindess, 1984). In an exploratory survey on commonsense notions about material possessions, respondents clearly thought – women even more so than men – that the symbolic aspects of possessions are more important than their practical functions. They disagreed with statements which proclaimed utility to be more significant than the symbolic features of material objects, such as 'The practical utility of the things one owns is more important than the people and events they remind one of', or 'Gifts mean a lot only when they are also useful' (Dittmar, 1988).[1] A recent analysis of consumer processes from an interdisciplinary perspective, combining anthropology with marketing, arrives at a similar conclusion:

> They [consumers] use the meaning of consumer goods to express cultural categories and principles, cultivate ideas, create and sustain lifestyles, construct notions of self, and create (and survive) social change . . . Consumption is thoroughly cultural in character. (McCracken, 1990, p. xi)

Even such thoroughly practical items as tools, kitchen appliances or watches are not devoid of symbolic connotations. Watches and kitchens can be dynamically modern, stylishly sparse or romantically old-fashioned. And most people's choice will be influenced by the images and qualities these objects convey and which, if we are to believe advertising, will magically transfer to the owner.

The starting point of this chapter is the view that, among the wide-ranging symbolic significance of material possessions, it is their relation to our sense of identity, and to the identity of others, that is particularly important. Serving as an introduction to further discussions of empirical work, it outlines a theoretical perspective which provides a conceptual analysis of the link between identity and material possessions. The broad approach adopted in this book is a social constructionist one which views material possessions as socially shared symbols for identity. The overall aim of this chapter is twofold. Firstly, it attempts to build a theoretical foundation for a clearer formulation of the link between possessions and identity, which may overcome some of the inconsistencies and fragmentation of earlier contributions on this topic. Secondly, it tries to develop a broader perspective in which material possessions as symbols of identity can be seen to play a role in a variety of aspects of everyday social life. These aspects are investigated in traditionally separate areas of social psychological theory and research, such as stereotypes, social categories or person perception.

It needs to be stressed that the argument put forward in this chapter only makes sense against the backdrop of historical changes in the definition of identity, sketched in the introductory chapter: the change from an identity broadly *ascribed* on the basis of kinship relations and associated duties to one that is supposed to be personally *achieved*, not least through consumption and ownership of material artefacts. In a society in which material possessions have become increasingly important for expressing 'who somebody is', it should not be surprising that self-assessments and judgments about others are profoundly influenced by material symbols.

From a social constructionist perspective, the meanings of material possessions for identity are viewed as socially constituted and socially shared. In other words, the focus of interest is on people's everyday understanding of themselves and others with respect to the objects they own. Social constructionism is not a theoretical framework as such, but constitutes a meta-theory or a 'policy statement' (Semin, 1990) about how to look at social reality. In particular, it stresses the social origins and social nature of all knowledge. The term *constructionism* will be used throughout to refer to this perspective, rather than the equally commonly employed *constructivism*. As Gergen (1985) points out, not only does constructionism stress the theoretical continuity with Berger and Luckmann's (1967) *The Social Construction of Reality*, it is more precise than constructivism. The latter term has also been used in conjunction with child development in Piagetian theory, a modern art movement and a particular psychological approach to perception.

This chapter begins with a brief general outline of the social constructionist perspective, its main theoretical aspects and implications. But as Billig *et al.* (1988) put it, 'it is one thing to outline a general theoretical approach, but it is quite another to say how it might be applied to the study of [particular] social phenomena' (p. 20). Such an application of a social constructionist perspective to the study of material possessions and identity will subsequently be attempted by drawing on Mead's symbolic interactionism.

The social constructionist perspective

Social constructionism is neither a recent development, nor does it constitute a singular approach with sharply delineated boundaries. Rather, it is best viewed as consisting of converging orientations which have historical links to such diverse fields as the sociology of knowledge (e.g., Berger, 1966; Berger and Luckmann, 1967; Goff, 1980), phenomenological sociology (e.g., Schütz, 1972), philosophy of language (e.g., Winch, 1958; Wittgenstein, 1963), Soviet socio-cultural psychology (e.g., Vygotsky, 1978; see also Wertsch, 1985), and particularly the social behaviourism of the Chicago school later termed symbolic interactionism (e.g., Mead, 1934, 1938). Despite its long history, it is only during the last decade that this approach has gained sufficient recognition to be referred to as the 'social constructionist movement in modern psychology' (Gergen, 1985).

A somewhat oversimplified, but nevertheless poignant, location of social constructionist formulations as theoretical frameworks can be derived from a contribution by Shweder and Miller (1985). We do not experience our environment as a chaotic and overwhelming mass of impressions, but as an ordered and comprehensible world. Shweder and Miller (1985) argue that theories of social cognition which deal with how this order comes about can be roughly divided into three kinds. Firstly, *realist* theories argue that people perceive the world the way they do 'because that's the way the world is', implying some form of environmental determinism. Secondly, *innatist* theories argue that people perceive the world the way they do because that's the way people are, assuming the determining influence of intra-individual biological or perceptual processes. And thirdly, we have *social construction* theories which differ in important ways from the other two approaches. Firstly, they reject *unilinear determinism* and, secondly, they stress the *social origins of knowledge*. These theories argue that people perceive the world the way they do because they participate in socially shared practices and interact with the world in terms of meaning systems which are simultaneously transmitted, reproduced and transformed in direct and symbolic social interchanges. These points need brief elaboration.

With respect to realist theories, research evidence has not favoured the traditional empiricist claim that people's cognitive system – their knowledge, concepts, categories, beliefs – is a straightforward reflection of the external world. A prominent example is the failure of Skinnerian behaviourism to give a satisfactory account of language learning through environmental conditioning alone (cf. Wertsch, 1985). Rather, it seems to be the case that people select the aspects of 'reality' they attend to and act upon: their knowledge and concepts form the basis for how they understand their environment. Thus, the outside world cannot be perceived and understood in a direct and decontextualized way, but is *constructed* in the sense that any observation can only become meaningful through the categories and concepts a person uses to understand the world.

But if it is accepted that '[r]ather than reality driving the conceptual system, the conceptual system is said to determine what is taken as real' (Semin and Gergen, 1990, p. 7), the question arises of where this conceptual system originates from. The answer given by innatist theories is that people's categories, schemas and concepts are internally generated. Perception and thought are patterned by fixed, fundamental processes which, by default, take on a universal and transhistorical character: their structural organization and functions remain, only the contents of beliefs may vary. Semin and Gergen (1990) pointedly state that 'by avoiding the Scylla of everyday understanding as built up or produced by the environment, theorists run headlong into the Charybdis of knowledge as internally generated' (p. 8). To give just two examples, such an asocial and ahistorical perspective can be questioned with respect to everyday emotional experience and notions of person-hood or identity. Various studies illustrate not only that emotions are thought and talked about differently in different cultures (e.g., Averill, 1982; Harré, 1986), but that social influences shape how they are experienced (e.g., Hochschild, 1979, 1983; Papadopoulous, 1990; Shott, 1979). People's concepts of self and personhood vary socially and culturally, too (see chapter 8). Moreover, Miller (1984) demonstrated that American and Indian children start off with similar sets of explanations for social behaviour, but gradually diverge towards cultur-ally prevalent accounts in terms of either an individual's stable personal-ity traits (America) or her or his social roles and duties (India).

The solution adopted here is that the origins of everyday knowledge and understanding are *social*. Reality construction is thus viewed not as an individual but as a social process, because it is based on social interaction – direct and symbolic. Proponents of a social constructionist perspective argue that the world is perceived in terms of socially shared meaning systems and that society as we know it could not exist if individuals did not share such a common underlying symbolic order of rules, beliefs and understanding (e.g., Hallowell, 1955; Lock, 1981). Our subjective consciousness is permeated, maintained and reproduced by social processes (e.g., Adoni and Mane, 1984; Berger, 1966; Gergen, 1982, 1985; Gergen and Davis, 1985; Mead, 1934; Semin and Gergen, 1990). Bourdieu (1979) speaks of 'incorporated' culture to designate that part of overall society which has rooted itself in the individual, shaping our thoughts and actions. Thus,

> the world of everyday experience . . . presents itself to the senses of the individual, fully shaped and constituted by the beliefs and assumptions of his or her culture. This world has been constituted by culture in two ways. Culture is the 'lens' through which all phenomena are seen . . . Second, culture is the 'blueprint' of human activity, . . . specifying the behaviors and objects that issue from [it]. (McCracken, 1990, pp. 72–3)

However, society does not determine the individual in any simple sense; the process is a reciprocal, circular one in which individuals are both the products and the transformers of their social world. Societal structures, practices and conventions pre-exist individuals who learn and re-appropriate them throughout their lifetime via symbol systems with commonly agreed meanings. But, at the same time, by doing so they simultaneously reproduce or even transform these structures and prac-tices (e.g., Bhaskar, 1979, 1989).

An example of this interaction particularly relevant to this book concerns the representation and reproduction of socio-cultural categor-ies through material symbols. These categories can be thought of as the basic distinctions a culture uses to carve up the perceived world, such as time, space or the human social categories of class, gender, age, occupation or status. Such categories have no existence outside of social activity, and would be invisible were they not being constantly substantiated and reproduced by human practice. Material goods play a particular role here, in the sense that gender, class and status are clearly marked by certain kinds of possession and dress. During socialization, we learn to understand the map of our social environment in terms of which material possessions signify which social categories. At the same time, our own constant display and use of goods and possessions reproduces and maintains social categories. McCracken (1990) puts it this way:

> The meanings of consumer goods and the meaning creation accomplished
> by consumer processes are important parts of the scaffolding of our
> present realities. Without consumer goods, certain acts of self-definition
> and collective definition in this culture would be impossible. (p. ix)

Although predominantly supporting the status quo, modes of consumption or dress can also potentially be used for social change. For example, the padded shoulder 'power-dressing' of professional women can be analysed as an attempt to transform traditional gender roles at work (see Chapter 6).

So far, some of the core notions of social constructionism have been sketched, but, as a theoretical perspective, it carries further corollaries and implications. Because it assumes that reality construction is a social process, it criticizes the positivist-empiricist conception of knowledge underlying most sciences which, put crudely, holds that reality can be perceived and understood in a direct and decontextualized way. The data scientists collect are seen as unproblematic reflections of that reality, whereas theories are interpretations of those data which can be subjected to rigorous empirical (in)validation. Without going into detail, these assumptions are inherently problematic and have a long and complex history in philosophical controversies. Recently, the notions of absolute truth and cumulative scientific progress have come under critical attack even with respect to the so-called epitome of objective knowledge, the natural sciences (e.g., Feyerabend, 1975; Kuhn, 1962; Lakatos, 1970).

In place of the dominant positivist-empiricist science exemplified by most psychological theory and research, a good number of advocates of the 'new' psychology are advancing versions of social constructionist theory in which knowledge is seen as a historically and culturally specific construction, the dominant forms of which are used to legitimate the existing social order. Thus the difference between scientific beliefs and everyday understanding is less compelling and becomes problematic:

> Within the constructionist framework . . . the researcher is not credited with any special access to 'the truth', and her role is not to unveil objective facts about the nature of reality, but only to describe the different ways in which people construct their realities. (Kitzinger, 1986, p. 152)

What is important in the context of this book is that the interdependence between social process and individual reality implies that the description and study of meaning systems shared by members of a society become interesting and important in their own right. These systems are seen as constituting an actual environment which forms and is formed by human thought and action, a point also highlighted by the French social representations movement (e.g., Moscovici, 1981, 1984, 1988). Such socially shared beliefs and notions are 'in the world' as well as being 'in the head' (Farr, 1987). In a way foreshadowed by Gergen's (1973) seminal paper on social psychology as history, Semin (1987) therefore describes one of the major tasks of social psychological work as 'accessing socially, i.e. historically and culturally constituted . . . representations' (p. 321). A further corollary of this view is that all thought is socio-culturally and historically embedded. Amongst other things, this means that psychological theories bear a relationship to the consensual universe in which they were formulated. This is illustrated, for instance, by several contributions which emphasize the convergence of scientific and commonsense theories about personality (e.g., Hampson, 1988; Semin, 1987, 1990).

A further implication for social psychological theory and research, which has not yet been addressed prominently by social constructionists in the psychological field, stems from the assertion that

> [t]he degree to which a given form of understanding *prevails* . . . is not fundamentally dependent on the empirical validity of the perspective in question, but on the vicissitudes of social processes (e.g., communication, conflict . . .). (Gergen, 1985, p. 268, emphasis added)

Such an argument clearly suggests not only that social knowledge is communicated and reproduced in face-to-face interactions, but also that societal power relations are bound to be reflected in the symbolic universe we share (cf. Deschamps, 1982). Amongst the variety of available representations some are more prevalent and dominant than others. This aspect of social reality is usually dealt with under the umbrella term ideology (cf. Billig *et al.*, 1988; Sampson, 1981; Thompson, 1986). Despite the various ways in which ideology has been conceptualized, authors tend to agree on a broad double meaning:

ideology as the glue which binds a culture together and ideology as a reflection of power and dominance. Ideology in this latter sense implies that the reproduction of dominant meaning systems is intricately linked to the maintenance of the social composition of a society (e.g., Adorno, 1967, 1968; Goff, 1980; Hall, 1986; Marx and Engels, 1965; Sampson, 1983, 1989). This would mean that everyday, social knowledge is informed by ideological, dominant representations, and that this issue should be addressed within social psychological work concerned with social constructionism (see also Bouton, 1984).

Finally, this focus on human beings as simultaneous creators and products of the social world necessarily implies the interdependence of social process and individual psychological reality and self-definition. Berger's (1966) analysis of the social individual (see also Semin, 1986) remains both relevant and succinct:

> Self and society are inextricably interwoven entities. Their relationship is dialectical because the self . . . may act back in its turn upon the society that shaped it. The self exists by virtue of society, but society is only possible as many selves continue to apprehend themselves and each other with reference to it. Every society contains a repertoire of identities that is part of the 'objective knowledge' of its members . . . As the individual is socialized, these identities are 'internalized' . . . The objective reality, as defined by society, is subjectively appropriated . . . This dialectic between social structure and psychological reality may be called the fundamental proposition of any social psychology in the Meadian tradition . . . The individual *realizes* himself in society – that is he recognizes his identity in socially defined terms and these definitions *become reality* as he lives in society . . . *One identifies oneself, as one is identified by others, by being located in a common world.* (pp. 107-9, emphases in original)

In this early contribution Berger starts from the general notion that individual consciousness is essentially social, but then pays particular attention to identity: how people perceive and construe themselves and others. Identity is thus located at the individual–society interface, in the sense that it is part of each individual's subjective reality but can only arise in a social, and thus socio-cultural, context: 'The individual constitutes society as genuinely as society constitutes the individual' (Mead, 1934, p. 15). Such a conception of identity both potentially dissolves the traditional dichotomy between the individual and society and simultaneously avoids the innatist or environmental unilinear determinism which tends to accompany this dichotomy (see also Gergen's discussion of exogenic versus endogenic perspectives in psychology, 1985).

The concept of identity

At this point, a brief explanatory note about the term 'identity' may be in order. Given that it is an endlessly contestable concept, this aside is nothing more than a clarification of how identity is understood and used in this book. Robbins (1973) distinguishes three types of investigations on identity. The first one is an *identity-health* model which focuses on the psychopathology of identity and the development of a healthy personality. The second model uses an *identity-interaction* approach which analyses identity through face-to-face interaction. The third framework employs an *identity-world-view* model, which interprets identity as an accumulation of knowledge, codes, values, stores of experiences and guiding principles of action, i.e. as a set of social-cognitive representations. Identity is employed here in this third, broad sense to encompass both personal and social characteristics of people as understood by themselves and others. It can therefore be used inter-changeably with self or personhood. But it has been argued by social psychologists that identity should be distinguished from self because it refers to *situated*, socially located aspects of the person:

> identity establishes *what* and *where* the person is in social terms. It is not a substitute word for 'self' . . . One's identity is established when others *place* him as a social object by assigning him the same words or identity that he appropriates for himself. (Stone, 1962, p. 93, emphases in original)

Within a social constructionist perspective on self, the social 'place-ment' by others which Stone describes as the essence of identity is also the major hallmark of a sense of self. It appears therefore that to draw a distinction between self and identity, such as that in the above quotation, may run the risk of implying a non-social conception of self which is rejected here. A more useful distinction may be drawn between more personal and more public aspects of identity. Weigart (1983) offers a useful definition of such a distinction in his review of the development of the concept of 'identity' in social psychology:

> At the micro level, identity is considered in terms of multiple categorizations of the individual by self and others that . . . constitute life's meanings. At the macro level, identity reflects a positional definition within institutions and entire societies. (p. 200)

In this book, particular emphasis will be placed on personal and interactional qualities as indicators and manifestations of identity, both at the personal 'micro' and the social 'macro' level.

Abandoning 'absolute truth' does not mean 'anything goes'

Because of its main tenet that all knowledge is socially, culturally and historically embedded, social constructionism has been attacked for its apparent rampant relativism, a discussion of which is well beyond the scope of this brief treatment. However, the issue of relativity can be usefully considered in Armon-Jones's (1986) terms of a *strong* and a *weak* version of social constructionism. The strong version holds that everything is nothing but an irreducibly socio-cultural product, which essentially means that any description of the world is equally compatible with any experience of it. Gergen's (e.g., 1985, 1986) avowal of the strong position moreover entails a radical anti-empiricism which rejects any claim that observation should or could decide whether statements about the world are accepted or rejected. Put crudely, science becomes a field in which social processes alone – negotiation, conflict and power struggles – determine what are regarded as scientific beliefs. In contrast, the weaker version allows for social constructions to be elaborations and/or interpretations of either instinctive responses or environmental objects. It, too, abandons the idea of objective truth, but maintains that observations can play a role in selecting one among several descriptions of the world, provided they are considered with respect to the theoretical perspective from which data has been collected. Accepting that we 'appreciate . . . parts of the world through concepts that are . . . time- and culturebound and hence endlessly contestable' (Nettler, 1986, p. 480) does not preclude that such concepts can – to some extent – be verified through repeated experience on the one hand and intersubjective agreement on the other (see also Stroebe and Kruglanski, 1989).

Although social constructionism does not subscribe to the idea of 'truth through method', as if empirical methodology were some form of meat grinder from which [objective] truth could be turned out like so many sausages' (Gergen, 1985, p. 273), this acknowledgement that research cannot produce ultimate truth has sometimes led to an anti-empirical stance, particularly in the rapidly growing domain of discourse analysis (e.g., Potter and Wetherell, 1987). In contrast, I view systematic and controlled data-collection as a fruitful avenue for an exposition of representations about possessions and identity. A rejection of traditional empiricism does not need to be tantamount to a rejection of empirical research. Overall, what has been presented under the heading of weak social constructionism appears preferable because it does not compromise the major tenets of the theoretical perspective, but does escape the uncomfortable vision of our living in some 'mentalistic netherland' (Rochberg-Halton, 1984) where the relations between meaning systems and the environment are completely arbitrary, and where criteria for choosing between different theoretical standpoints appear abandoned.

The next section presents an attempt to lay a social constructionist foundation for viewing identity in its material context. It does so by drawing on George Herbert Mead's symbolic interactionism. For this reason, some general considerations about his work will serve as an introduction into the theoretical approach put forward in this book.

A symbolic interactionist view of material identity

The body of thought outlined by George Herbert Mead (1913, 1924–25, 1934, 1938, 1968, 1982) has significantly influenced the development of the social constructionist perspective and can be viewed as a theoretical framework that is clearly compatible with it. Mead's formulation is now commonly referred to as *symbolic interactionism* (e.g., Blumer, 1969; Hewitt, 1979; Rock, 1979). It is sometimes difficult to uncover Mead's exact position on subtle theoretical points, given that his main contributions consist of unfinished, often fragmentary papers and posthumous reconstructions from his students' lecture notes. Not surprisingly, emerging ambiguities have fuelled critical appraisals of his conceptualization of identity and society (e.g., Kolb, 1944; Lichtman, 1970; Wrong, 1961). But a good number of authors have argued that his framework is both coherent and truly dialectical (e.g., Bouton, 1984; Cottrell, 1978; Cronk, 1973; Goff, 1980; Joas, 1985; Lewis, 1979; Rochberg-Halton, 1982, 1984; Ropers, 1973; Stryker, 1980).

At the core of symbolic interactionism is the notion that developing a sense of identity stems from the human ability for self-reflexivity or, in Mead's terms, viewing oneself from the *perspective of the other*. Self-awareness means that the self becomes the object of reflection. This requires the capacity for self-reference and the development of role-taking abilities, both of which become possible only in the context of socially shared meaning systems where self, others and objects in the environment can be designated and represented symbolically. The potential of a Meadian perspective for coming to grips with the symbolic significance of material possessions for identity has been acknowledged in various contributions (Csikszentmihalyi and Rochberg-Halton, 1981; Rochberg-Halton, 1984; Solomon, 1983), but none of them offers more than brief sketches. Here, fundamental theoretical elements of symbolic interactionism are discussed only in a cursory fashion, with the main focus on their relevance to material symbols. Detailed expositions and appraisals of Mead's position can be found in, for example, Goff (1980), Hewitt (1979), Joas (1985), Rock (1979) or Stryker (1980).

A useful way of giving structure to an account of material symbols and identity which draws on Mead and other sources is to discuss relevant concepts with respect to three types of social reality (see Adoni and Mane, 1984). Social reality is used here in a broad sense to emphasize that people's knowledge and perception of reality are socially constituted. These three kinds of social reality are, of course, related to each other and the following distinction is drawn purely for analytical purposes. Firstly, people share an *objective social reality* which they experience as the objective world existing outside the individual. Here objects are seen to possess 'hard' quantitative dimensions, but also various qualitative characteristics. The second kind of reality is *symbolic social reality*, which consists of any form of symbolic expression of the world we live in. This type of social reality encompasses at least three important symbol systems: language, non-verbal communication and material objects (e.g., McCarthy, 1984), although language is usually treated as *the* symbolic system par excellence to the detriment of the other two (e.g., Rochberg-Halton, 1984; Solomon, 1983). Thirdly, there is *subjective social reality*, where both objective and symbolic worlds are internalized and represented in terms of each individual's awareness and understanding. Thus, by integrating the objective and symbolic aspects of material objects in their own representations, individuals come to regard their own and other people's possessions as symbols of identity. This can be represented in the form shown in Figure 4.1.

The following subsections first of all discuss the role of material artefacts in early objective reality construction. Subsequently, I con-

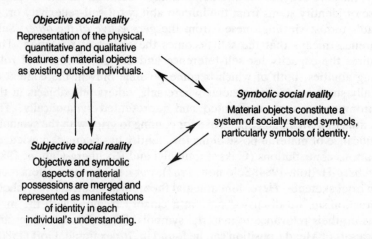

Figure 4.1 Material possessions in three types of social reality

sider how people may come to understand and socially share the symbolic meanings of material objects, particularly with reference to identity. Finally, and most importantly, the relationship between material symbols and identity as it emerges in subjective social reality is examined.

Material objects and early self-awareness

McCarthy (1984) argues that Mead had much to say about the relationship between people and their physical environment, but that this particular aspect of his work has been sorely neglected. She presents a Meadian account of early objective reality construction which deals with physical surroundings in general, but can also be used to lay a useful foundation for an understanding of the close association between people and their possessions. According to McCarthy (1984), infants' early exploration and dawning understanding of their physical surroundings constitute a crucial stage of development. In particular, she stresses the importance of early tactile contact with objects for the emergence of self-awareness. Exploration of physical artefacts is vital for the individual's recognition of boundaries, for coming to comprehend the 'landscape' of the environment. And that landscape includes the discovery of the bodily boundedness of self, and thus a rudimentary awareness of self. Furthermore, the infant enters into a social relation with the environment which establishes a lasting continuity between the individual and the object world.

This notion of a social relation is based on Mead's concept of *taking the perspective of the other*. He states that we 'must be others if we are to be ourselves' (1913, p. 276). Put simply, what he means by this statement is that becoming aware of ourselves depends on our capacity to imagine how we appear from the standpoint of others. But objects, too, can serve as imaginary points of view from which to see the self, initially because of their physical resistance and solidity. Feeling the boundaries of a physical object means having a *simultaneous* perspective: the sense of self touching the object and the object's rigidity against which the hand rests (Mead, 1934, pp. 182–4). In that sense, experiencing material objects and experiencing oneself are closely linked. The continuity between individuals and objects is thus seen as located in early self-perception from the *point of view* of the object.

A series of studies by Irwin and colleagues (Irwin *et al.*, 1943; Irwin and Gebhard, 1946) provides an interesting illustration of the fact that owning objects – as opposed to simply interacting with them – creates even more 'psychological nearness'. This nearness implies that self and possessions can be essentially fused. Their respondents, children and adults, always preferred objects they were given to keep, even when presented with the same object new, but not owned.

But early interactions with objects cannot, of course, be divorced from the social interactions in which the child engages, and in which the meanings of material objects and possessions are established and internalized. The continuity between self and objects which emerges in early tactile encounters is soon overlaid by a symbolic dimension. This means that the objective and symbolic reality of material possessions become progressively more interrelated.

The symbolic dimension of material objects

Mead stresses the supreme role of symbols and their socially shared meanings for the development of a sense of identity. As already indicated, this development is synonymous with coming to know ourselves through adopting the viewpoints of others. But how do we 'get inside' their perspective?

The first step in answering this question is to be found in the Meadian notion of significant symbols. A symbol is significant when it means approximately the same thing to its user and the perceiver. An obvious example is language, where the spoken word 'calls out the same response' in the speaker and listener. It is through the commonly shared meanings of symbols, such as language, that human beings are able to have a simultaneous perspective on how they are acting *and* on how this behaviour appears to and affects others. For instance, saying 'I am angry' means drawing on the shared meaning of that phrase, knowing how others view one as an angry person, and thus being able to think of oneself as an angry person. So it is through symbolic communication that we can become aware of ourselves, and develop and maintain an identity.

The meaning of any kind of symbol or object is neither intrinsic nor idiosyncratic, but social. Initially, meaning is inferred from observing the conduct of others towards an object. By imaginatively adopting their perspectives, an individual gradually comes to understand and thus internalize their 'attitudes' or, in other words, to learn the meaning of that particular symbol or object. This is not a process of simple imitation but involves making others' perspectives one's own.

Reference was made above to language as a means of symbolic communication, but Mead was aware that other forms of communication exist, such as that provided by the symbolic dimensions of material objects. A symbol is an entity that represents some other entity, and viewing material objects as symbols means focusing on their meanings beyond their tangible, physical characteristics. It is also clear that, for an object to function as a symbol, it must have a shared reality among people. Having a 'fashion' wrist-watch cannot be an effective symbol of being 'up to date' unless others in the relevant social reference group share the wearer's belief that the watch is, indeed, fashionable. The introductory chapter indicated a wide range of such symbolic meanings, including presents as tokens of friendship, goods which mark the passage of important events, such as birthdays or anniversaries, or objects which signify female and male spaces in the family home. Even the thrown away remnants of consumption goods – household refuse – have been examined in various 'garbage projects' as indicators of values, lifestyle and social stratification (see Hudson, 1984).

But it appears that examples of the symbolic dimension of material goods come most readily to mind with reference to the characteristics of people: their identity. Material objects can symbolically communicate the personal qualities of individuals; that they are, for instance, artistic, extroverted, conventional, adventurous or open-minded. They can also serve as signs of political values, group membership or broad social categories, such as class or gender. Therefore I suggest that material objects have socially shared, symbolic meanings through which a variety of identity aspects can be communicated. In part at least, people express who they are through their material symbols, and understand and judge who others are through the possessions these individuals own. But from what has been argued so far, it is clear that the meanings of material possessions with respect to the owner's identity must be *socially shared* in order to function as symbols.

Socially shared meaning systems

Drawing on the introductory chapter and the previous subsections in combination, it may be argued that part of the symbolic social reality we all share is constituted by a system of symbolic meanings of material possessions. A significant part of these meanings refers to various aspects of the owner's identity. Such meaning systems can be viewed as a kind of quasi-autonomous environment which informs individual thought and knowledge. But meaning systems, or socially shared representations,[2] are not static – they are continuously produced and reproduced during interactions between people. This symbolic environment *pre-dates* individuals and thus provides the *context* within which their subjective reality is constructed. This means that children develop their representations of society through social sources, such as family, school, friends and the mass media. Moreover, this process of subject-ively appropriating, reproducing and transforming socially shared meaning systems carries on throughout the lifespan. As a consequence, knowledge is inescapably social in nature.

Mead uses the term *generalized other* to refer to such collective, or socially shared, representations:

> The organized community or social group which gives to the individual his unity of self may be called the 'generalized other' . . . It is in the form of the generalized other . . . that the community exercises control over the conduct of its individual members; for it is in this form that the social process enters as a determining factor into the individual's thinking. (1934, pp. 154-5)

It may be argued that this statement carries two implications. On the one hand, it suggests that those groups of individuals who frequently share conversations and communications will also share representations of the world (which includes material objects), and that other groups of people may come to develop different representations. But, on the other hand, it also talks about the 'organized community' as a whole. Particularly in modern, technological societies like our own, the symbolic universe is informed by the mass media and widely shared beliefs (e.g., Adoni and Mane, 1984). As already discussed in the section on the social constructionist perspective, some sets of socially shared representations may be described as more dominant than others and could therefore be described as ideological in nature – which may be particularly relevant for material symbols of identity. In fact, a recent paper by Bouton (1984) criticizes work derived from a Meadian perspective for tending to concentrate on face-to-face interactions, and thus neglecting the importance of ideological, dominant representations for individual thought and belief systems.

The notion that material symbols may reflect dominant social arrangements appears in Kuper's (1973) work, for instance, which examined the role of clothes in colonial southeast Africa and demon-strated that they were used both as instruments of the hegemonic influence of the West and as indigenous attempts to resist that influence. McCracken (1990) presents a theoretical model in which the symbolic properties of consumer goods have three main locations: the culturally constituted world, consumer goods and individual consumers. Two planes of meaning transfer exist. The first one is good-to-individual, where consumers appropriate the meanings of material goods through various social rituals (see next section). But, more importantly here, the second plane, world-to-good, is one which reproduces dominant rep-resentations in the sense that designers, advertisers and other culture creators 'unhook' meanings and beliefs prevailing in the society in question and transfer them to inanimate objects through appropriate imagery.

The general processes through which cultural categories and principles are expressed in clothing, housing or art has been described by some anthropologists. They, too, analyse material symbols as a means of communication because of their expressive potential and features, but their theoretical starting point tends to be a more or less explicit analogy with language. For example, Bogatyrev's (1971) analysis of folk costumes in Moravian Slovakia reveals that their system of categorizing people by age is reflected in the costumes worn by each Moravian age group through differences in colouring, shape and so on. But it seems that the ease with which we speak of the *language* of clothing or the *language* of houses can be deceptive.

Overstretching the language metaphor

A good portion of structural, symbolic and semiotic anthropological analyses of material culture have assumed, as their theoretical foundation, that there is an essential similarity between language and inanimate objects. The strength of these contributions, inspired by the seminal work of Lévi-Strauss (1968), lies in emphasizing the symbolic properties of material goods. But there seem to be reasons for suspecting that the unreserved adoption of a linguistic model may be potentially misleading in terms of the nature and use of these symbolic properties. Put simply, structural linguistics is based on two main principles: the *selection* of speech units from particular categories of equivalent items and the *linear combination* of these units into systematic chains. At the level of single sounds or syllables, the speaker is relatively constrained in selection and combination by her or his language community, but at the level of sentences and longer utterances, there is greater expressive scope. In that sense, language is characterized by an 'ascending scale of freedom'. The greater the freedom in combinatorial activity, the more expressive and meaningful a speaker's message should become.

In order to examine whether material goods have communicative properties which follow this logic, McCracken (1990) carried out a series of studies on how observers interpret, or *decode*, clothing. He showed slides which portrayed individuals photographed in Vancouver city to respondents and carried out non-directive interviews, starting with the question: 'What can you tell me about this person on the basis of their clothing?'. The outfits shown fell roughly into three categories: 1. conventional, 2. outfits which combined conventional items of clothing not usually seen together (e.g., business suit jacket with casual trousers), and 3. fairly idiosyncratic or bizarre ensembles. For the first, conventional, clothing category, respondents answered instantaneously, using a fairly limited vocabulary of social types such as 'hippie', 'housewife' or 'businessman', sometimes qualified with adjectives like 'middle-class' or 'uneducated'. Slides in the second category, showing unusual combinations, were met with hesitation, careful study and complaints that the outfit 'does not really go together'. Typically, people would either concentrate on just one salient piece of clothing or invent some sort of explanatory account, trying to reconcile the contradictions they perceived in the clothing: 'Well, he wears that jacket because he used to be a businessman, but it doesn't fit with the pants and shoes because he's lost his job and is on the skids' (response quoted by McCracken, 1990, p. 65). The even more anomalous outfits in the third category also produced uncertainty, but after trying various interpretations, people would typically give up altogether, often with a comment that this person 'could be anybody' since they did not fit any prescribed look at all.

Extrapolating from these findings, McCracken (1990) outlines important differences between language and clothing as communicative devices. The more clothing elements were grouped into novel combinations, the less sense people were able to make of the resulting message. The meaning of apparel seems to be prefabricated: if an assortment of items violates what is usually thought to characterize particular social categories of people, it does not provide meaningful information to an onlooker. The rules of combination which govern language do not seem applicable to clothes, because heterogeneous items make interpretation difficult rather than offering a complex message created by combinatorial freedom. Clothes, and most probably other material symbols, *are* a collection of messages, not a means for the creation and combination of messages. Moreover, the 'linear discursive quality' of language was not echoed by respondents, as they did not describe separate clothing items in an additive way, but seemed to have formed a holistic picture of the whole clothing 'ensemble'.

McCracken's warning against overstretching the language metaphor ends with five tentative observations, which are reported here because they are likely to apply to other material possessions as well as to clothes and because they will be picked up again in the concluding chapter. They are as follows:

1. Material symbols are limited in the *number* and *range* of things they can communicate.
2. The messages they convey are less overt and interpretation may often not be conscious and deliberate.

3. The symbolic meanings of some objects may have different meanings for different social or cultural groups, rather than be understood at a societal level.
4. Material symbols circumvent *explicit* messages about stratification, but nevertheless depict and reinforce status, wealth and power differentials.
5. Material symbols allow for the *representation* of social categories and processes more than for their innovative manipulation, and thus form a *conservative code* which puts on display information that is not easily transformed.

Following on from these comments on some aspects of material symbols as socially shared representations, the next section is concerned with the development of the link between material objects and identity, and with how the symbolic significance of material possessions for identity comes to be represented in the subjective social reality of individuals.

The possessions–identity link

Early tactile contact with material objects plays a role in the development of self-awareness. Their objective reality is thus linked to a rudimentary sense of self. At the same time, we share a symbolic social reality in which material possessions are seen as symbols of identity. The previous subsections have laid some foundations for addressing the question of most interest in the present context: how does the early continuity between people and objects become overlaid by the symbolic significance of material possessions for identity in individuals' subjective awareness?

In Meadian terms, people gain a sense of identity through seeing themselves through the eyes of others:

> The individual experiences himself as such, not directly, but only indirectly, from the particular standpoints of other individual members of the same social group, or from the generalized standpoint of the social group as a whole to which he belongs. (Mead, 1934, p. 138)

However, identity is more than simply a passively internalized set of societal attitudes and prescriptions. This particular point has been hotly debated, with Mead being accused of social determinism (see, for example, Lichtman, 1970; Wrong, 1961). This may be due, at least in part, to misunderstandings resulting from his rather hazy distinction between two aspects of self or identity – the 'me' (internalized sets of attitudes) and the 'I' (some more spontaneous form of thought). A variety of contributions discuss the 'I' and the 'me' (e.g., Goff, 1980; Kolb, 1944; Ropers, 1973). Franks (1985) concludes:

> It is important to see the generalized other as the *creative emergent result* of the process of the 'I' and the 'me'. As such it refers to the actor's unique organization of a multiplicity of roles representing complex collectivities. (p. 51, emphasis added)

Put differently, this means that individual reality is a social product, but not a passive replica of beliefs and attitudes transmitted by socialization agents. Rather, it consists of a unique intersection of perspectives which are integrated and transformed during social interaction, but which nevertheless reflect 'the unity and structure of the social process as a whole' (Mead, 1934, p. 144).

The process of developing an identity is a gradual one, progressing in stages. Early on, a child can only adopt the perspective of a specific person with whom s/he interacts directly, and thus internalize the attitudes of that individual. Subsequently, the child is able to adopt the perspective of several specific others simultaneously and thus comes to see herself or himself from the viewpoint of, for example, her or his whole family or group of playmates all at once. Consequently, self-attitudes become more complex and integrated. But Mead speaks of a fully developed self only when particular attitudes of specific others towards the individual are generalized into an internalized set of representations of larger social units and society as a whole. All encountered and imaginatively taken attitudes are integrated into an impersonal unit – the *generalized other* – which serves as a basis for organizing thought and action independently of the physical presence of others.

I propose that this kind of process can equally be applied to the link between material possessions and identity. Initially, young children learn the range of meanings of material possessions through observing and imaginatively taking part in others' interactions with their possessions, or hearing comments about them. They do not only learn their functional uses, but also observe people acting towards others in terms of material symbols. For example, a mother may show her child a picture book and comment that the man who owns this beautiful, large house is very clever and successful. In this way, children may be introduced to the idea that possessions can provide information about the characteristics of the owner. But they will also experience that other people react to them in terms of the material possessions they have, such as their toys. Traditionally, a girl playing with her miniature dinner set may well hear comments from family or visitors about what a nice and generous young lady she is, serving (imaginary) cups of tea to everybody. A little boy with his plastic hammer and screwdriver may well be told how strong and skilled he is, just like his dad at work. It may therefore be argued that these toys can come to signify particular personal qualities and, in a rudimentary fashion, broader sets of values associated with social categories, such as traditional gender roles in these examples.

Through social interaction and communication, such as in the family and in peer groups, children may soon develop a more integrated and complex representation of their material objects as part of their identity. Their toys come to

> act as essential models for certain roles in the socialization process. A model rocket, doll house or video game can signify to a child certain values of the culture that can be personified and internalized through fantasy and play activities. (Rochberg-Halton, 1984, p. 338)

To give a simple example, as the little girl comes to understand what it means to be a mother through enacting this role with her dolls, the dolls become embodiments of the cultural meanings of motherhood: the social role of mother and the personal attributes of a mother. This, in fact, is the primary meaning of the term 'role model' for Mead, 'a representation of the community that becomes internalized as the generalized other' (Rochberg-Halton, 1984, p. 338), and not the much narrower notion of characteristic behavioural patterns of actual persons (see Reber, 1985, for a definition of role as usually accepted in psychology). Role models can be 'objectified' as much as 'personified'.

So personal possessions come to objectify aspects of self-definition. In the example of the girl given above, it was indicated how gender identity is developed and maintained, in part, through the symbolic meanings of material possessions. Another example might be the use of macho symbols by adolescent males (e.g., motorbikes, leather clothing) to bolster their developing masculine self-concept.

Willis's (1978) study of the 'motor-bike boys' provides a still valid, detailed insight into some of the qualities of these material objects, which rub off on the driver and make for a 'tough' male identity:

> Not only is the ontological security of the motor-bike boys demonstrated in their mastery of the motor-bike, but the qualities and function of the machine itself express their sense of concrete identity. . . . The motor-bike boys' style was masculine in more developed ways than the simply violent. . . . The motor-cycle gear both looked tough, with its leather, studs and denim, and by association with the motor-bike, took over some of the intimidating quality of the machine. (pp. 16, 20)

Within such a perspective on possessions as reflections of social categorizations such as gender, it is important not to overlook their symbolization of personal qualities and attributes. Other people respond to individuals in terms of the material objects that surround them. By simultaneously taking the perspectives of self and these others, individuals come to understand the meanings of their own possessions as parts of their identity. For instance, people may accord their neighbour respect on the basis of his expensive car, which he can then interpret for himself as a symbol of his status and social standing. If it is a streamlined, sporty car it may signify self-assuredness to others and, reflexively, to the owner, too. Feedback that individuals receive from reflecting on others' estimated appraisals leads to an affirmation of who they are at that point in time:

> The individual's reflexive evaluation of the meaning assigned by others to self is influenced by the material possessions with which the self is surrounded. The (real or imagined) appraisal by significant others is . . . incorporated into self-definition. (Solomon, 1983, p. 323)

During an individual's development of identity, this *triadic* nature of the identity–possessions link – self, other, object – is gradually extended beyond the reflected appraisals of specific others. With the emergence of a fully developed identity, reflexive evaluation in terms of possessions derives from a generalized set of internalized cultural meanings, transmitted not only in direct social interaction but also through social institutions, such as schools or the media. Identity is significantly affected by an evaluation of the total symbolic significance of one's own possessions. Instead of isolated artefacts with sharply delineated meanings, they form a sign-complex – a symbolic *Gestalt* – of identity (e.g., Belk, 1988; Rochberg-Halton, 1984; Solomon, 1983). Mead's reflexive evaluation construct implies that the process of incorporating others' appraisals of self in terms of material possessions can be viewed initially as a process in which others, and society as a whole, are the 'senders' of symbolic communication and the self the 'receiver' (cf. Solomon, 1983). Through the internalization of cultural meanings of material symbols, this process also comes to take place within the individual, in the sense that the *dyad* of sender and receiver may be one and the same person. Through interacting with, and reflecting upon, our material possessions, we evaluate ourselves on the basis of their symbolic meanings without requiring the physical presence of others. In other words, '[t]ransactions with cherished possessions are communicative dialogues with ourselves' (Rochberg-Halton, 1984, p. 347). This means that, in part, our sense of identity, our self-definitions, are established, maintained, reproduced and transformed in our relations with our possessions. In terms of the framework I have advanced, individuals can take the *perspective* of the objects they own to gain a view of themselves through the symbolic meanings of their possessions. But what has been argued so far also indicates that people can understand and evaluate others in terms of their material possessions. In this way, the identity of other people becomes visible in objectified form, too.

The bare essence of the framework I have just outlined is contained in brief and rudimentary form in the following, rather obscure, passage of Mead's writings (1934), provided that it is interpreted in the context of his work as a whole:

> It is possible for *inanimate* objects, no less than for other human
> organisms, to form parts of the generalized and organized – the
> completely socialized – other for any given human individual . . . Any
> thing – *any object or set of objects, whether animate or inanimate, human
> or animal, or merely physical* – towards which he acts, or to which he
> responds, socially, is an element in what for him is the generalized other;
> by taking the attitudes of which toward himself he becomes conscious of
> himself as an object or individual and thus develops a self or personality
> . . . and in this way . . . the environment becomes part of the total
> generalized other for each of the individual members of a given social
> group or community. (p. 154, emphases added)

What this also means is that establishing, expressing and transforming identity through material symbols is a process which continues throughout adolescence and adulthood. McCracken (1990) argues that people transfer the symbolic meanings of material goods to themselves by various social practices. He agrees that '[o]ne of the ways individuals satisfy the freedom and fulfil the responsibility of self-definition is through the systematic appropriation of the meaningful properties of goods' (McCracken, 1986, p. 90), and identifies four types of rituals in particular. The first one is exchange, in which gifts, for instance, are chosen because they possess symbolic qualities the giver wishes the recipient to have, or qualities they think reinforce the recipient's character. The presents given by parents to their children, such as cricket or baseball equipment selected by sports-enthusiastic fathers for their sons, are evocative examples. Another ritual is 'grooming', whereby the special attention given to pieces of clothing, for example, supercharges them as objects which can then give special heightened properties and significance to the 'dressed up' wearer. Because of the association between objects and owners' personal qualities, there are rituals aimed at erasing meanings of an object associated with its previous owner, such as cleaning and decorating houses or flats before moving in. Objects are usually depersonalized, emptied of meaning, before they are given away or sold, such as cars returned to near-perfect anonymity even for private sales.

People spend a good deal of time handling, comparing, discussing, thinking about or photographing their possessions, particularly newly acquired ones. Most people have to talk about and use their new stereo for a few days before it 'feels' theirs. Such practices can be viewed as an attempt to claim from those objects their symbolic properties: they personalize them. Saunders (1990) notes the time, effort and money that British home-owners lavish on 'improving' their houses or flats, and other authors argue that housing serves as a 'cultivator' of the self, as it is a vital source of memories, a place of get-togethers and traditions, and a shelter for those persons and objects which define the self (Cooper, 1976; Csikszentmihalyi and Rochberg-Halton, 1981; Kron, 1983). After holidays or other longer absences, people can be seen to 'reclaim' their home and the things within them, by touching and rearranging their personal possessions. In other words, it is these various acts of personalizing mostly anonymous, mass-produced material objects which turn them into personal possessions that symbolically reflect self and others.

A symbolic-communicational model of possessions and identity

The perspective on the link between material possessions and identity developed in this chapter is a *symbolic-communicational* one. It is through their symbolic meanings that material objects can communicate aspects of the owner's identity to self and to others. The notion that possessions serve as symbols of identity also implies that people's perceptions of social reality are partly structured in terms of material signs.

Of course, not all the meanings and functions of possessions are symbolic. They also serve purely *instrumental* purposes in terms of their functional uses and by helping people to exert direct control over their environment. Examples are tools or kitchen appliances. However, any simple instrumental–symbolic dichotomy would be misplaced, given that even functional, utilitarian aspects are also (at least potentially) symbolic and communicative. People with the latest labour-saving device may well think of themselves, and be seen by others, as capable, in control, and free to act in ways they want to and others may not be able to. Also on a practical level, possessions make possible a variety of activities. The activities themselves are self-explanatory – people can use their cars to drive to work, or to keep in touch with friends. But these *use-related* features combine functional and symbolic elements, in the sense that the car makes possible these activities, but also signifies the owner's freedom to engage in them. It can even come to stand as a symbol for work-related and social contacts. A similar argument can be put forward with respect to more emotionally toned aspects of possessions. Listening to different kinds of music makes hi-fi equipment a means for relaxation, comfort or mood change, but tapes and records can also become symbols of particular emotional states and experiences.

Of most interest for the concerns of this book is the fact that material objects serve as *symbolic expressions of who we are*. We all choose particular kinds of object to express something about ourselves, such as our clothes, the way we decorate and furnish our rooms or houses, the car we buy and so on. The symbolic functions of possessions can be further subdivided into categorical ones, which enable us to express our social standing, wealth or status. They signify the broad social categories we belong to (such as class or gender), as well as the smaller groups or subcultures we identify with. Self-expressive functions concern individuals' uniqueness and their attitudes, values and personal qualities. What we accumulate during our lifetime becomes a symbolic, yet concrete, collage of our personal history, and of our personal and social relationships. However, this distinction between the categorical and self-expressive meanings of material possessions is an analytical rather than an absolute one. For example, somebody's living-room furniture may symbolize their personal history as well as their class background. This range of meanings of possessions for identity can be laid out as a schematic model,[3] displayed in Figure 4.2.

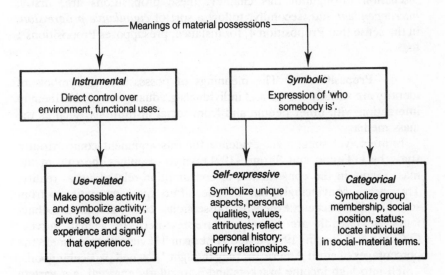

Figure 4.2 Meanings of material possessions for identity

In conclusion, to conceptualize material possessions as symbolic mediators of identity between self and others means two things. Firstly, from the perspective of individual owners, their possessions play a role as symbols for their own personal qualities as well as for their group memberships and general social standing. To an extent, both personal and social aspects of identity are confirmed, maintained and expressed through material symbols. But expression and maintenance of identity depend on the appraisals of others as well as on a more generalized perspective on one's self through societal meanings of possessions. Secondly, when people form impressions of others from an 'observer' perspective, they also draw on the symbolic meanings of possessions to make inferences about idiosyncratic, personal aspects of their identities and to locate them as belonging to particular social groups, categories and strata.

The earlier considerations of objective, symbolic and subjective social realities with respect to material symbols, and the model of their meanings outlined above, are an attempt to sketch a social constructionist perspective that is tailored towards possessions and identity. It does so by drawing on George Herbert Mead's symbolic interactionism, which is based on two main axioms: that a sense of identity is gained and maintained by viewing oneself 'through the eyes of others' (i.e., self-objectification) and that this is only possible in the context of socially shared symbol systems. This outline can be summarized in five tentative propositions, discussed in turn. As should have become clear in the discussion throughout this chapter, these propositions are, firstly, *interdependent* and, secondly, follow a sort of *cumulative progression*, in the sense that Proposition 4, for instance, presupposes Propositions 1 to 3.

Proposition 1: The meanings of possessions as symbols of identity are socially shared and individuals gradually internalize them in interaction with other people and from social institutions, such as the mass media.

Indirect, yet suggestive, evidence for this argument comes from a study by O'Guinn and Shrum (1991) which examines the role of the mass media in the construction of consumption-related social reality. They argue convincingly that TV life differs quite dramatically from social reality because expensive possessions, costly consumer behaviours and wealth are heavily overrepresented. In a mail survey, O'Guinn and Shrum (1991) asked American TV viewers to estimate the percentages of adult Americans they thought 1. owned particular goods, 2. fell into high income brackets and 3. regularly engaged in a variety of consumption behaviours. The more television people watched, the more they tended to overestimate all the above percentages. For example, hours of TV watching went hand in hand with overestimating the incidence of such overrepresented possessions as tennis courts, convertibles and car telephones, or overestimating the percentage of American adults who are millionaires. Therefore, the mass media appear to play a significant role in how individuals construct their own versions of consumption norms, no matter whether they are asked about income distributions, consumer behaviour or ownership of material goods.

Proposition 2:   Other people respond to an individual in terms of the material possessions that surround her or him. Thus, an individual's evaluation of meaning assigned by others to self is influenced by the possessions owned.

'Taken together our possessions add up to an integrated expression of ourselves' (Saunders, 1990, pp. 81-2), an argument echoed by the agreement respondents expressed with a self-extension scale (a mean of 5 on a 7-point scale) in a study on commonsense notions about possessions, comprising statements such as 'What a person possesses is a reflection of their personality', or 'Possessions give people a sense of identity' (Dittmar, 1989).

Proposition 3:   The implication of the first two propositions taken together is that a person comes to take the *perspective* of the objects they own to gain a view of *who they are* through the symbolic meanings of their possessions.

This symbolic-communicational approach questions the idea (still prevalent in common sense and much consumer research) that possessions are mere *responses*, in the sense that individuals choose a constellation of material symbols that is consistent with an already developed and static set of attitudes, values and beliefs. In contrast, it would appear that possessions are *active* components of identity in the sense that material symbols are involved in the maintenance, transformation and communication of identity (see also Solomon, 1983). In short, they are constitutive and integral parts of identity.

Proposition 4:   The identity of others is visible in objectified form, as well as one's own.

Other individuals are *placed* and *evaluated* in a social nexus in which possessions form a significant segment. The necessary corollary of the argument that reflexive self-evaluation is influenced by an appraisal of the symbolic significance of one's *own* possessions is that, to a degree, people base their impressions of others on the material objects they own – especially in the absence of other information. And this may be particularly pronounced in modern Western societies where many interpersonal contacts have become increasingly contractual and impersonal. Material goods are used to make inferences about others' identities – about their social class, lifestyle, occupation, personal qualities and values – because judging others in material terms fulfils an important function in orienting people in their social worlds so that they can anticipate what kind of interaction to enter into. In particular, because of our heavily stratified society, material possessions are used to *locate* others in a social-material hierarchy. Wallendorf and Arnould (1988) complement this point by referring to three social processes in which possessions play a profound role: differentiation from others, comparison with others and integration into social groups.

Proposition 5: Meanings of material objects are established through social processes. The socially constituted and socially shared meanings of possessions as symbols of identity reflect social power relationships.

In some ways this last proposition may be the most speculative, but it does find some support in anthropological research (e.g., Kuper, 1973). It can therefore be argued that, to a considerable extent, Western society is sustained by consumption, whereby material goods function as key instruments for the representation, reproduction and manipulation of culture, not only for individuals but for society and its institutions (cf. Cushman, 1990). This notion is discussed further in the concluding chapter.

These five propositions are not, of course, 'provable' by conclusive evidence, but the body of research discussed in this book, including the author's own empirical studies, does provide illustrative support. Apart from their plausibility, the most significant advantage this set of propositions offers is a change of focus towards questions which would not have been asked from other perspectives. The main question of the biological approach – 'Why do people possess?'- is embedded in a nature–nurture controversy which leaves little space for considering any social functions of possessions. And the main concern of the individual-centred approach – 'What functions do possessions fulfil for individuals?' – remains asocial in emphasis, too.

Concluding comments

An important implication of this social constructionist approach to possessions and identity is that the meanings of possessions will vary historically and socio-culturally. Their study thus needs to take account of specific contexts, and we should be wary of exporting our Anglo-

American and Western findings to other parts of the world (e.g., Wallendorf and Arnould, 1988). But the main preliminary conclusion to be drawn from this discussion is that a *domain-specific* theory of material possessions, i.e., a circumscribed theory concerned with material possessions *per se*, is neither a useful nor an achievable aim. Material symbols play a significant role in a variety of areas of self-definition and other-perception for which established social psychological theories exist. These include stereotypes, gender identity, person perception, social interaction and social categorization. They offer fertile ground for application to the possessions–identity link, and some empirical results of initial undertakings in this direction by the author are presented in Chapters 6 and 7. Rather than specific 'miniature' theories, the social constructionist approach hopes to present a *meta-theoretical framework* within which material context is considered an important influence on various areas of everyday understanding.

What is needed is further work to transcend the microcosmic perspective and the use of predominantly individualistic forms of methodology of the earlier work in psychology, in order to consider larger social and cultural aspects, and to examine systems and contexts of material possessions and goods. In his critique of conventional market research, McCracken (1990) terms this a necessary 'Dürk-heimian shift' towards considering 'collective representations', which deal with 'supra-individual characteristics of consumption'.

If it were addressing Erich Fromm's question *To Have or To Be?*, the answer provided by this chapter would be that, in many important respects, to have *is* to be. If we accept for a minute the proposal that material objects play such a profound role in reflecting and shaping our social world, the question arises of whether we are dealing with the maligned devil of materialism here, and so should view the role of material symbols in an entirely negative light. As argued earlier, they can be seen as vital means of individual and collective self-definition and therefore have positive aspects, namely that they create and maintain socio-cultural order. Moreover, Kron (1983) suggests that identities 'flicker and fade' in our multifaceted, industrialized society where everybody assumes a multitude of temporary and changeable roles. Due to their concreteness and physical stability, belongings may thus have come to be important self-reinforcers in almost a literal sense: they keep people from feeling disoriented, counteract a sense of *fragmentation* of self and provide historical continuity (see also Cushman, 1990). But, on the negative side, we now have *consumption pathologies* as misplaced pursuits of success and happiness (cf. Nataraajan and Goff, 1991). Moreover, if the symbolic meanings of possessions reinforce the cultural order, they must also reproduce social constraints. The transmission of traditional gender roles via toys is a pertinent example. The even broader question of whether material possessions can possibly deliver the means for *satisfactory* self-expression and *healthy* socio-psychological development remains controversial, and any attempt at an answer is beyond the scope of this book. But some of the issues just sketched are picked up in the subsequent chapter, which reviews research more directly concerned with material possessions as symbols for identity.

Notes

1. The overall mean was 3 on a 7-point agreement scale. These findings are part of the study on beliefs about possessions already introduced in Chapter 3.
2. The term 'socially shared representation' is employed throughout this book rather than 'social representation' in order to indicate that the approach adopted here is not directly derived from Moscovici's social representations model (e.g., 1981, 1984, 1988), although it shares the latter's concern with socially constituted and reproduced meaning systems. The exact definition of a social representation as well as the theoretical novelty and credibility of Moscovici's approach have been the bone of some contention (e.g., Harré, 1984; Jahoda, 1988; McKinlay and Potter, 1987; Potter and Litton, 1985). But a substantial portion of this bone appears to revolve around the question of whether any set of commonsense beliefs constitutes a social representation or whether the term should be interpreted in a more specific sense as the commonsense translation of scientific knowledge (Billig, 1988). Moscovici describes two processes by which social representations are generated. The process of *anchoring* refers to the understanding of novel aspects of social reality in terms of already existing meaning systems and could thus be said to characterize commonsense notions in general. But *objectification* describes the translation of abstract notions, such as the Freudian super-ego, into concretely perceivable entities. Billig (1988) argues that *objectification* appears to apply predominantly to the translation of scientific concepts into notions used in everyday conversations. For this reason, he argues, it may be the case that the study of social representations is best applied in the context of lay conceptions of scientific formulations (Billig, 1988). Shared meanings of material symbols do not seem to fall under this heading.
3. This figure was published in a slightly modified form in Dittmar, 1991b.

5

Possessions as symbolic expressions of identity

The bulk of earlier studies concerned with possessions from what can broadly be termed a psychological angle is primarily concerned with the *intra-individual* and *interpersonal* functions material possessions fulfil (as we saw in Chapter 3). In contrast, some recent investigations have begun, directly or indirectly, to examine whether material objects form part of the owner's extended self by constituting symbols for personal and social aspects of identity. The theoretical approach adopted in this book – outlined in the previous chapter – explicitly conceptualizes possessions as symbols of identity by viewing their meanings as socially constituted. Evidence which supports the proposition that possessions function as self-extensions because they symbolize aspects of our identity can be drawn from such diverse fields as sociology, abnormal and social psychology, criminology, gerontology, anthropology and consumer research.

The main argument of the previous chapter has been the contention that not only do possessions fulfil instrumental and utilitarian functions, but their symbolic dimensions also have important implications for the personal and social identity of their owners. Lévi-Strauss emphasized a quarter of a century ago that 'goods are not only economic commodities but vehicles and instruments for realities of another order: influence, power, sympathy, status, emotion' (1965, p. 76). Possessions can provide actual and perceived control and mastery, a source of comfort and emotional adjustment, a concrete record of our achievements, past experiences or future goals, and a reminder of our relationships with others. The notion of socially shared representations about material objects as symbolic manifestations of identity means that people express who they are through material possessions, both to themselves and to

others. It also means that we make inferences about others on the basis
of their possessions.

This chapter discusses the rather disjointed empirical work which is
either directly concerned with material objects as symbols of identity, or
relevant in other ways to a symbolic-communicational account of
possessions. It is concerned exclusively with the expression and maintenance of our own identity. The rather sparse literature relevant to how
people form impressions about the *identity of others* from material
surroundings is considered in the next chapter.

Status symbols

A clear expression of one's position in society's social-material hierarchy is material possessions which serve as status symbols, an area
usually investigated by sociologists. Inspired by Veblen's (1899) seminal
essay on conspicuous and wasteful consumption of time and goods as an
expression and marker of high social status, Chapin (1928, 1959/1935)
constructed a measure for a family's social class based on an inventory
of their living-room interior, which proved reliable and valid. Laumann
and House (1970) investigated living-room styles in relation to various
social attributes and found that they expressed not only a household's
socio-economic status (SES) and income, but also goals such as upward
mobility, and beliefs concerning religion, party political preference and
sex-role characteristics. In this sense, '[o]ne's position in the social order
is an integral part of who one is, thus the signs of status are important
ingredients of the self' (Csikszentmihalyi and Rochberg-Halton, 1981,
p. 17). Goffman (1951) offers a theoretical analysis of status symbols
and argues that they carry *categorical* significance which identifies the
social position of the owner, but also *expressive* significance for the
owner's style of life and personal and cultural values. Sociologists
further imply that status symbols serve to maintain social order (and the
status quo) by supporting and making visible hierarchical differentiation
and stratification among people.

Old symbols for class status are discarded once they fail to differentiate between class backgrounds, and Blumberg (1974) actually traces
changes in objects which cease to serve as status symbols, once they
come to be shared too widely to denote exclusiveness. For example,
whereas 'once a television was a symbol of affluence, now its near
saturation makes its absence a sign of poverty' (Lunt and Livingstone,
1991, p. 1). Blumberg (1974) also argues that the informative significance of traditional status symbols has declined over the last decades,
due to greater abundance of, and access to, material goods. Dellinger

(1977) even talks about a 'status pandemonium' because status symbols now become obsolete and are replaced at a truly remarkable pace. It has become harder than ever to 'keep tabs on the Joneses'. In a similar vein, Felson (1978) claimed to have demonstrated empirically that social class judgments based on car, residential area and dress are no longer consensual. But relevant discussions (e.g., Belk, 1978; Holman, 1981; Sirgy, 1982) indicate that his research was flawed methodologically. Moreover, the argument that *certain* material possessions may no longer serve as strong symbols for social status does not imply that consensual beliefs about others' possessions based on their social-material position no longer exist.

With respect to the processes which may underlie changes in status symbols, the German sociologist Simmel was one of the first to formulate a 'trickle-down' theory of changing fashions at the turn of this century which, by implication, also applies to other material symbols (cf. Frisby, 1984). Low-status, yet aspiring, social groups imitate and adopt the status symbols of those groups slightly more affluent than they are and, as a consequence, these markers are discarded and new ones adopted by higher-status groups to differentiate themselves, and so on. So status symbols move 'downwards' from well-off to increasingly lower-status groups; on the other hand, it has been recognized fairly recently that social groups are also constantly engaged in 'upwards' selection of new status symbols (e.g., Blumberg, 1974). Modern critiques of the 'trickle-down' approach emphasize that formerly elitist fashion has been supplanted by an advertising-driven mass fashion, which simultaneously informs social groups at all levels of the social-material hierarchy (e.g., Solomon, 1985). However, it seems that by taking additional demographic boundaries into account, such as gender or ethnicity, 'trickle-down' as well as 'trickle-up' phenomena can still be observed (e.g., McCracken, 1990).

It can be concluded that certain material possessions, individually and in combination, express an individual's social standing. This implies that they serve a *locatory* function, and a more substantial body of research has focused on how we make judgments about the social standing of others on the basis of material symbols (addressed in Chapter 7).

Gift-giving: accepting and imposing identities

Lévi-Strauss (1965) is concerned with material objects as symbols of status, power and influence, too, but he draws particular attention to the 'skilful game of exchange' of objects, particularly gifts, as a 'complex totality of maneuvers, conscious or unconscious, in order to gain security and to fortify one's self against risks incurred through alliances and rivalry' (p. 76). Status and achievement gifts can be regarded as concrete symbols, or objectifications, of past and present social relationships. A related example, particularly pertinent for English culture, is the custom of displaying one's Christmas cards on the mantelpiece and of draping the excess over pieces of string spanning the living-room. Incredible sums are spent each year on buying and sending Christmas cards, and the ones received are often counted, coveted and proudly shown to visitors as the tangible, visible manifestation of the strength and size of one's social network of family, friends and acquaintances. Schwartz (1967) put it succinctly: 'The presentation of self, then, is often made with symbols of one's connections to others' (p. 8).

Schwartz (1967) proposes that the giving of gifts involves more than its significance as a token or symbol of the relationship between two or more people. Rather the presentation of a gift can be likened to an *imposition of an identity*, in the sense that not only is it one of the ways by which we announce and transmit the image we have of somebody, but also we publicly define ourselves in our choice of present. Accepting a gift is in a sense an acceptance of the giver's ideas about what we want and need – an identity. With respect to clothing, McCracken (1986) remarks that

> the woman who receives a particular kind of dress is also made the recipient of a particular concept of herself as a woman. The dress contains this concept and the giver invites the recipient to define herself in its terms. (p. 78)

Therefore, to reject a gift means to reject the giver's definition of yourself and her or his conception of the relationship s/he has with you, which may be a major reason why being handed back a refused gift is experienced as so hurtful. In short, the symbolic properties of gifts exchanged involve the acceptance, negotiation and imposition of different identities.

Consumer goods revisited

During most of our waking hours we are bombarded with all kinds of advert for consumer goods. The images used lure us with the promise that we will become a different person – successful, exciting, stunningly attractive, socially well placed – if only we start to use product X. It is in the area of consumption that the significance of the symbolic functions of possessions has been spelt out most clearly (e.g., Holman, 1983). Levy's (1959) early article draws attention to the self-referent meanings of products which serve as symbols for personal qualities, attitudes and values on the one hand, and as markers for social affiliations and position on the other. This analytical distinction between the *expressive* and *categorical* significance of possessions can also be found in Stone's (1962) social psychological investigation on dress, and echoes that which is drawn in Goffman's (1951) writings on status symbols.

There is suggestive evidence that the symbolic dimensions of consumer products are recognized at the surprisingly early age of around 5 or 6 years, and that they are fully understood by the time children reach 10 or 11 years (e.g., Belk *et al.*, 1982). The symbolic or *significative* properties of products have been investigated empirically in quite a number of consumer research studies which produced some illuminating findings. However, their emphasis on implications for purchase behaviour and marketing strategies have tended to limit severely their theoretical relevance for an analytical treatment of the role of possessions in everyday social life (see also Solomon, 1983).

As we saw in Chapter 3, early market research focused on purchase decisions as reflections of 'objectively' existing personality traits, but failed to find convincing empirical support. A first breakthrough occurred with the introduction of *image*, as a summary of qualities which apply to a product, but which can also form part of a consumer's self-concept. By comparing product-images with images of self, increasingly sophisticated analyses of the congruity between object-perception and self-perception emerged, although this work still tends to concentrate on single objects or brands, and seems to treat 'product-images' unproblematically as interpretations made by individual consumers.

However, neither self-images nor product-images have individualistically defined meanings, but are clearly subject to social influences. For example, Grubb and Hupp (1968) showed that consumers try to match their self-image with the image of a *typical* user of a product. This finding indicates the existence of product user stereotypes. Several studies investigate a kind of looking glass measure of self which focuses on people's concern with how they think they are being perceived by others, given their particular product choices (e.g., Munson and Spivey, 1980). The relationship between self-image and brand-image also appears to be related to broad social dimensions, such as gender. For example, Orpen and Low (1973) found that the more masculine an individual's self-image, the more masculine the image of their most liked cigarette brand and type of car. A recent review of market research on women's portrayal in advertising concludes that, for an advert to be effective, the gender of the model should match the image of the product, its environment and the product's benefits, as perceived by consumers (Whipple and Courtney, 1985).

A smaller number of consumer studies addresses the expression of group affiliations and social standing through material possessions. Investigations on how self and social reference groups are perceived in terms of products (e.g., Sommers, 1964; Sommers and Bruce, 1969) show that members of one social stratum describe themselves and their reference group in similar product-anchored terms, and depict members of other social groups in terms of rather different product profiles. Cocanougher and Bruce (1971) report that aspirations towards certain reference groups are expressed by choosing goods for oneself which are congruent with those selected by typical reference group members. Concentrating on different social and political spheres, Buckley and Roach (1974), Cassell (1974) and Holman (1980) illustrate that dress also serves as an expression of group membership.

But even the more social orientation of the investigations just mentioned is still a far cry from recent arguments that consumer research has to be seen as situated within its Western context (e.g., Engel, 1985) and, moreover, needs to develop a broader theoretical framework which allows an analysis of product symbolism as a *socially shared reality*, with profound implications for all aspects of consumer behaviour (e.g., Belk, 1988; McCracken, 1985, 1990; Solomon, 1983). An example of the move in this direction that is beginning is Hirschman's (1980) research, which examines the commonsense meanings and symbolic properties of four types of consumer goods: transport, food, clothes and entertainment. Giving her respondents labels of goods at different levels of abstraction – such as food, meat, hamburger, McDonald's hamburger – she simply asked them to free-associate in response to each label. Although she found a fair degree of idiosyncratic meanings at all levels of abstraction, about 50 per cent of the most frequently given associations were shared, implying a stock of socially shared images and ideas about material goods. Her findings indicate a continuum from individual to increasingly consensual meanings of goods: idiosyncratic, subcultural, cultural and tangible (i.e. physical) attributes.

The work by Belk (e.g., 1984b, 1987, 1988, 1991), McCracken (1986, 1990) and Solomon (e.g., 1983, 1985) is probably the most prominent which evidences a *rapprochement* between consumer research and perspectives of other disciplines, such as psychology, sociology or anthropology. The following four features characterize these latest developments, which allow for the study of material goods in a broader social and cultural context (cf. McCracken, 1990; Solomon, 1983). Firstly, they widen the traditional definition of consumer behaviour as 'purchase behaviour' to a beginning consideration of all the interaction between consumer and goods, before and after purchase. Secondly, they have departed from the long-standing preoccupation with decision-making processes about what and when to buy, by examining, for instance, the symbolic and emotional aspects of products. Thirdly, in terms of the methods they employ, they start to move beyond the individualistic and narrow focus inherited from psychology to consider social and cultural aspects of consumption. Finally, the import and legitimacy of studying topics not directly relevant for marketing concerns is acknowledged.

What is starting to emerge in some quarters of consumer research is a much broader perspective on material goods as symbolic means for defining self and the social world, which makes a consideration of market research under a separate heading increasingly implausible. For this reason, further relevant contributions are considered in the remainder of this chapter in terms of the specific topics they address.

Symbolic self-completion

The notion that material symbols help to establish an identity led Wicklund and Gollwitzer (1980, 1982, 1985) to propose that people employ material possessions, among other strategies, to compensate for perceived inadequacies in their concepts of self: they engage in 'symbolic self-completion'. Material symbols have identity-creating and identity-enhancing features because of their communicative power:

> Symbols of completion are all indicators of achieving a goal which is important for the self of individuals . . . [who] can increase the social reality of their symbols by making sure that they are noticed by other people . . . Positive self-description therefore produces a feeling of being complete to the extent to which it can be communicated to other people. (Wicklund and Gollwitzer, 1985, p. 59, my translation from German original)

They demonstrated empirically that business students who had a weak symbolic basis for a business career, in the sense that they lacked good qualifications, for instance, tended to display more relevant symbols, such as an expensive watch, briefcase or business suit, than students with better career prospects. In other words, if people doubt particular aspects of their identity, they will tend to display more relevant material symbols in order not only to enhance those aspects for themselves, but also to communicate them to others.

A later series of studies reported by Braun and Wicklund (1989) examines the assumption that a compensatory relationship exists between lack of experience, expertise or competence in occupational, domestic or ideological identity domains on the one hand, and increased use of material symbols of those particular aspects of identity on the other. They showed that law students attached more importance to the outer manifestations of their professional identity (car, clothing, etc.) than practising attorneys, and that first-year students reported buying more university-related attire and accessories than students further advanced in their studies. Laying claim to relevant material symbols is explained for both junior groups by insecurity in their identities. However, symbolic self-completion presupposes that people have a personal commitment to particular identity domains, an issue not addressed in these studies. A further four investigations with students studying different subjects and tennis players, in which commitment was measured rather than assumed, showed that the compensatory relationship between recent entry into an identity and increased use of material symbols held only for those people who were committed to their career or sport.

All of these studies are intriguing, but do not seem to substantiate fully the theoretical framework of symbolic self-completion as outlined by Wicklund and Gollwitzer (1982, 1985). The definition, or rather operationalization, of 'identity deficit' is not entirely clear. In the research described, it was not ascertained either directly or indirectly whether respondents (or their peers) actually felt that their identity was either complete or lacking in some respects. This allows for the alternative explanations that the law students, first-year students, and so on, made more use of material symbols either because of peer pressure, or because of their preconceived notions about what 'belongs' to a certain identity, which later on they did not find substantiated. These explanations do not contradict a broad notion of self-completion, but rather than presupposing a particular intra-psychic state of incompleteness, they focus on social motivations and pressures to conform. A related, and as yet unresolved, question revolves around the extent to which material symbols need to be displayed publicly, and appreciated by other people, for any self-completion to work. Wicklund and Gollwitzer (1985) seem to imply that self-completion is an intra-individual, cognitive process, for which social mediation is only relevant to the extent that people select those material symbols which are consensually recognized as significant for the identity they want to convey. Their assertion that we are not concerned with the opinions and appraisals of others *while* we engage in self-symbolic actions sits uneasily with their premise that self-enhancement occurs only if the desired image is communicated to others. This ambiguity could potentially be resolved by conceiving of self-completion as a thoroughly social process which dissolves an artificial public–private dichotomy, namely as a kind of dialogue with self and others via the symbolic properties of material objects.

A recent experimental study has taken a slightly different and more narrowly focused approach to self-completion (Beggan, 1991b). Here the motivation to have control was seen as a self-defining personal quality. Experimentally induced lack of control should therefore lead individuals to compensate with their possessions, if given that option. This relationship should be tempered by locus of control beliefs, i.e., beliefs about whether or not we *actually have* control over ourselves and our environment. Beggan's (1991b) findings were quite complex, but essentially he showed that 'control deprivation' led those who believed they usually had control over their lives (internals) to compensate by overemphasizing the extent to which they judged their possessions to give them control, and make them efficient and well-adjusted people. In contrast to the work discussed above, Beggan (1991b) has opened the arena for considering a whole array of possessions as symbolic manifestations of the owner's personal qualities, rather than particular items signifying occupational or other group identities.

If some form of symbolic self-completion is a frequent motivational force underlying possessive or consumer behaviour, a rather important issue not addressed so far in this area is whether or not it is successful or, at least, is perceived to be so by those who engage in it. However, this question has been posed and addressed in a much more general way, outside the self-completion framework outlined above. If material goods supply people with the materials with which to concretize their ideas of what it means to be middle-class, an academic, a woman, a radical or a punk, then people are engaged in a much broader fashion than suggested above in long-ranging projects to complete their selves symbolically and compensate for perceived inadequacies (see also Gronmo, 1984).

It is then possible to ask whether acquiring material goods, and particularly those possessions we have wanted for a long time, does make us feel more positive about ourselves or the world. Alternatively, the question has been posed as to whether a strong commitment to material things is linked with life satisfaction, either positively or negatively.

Is enough ever enough?

A cross-cultural study in the United States and Niger on the meanings of favourite possessions addressed the question of whether objects fill the void of alienation from other people, but found that possessiveness is not a substitute for a lack of personal relationships. On the contrary, they found in both societies that those people who had a strong and meaningful attachment to a favourite object were also those who had more social contact points and a better social network (Wallendorf and Arnould, 1988). It appears that at least highly treasured possessions may serve to represent meaningful social ties rather than their absence (see also Csikszentmihalyi and Rochberg-Halton, 1981).

Focusing on material possessions in general rather than on single treasured items, other theorists view the ways in which we are attached to material goods in a much more critical light. On the one hand, material objects play an important role in giving people a means firstly to symbolize ideals and hopes and, secondly, to move closer towards them by acquiring them as possessions. But, on the other hand, while those symbols of values, hopes and future goals may help to explain the irrational and fetishistic ways in which some people are attached to their material objects, these symbolic aspects may also shed some light on why so many people never appear to reach a state where their possessions are sufficient. They continue to acquire and consume in endless progression, as if ruled by the maxim: 'I shop, therefore I am'.

In an attempt to offer an explanation for the fact that enough never appears to be enough, McCracken (1990) refers to the concept of *displaced ideal*. Personal ideals, such as happiness or good relationships with others, and political ideals like true democracy or collective property are often removed from daily reality to a different place and time, such as an earlier golden age, a different society or to a promising future, or to 'ideal' people, such as film stars or political personalities. Material goods, in particular, serve as bridges to these displaced ideals. Before one buys new possessions, there is the anticipation that they will provide access to certain ideal circumstances that at the time still exist in the dim distance. For example, the 'rose-covered cottage' is not just an ideal house to live in, but comes with a whole set of relationships and circumstances that go with having it: high income level, a desirable partner, social contacts, certain domestic arrangements, a more active outdoor life, and so on. Once we actually buy a possession long wanted, we often only acquire a small, anticipatory part of the bridge, a tiny, concretized piece of the way of life we really aspire to. Thus, the larger configuration of the ideal way of life remains intact, even if buying what we wanted turns out to be a disappointment. The ideal is not abandoned or judged unrealistic because of our disappointment but, instead, what follows is a successive series of transfers of ideals and hopes to other, increasingly more expensive, sets of goods and objects. Advertising quite obviously fuels this 'consumption appetite', which is considered vital for a thriving economy.

Various aspects of material objects make them especially suitable for this symbolic pursuit of ideals. Because material possessions are concrete and enduring symbols, the very property of concreteness seems to pass from the object to the ideal in question: 'concrete signs help encourage the fiction that the intangibles for which they stand are indeed substantial and that they can be possessed concretely' (McCracken, 1990, p. 114). Goods represent an ideal in a part-for-whole manner and are similar to ideals because they are also desirable, yet difficult to obtain (albeit financially). Moreover, the variety and abundance of material goods means that the possibilities for movement up from one consumption level to the next are fairly extensive. At the upper levels, collecting what is scarce, unique and costly, such as original artwork, may require more than simple purchasing power, but it is still one of the solutions of the very rich for extending the consumption ladder (see also Formanek, 1991; Olmsted, 1991).

Some of these theoretical notions have been examined empirically by Richins (1991), who carried out research on materialism and materialists. For her, the construct of materialism has three central, interrelated themes:

1. Acquisition centrality: possessions and their acquisition are placed at the centre of one's life.
2. Acquisition as the pursuit of happiness: possessions are viewed as essential to satisfaction and well-being.
3. Possession-defined success: materialists tend to judge their own success and that of others by the number and quality of possessions accumulated.

She developed a materialism scale[1] to address the following question: does having more 'things' actually lead to happiness or improved well-being? On the positive side, possessions offer subsistence and survival, they aid the definition of self, labour-saving devices ease the burdens of everyday life and leisure objects help us to enjoy ourselves. At the opposite end of the spectrum, despite the hopes and wishes we attach to getting more possessions, we may be doomed to discontent because acquisition goals shift and rise endlessly, and because truly important satisfactions come from self-development and interpersonal relationships instead (see also Cushman, 1990). This latter, negative argument finds support in a series of studies (reported in Fournier and Richins, 1991; Richins, 1991). Negative correlations emerged between a highly materialistic outlook and general life-satisfaction. When studying the positive and negative emotions that accompany specific acquisitions and purchases, no differences were found between people who are high and low in materialism for the positive ones, such as happy or excited. However, materialists experience more negative emotions after having bought something, such as anger, anxiety, guilt or fear:

Because consumption is so important to them [materialists], they may
have higher expectations for what a new possession will accomplish in
their lives. With higher expectations, the chances for disappointment
increase, and indeed disappointment was greater among those high in
materialism. (Richins, 1991, p. 8)

A further study in this series examined the expectations people hold
about what new possessions will bring them. Materialists' strongest
expectations concern the increased fun and enjoyment they would have
in life if they owned more possessions. But they also believe that they
would feel differently about themselves: more successful, independent
and self-confident. On the social level, they expect that desired
possessions would improve their family life and that they would have
better relationships with others generally. Extending the concept of
commodity fetishism (Marx, 1930/1878), it seems reasonable to argue
that consumers assign possessions almost magical and fairly unrealistic
powers.

What has been argued so far leads to an interesting question: what
would happen to us if our material dreams could suddenly be purchased
wholesale and in full? There does not appear to be empirical research on
this question, but anecdotal evidence depicts rather disillusioned individuals, such as a woman who had gained sudden wealth through a lottery
win and thus could put all her ideals associated with acquiring the right
'things' to the test. She complained bitterly that a 'lot of fun is taken out
of life when you just go out and buy whatever you want' and that this
experience did not measure up at all to her joyful anticipation (cf.
McCracken, 1990). Ross (1991a, b) makes two related points, based on
his work as a clinical psychologist. Prestige, power and fame, other
people, even our knowledge, experiences and identities are constructs
which people often view as possessable. They have become 'things' that
can be accumulated in the same way one accumulates material possessions, with the belief that our lives are enhanced in proportion to what
we gather around us. Collecting non-material and material assets is
equated with self-development and personal fulfilment, which Ross
(1991a, b) views as his clients' ultimately doomed search for happiness
and an important cause of their separation from self-understanding,
resulting in anxiety and fear of loss:

Therefore, it is natural that people, accustomed to the notion of
quantifying and possessing virtually everything around them, even
unpossessable qualities and feelings, look to the acquisition of material
objects as a means of personal fulfilment. (1991b, p. 7)

The central idea in these contributions, namely that a good deal of
the motivation to acquire possessions is fuelled by an ill-fated attempt to

obtain qualities and lifestyles these objects express symbolically, can also be used to look at strange and compulsive acts of consumption. An example of the increasing concern with consumption pathologies is work on compulsive buying, with which people try temporarily to allay their feelings of frustration, lack of control and emotional emptiness (e.g., O'Guinn and Faber, 1989; see also Nataraajan and Goff, 1991). Even food consumption compulsions, more commonly referred to as eating disorders, can be conceptualized as the maladaptive pursuit of identity and the ideals of control and success (e.g., Dittmar and Bates, 1987). Moreover, the message that (controlled) food intake is intimately linked with success, beauty and control is fostered in TV advertising, particularly as perceived by women already troubled by eating problems (Blayney and Dittmar, 1991).

This section has concentrated on the overwhelmingly negative aspects of *expectations* about pursuing happiness, success and personal fulfilment through acquiring material symbols. The following sections are concerned with the *actual* effects of owning or not owning personal possessions on various aspects of identity, after some initial comments about pets.

Pets as self-extensions

For the sake of completeness and as an interesting sideline, the literature on pet ownership deserves a brief mention, although it is only partly relevant to the present concern with material, inanimate objects. But like possessions, pets also appear to be regarded as parts of the extended self (e.g., Levinson, 1972; see Belk, 1988, for a recent review of this literature from a self-extension perspective). In the series of studies (reported in Chapter 6) which asked people to list their five most important possessions, around 5–8 per cent of responses referred spontaneously to dogs, cats, goldfish and a host of other pets. Davis (1987) considered the relationship between having pets and the self-development of young adolescents, and concluded that the family dog plays a role similar to that of a best friend by being a source of reflected appraisal, i.e., an influence on how these adolescents thought they were viewed by others.

Most of the work on pet ownership, however, is more narrowly concerned with its psychological advantages or drawbacks. Some studies conclude that owning pets is psychologically beneficial because they are a source of unconditional affection and provide a sense of responsibility. Hyde *et al.*, (1983) compared young adults who did and did not own pets on a variety of self-related measures and found that pet owners scored higher on social sensitivity and interpersonal trust. Covert *et al.* (1985) discovered a positive relationship between self-esteem and owning pets. In contrast, two older studies argue that pet owners are less psychologically healthy than non-owners (Cameron *et al.*, 1966; Cameron and Mattson, 1972). They contend that pets can be used as maladaptive substitutes for personal relationships, given the societal myth of pets as perfect interaction partners, which may be detrimental to people forming effective social relationships. In terms of the role pets may play for the physical and psychological health of elderly people, Kidd and Feldmann (1981) found that pet owners were more self-confident and personally adjusted than non-owners, whereas two more recent American studies failed to find consistent relationships between having pets and psychological or physical well-being (Lawton *et al.*, 1984; Miller and Lago, 1990).

From a directly clinical angle, Levinson (1962) hailed the 'dog as co-therapist'. In a more theoretical vein, Rochberg-Halton (1985) has developed a social psychological model of the therapeutic value of pets in a study of psychiatrically disturbed adolescents engaged in voluntary work in 'Treehouse', a rescue home for cats. He analyses their interactions with the cats as a form of emotional dialogue with the self, which can resolve personal problems and provide a source of self-development. For example, one of the adolescents who was suffering from being rejected by her family chose to care for a cat which showed clear approach-avoidance behaviour, and therefore seemed to be an appropriate reflection of her own actions. On this basis, the issues of attachment and rejection could be usefully discussed in a therapeutic session.

Without intending to overstretch the similarities between pets and material possessions, it appears that people regard their animals as a part and a mirror of themselves, and in that sense they engage in a dialogue with themselves when interacting with their pets. This process is reminiscent of possessions symbolizing aspects of self.

Life in institutions

Goffman's seminal analysis of institutions such as prisons and mental hospitals (1961, 1968) offers a vivid account of the identity-maintaining features of personal possessions. He sharply criticizes the admission procedures used by such institutions because they take away most of the previous basis of people's self-identification. Although institutional principles have started to change quite dramatically, particularly in the psychiatric field, the procedures of being stripped of all personal belongings and issued with a 'uniform' are still not uncommon. Goffman argues not only that they are humiliating, but also that they deprive inmates of their 'identity kit', which includes clothing, make-up and other personal possessions: 'the boundary that the individual places between his being and the environment is invaded and the *embodiments* of self profaned' (1968, p. 271, emphasis in original). Here we find a clear statement that personal possessions are symbolic *constituents* of identity and are important for the maintenance of the owner's psychological integrity.

Similar conclusions can be found in empirical studies on the role that personal possessions fulfil for elderly, mentally retarded and psychiatric patients. Carroll's (1968) study on 'junk' collections among mentally retarded patients states that they derived a sense of personal worth as well as social status in the ward from the possessions they owned. Morgan and Cushing (1966) demonstrated the therapeutically beneficial effect of allowing long-term psychiatric patients to have personal possessions because they counteract Goffman's 'mortification of self'. Investigations concerned with elderly people (e.g., Kalymum, 1985; McCracken, 1987; Sherman and Newman, 1977) stress the importance of taking treasured personal possessions into old people's homes or sheltered accommodation, because they symbolize a person's life experiences and thus the historical continuity of self: 'The change in possessions that [often] accompanies relocation can contribute to a loss of continuity with life history, and a loss of a sense of self or identity' (McCracken, 1987, p. 14).

This kind of literature carries obvious implications for institutional policies, but it also highlights the symbolic aspects of possessions: they help people to maintain a general sense of identity and integrity, they can serve as locatory markers for status, and they provide a symbolic record of one's personal history.

Personal storehouses of meaning: life and beyond

Kamptner (1991a, b) carried out a broader investigation into the meanings of personal possessions throughout the life-span in the United States, but specifically considers their vital role for successful adaptation to old age (1989). She classifies the reasons why possessions are psychologically meaningful into five main categories: providing control and mastery, moderating emotions, cultivating the self, symbolizing ties with others and constituting a concrete history of one's past. On an emotional level, possessions can be like security blankets which provide feelings of comfort and low-intensity experiences of entertainment, escape and distraction (see also Sherman and Newman, 1977). The fact that possessions help to maintain a sense of mastery and social status probably has particular implications for nursing homes or psychiatric institutions, because they can partly counteract the lack of personal control patients or residents experience in other areas of their lives, leading to more positive attitudes and better rehabilitation (cf. Rodin and Langer, 1978).

As people get older, many of the usual markers of adult identity may be lost, through retirement from one's occupation, shrinkage of social networks and social roles, or physical deterioration. They may therefore develop a stronger emphasis on the past to reaffirm who they are – their identity – and in order to maintain a sense of self-continuity they may particularly need those possessions which are concrete reminders of past experiences and events. In this way, possessions do not only symbolize future goals and thus tell us who we are to become, they also tell us who we have been. They constitute a concretized, illustrated personal history: a series of snapshots of the past. Examining the role of material objects for remembering, Radley (1990) proposes that our material environment, including personal possessions, consists of markers of change: it is ordered in ways upon which people rely for a sense of temporal continuity. But objects do not just 'remind' people of past events, they are material settings which *shape* memory construction because they symbolize cultural categories, social groups, ideologies, and so on. '[R]emembering is something which occurs in a world of things, as well as words, . . . artefacts play a central role in the memories of cultures and individuals' (Radley, 1990, p. 19), especially for older people who engage in a review of their lives. They are particularly concerned with the development of an integrated and coherent personal history and a re-evaluation of their experiences over time. Possessions can be memories in a direct sense, as are literal documents and records (family trees, photograph albums), but others can serve similar functions as symbols and triggers for memories.

Moreover, if the personal possessions which function as symbols for ties with others are lost or cannot be taken into a nursing home, their lack could easily lead to an eroded sense of personal self. Kamptner (1989) found that when asked about the importance of family heir-looms, a full 83 per cent of her elderly respondents talked about interpersonal and familial associations, compared to 6 per cent who referred to intrinsic qualities, such as monetary value or aesthetic features.

In summary, Kamptner's (1989) main findings were that the possessions most treasured by the elderly were photos, jewellery and small appliances (TV, radio, etc.), with men preferring appliances and women jewellery and photos. The most frequent reasons were interpersonal-familial associations (49 per cent) and pleasant emotions (24 per cent). Men referred more to enjoyment, whereas women tended to be more concerned with the interpersonal realm. Thus it seems that a concern with interpersonal connectedness is even more central to older women's sense of self-continuity than to that of men. In an exploratory English survey, young and middle-aged adults responded to a personal history scale, consisting of items such as 'Photograph albums give me a sense of continuity', 'Sentimental items are a record of who and where one has been over the years', or 'The things we accumulate over time give us a sense of being connected to others'. As would be expected from a younger sample, possessions as symbols of one's history were not yet an overriding concern (overall mean of 4.5 on a 7-point scale), but gender differences were already apparent, with women agreeing more strongly with the questionnaire items (Dittmar, 1988).

Basing his view on open-ended interviews with twenty-five old people and an analysis of letters, mementos and conversations of the dying and their survivors, Unruh (1983) argues that the concern with self-continuity and identity preservation stretches even beyond the grave. Dying people use material objects to create in their survivors the kind of memory which they desire. They pass on treasured possessions which show marks of their personal attention because they were 'owned and used', and thus they engage in a form of identity preservation beyond death in the memories of their surviving family and friends: 'The dying . . . interpret and apportion their identities to survivors through the use of three strategies: solidifying identities, accumulating artefacts, and distributing artefacts' (Unruh, 1983, p. 342). These can be amplified as follows:

1. Solidifying identities: before dying, a period of intensive self-reflection, a heightened life review process, is evident, where people accentuate those portions of their personal history for which they would like to be remembered. Unruh (1983) gives the example of a man writing his life history with instructions that it be read at family and senior centre gatherings after his death.

2. Accumulating artefacts: throughout life, people acquire objects and imbue them with personal meanings which represent past accomplishments, talents, travels, or sentiments. Personal possessions are artefacts in which personal identities, feelings about oneself and shared biographies with our dearest are located, invested and stored. These objects often represent the last symbolic remnants of who and what the dying once were, and can therefore become objects of the survivors' reminiscences.

3. Distributing artefacts: wills and testaments used to apportion objects in which identity is stored select which identities should be remembered by whom. It is now common to leave one's personal estate to the surviving spouse or partner, implying that she or he was the major supplier of personal meaning and identity for the deceased. In addition, there are identity preservation strategies that the survivors engage in, such as sanctifying and idealizing often mundane objects or everyday implements, imbuing them with meanings symbolic of exemplary identities of the deceased. This can happen on a collective level, too. Unruh (1983) describes the collective sanctification surrounding what many fans perceived as the important identities of John Lennon. Fans donated plants, trees and stones for an area of Central Park, New York, to be called 'Strawberry Fields', objects which were intended to become a unified, sanctified symbol of Lennon's identities as working-class child, songwriter and social visionary.

In conclusion, it appears that possessions are an important and, in the Western world, possibly necessary part of people's selves which help to resolve the psycho-social challenges of late adulthood, old age and even impending death. For the dying, material objects are aids to carrying their selves into the future: they are concrete means of preserving their identity beyond the grave. Passing on treasured possessions is a strategic social action, rather than simply a personal process, as it is designed to exercise some control over inevitable mortality. Throughout life, material possessions can be a source of personal control, emotional relief, self-maintenance, social integration and lifetime continuity. For older people generally, particularly those in institutions, the loss of their personal objects would therefore mean losing the fabric of life and self. Whether living in a nursing home or owned flat, it is being surrounded by our possessions which makes where we live into a home.

The home as identity shell

> The home is a shelter for those persons and objects that define the self; thus, it becomes . . . an indispensable symbolic environment.
> (Csikszentmihalyi and Rochberg-Halton, 1981, p. 144)

Sadalla *et al.* (1987) set out to investigate 'identity symbolism in housing' and asked upper-middle-class house owners to rate themselves on a range of personality traits which had been selected as measures of personal and social identity. The main four dimensions of expressed identity were intellectual attributes, openness and warmth, individualism and extroversion. Students then rated all house owners in terms of these attributes on the basis of slides which showed the front exterior of the house in question and/or the interior of the living-room. The study was mainly concerned with how well other people could recognize how individuals express themselves through their material possessions, in this case house front and living-room furnishings. The authors conclude that 'observers showed consensus in their ratings of homeowner identity and discriminated between homeowners who rated themselves differently' (p. 580). This finding clearly indicates not only that house owners express a variety of personal attributes through their possessions and general living environment, but also that this identity symbolism is recognized by others with a reasonable degree of accuracy.

In describing and analysing social practices in Berber houses, Bourdieu (1973) describes a dark, nocturnal, lower part of the house where raw, green foodstuffs and objects are stored, where the domestic animals are stabled and where 'natural' human activities take place: sleep, sex or giving birth. In contrast, the upper part of the house is the place of human social activities, particularly entertaining guests, and it contains objects such as the fireplace, cooking utensils and the weaving loom. The whole house is arranged in relationships of oppositions, in terms of both material objects and social activities, and this opposition is partly associated with the division of labour between the sexes as well as with notions of gender identity: the low, dark part is the feminine space and the high, light part the masculine space. Thus the internal organization of the house reflects, symbolizes and reinforces Berber sex-role relationships. Artefacts in the home are also important influences on relationships in the industrialized West. Olson (1985) carried out in-depth interviews with six couples and asked them what the various objects in their homes meant to them. Of particular interest were those which were seen as embodiments of the relationship: family reminders, or historical records of the various stages of development the couple had gone through. Artefacts thus create a setting for remembering and communication shared by a couple, symbolically representing their relationship. A study which contrasted two families with diametrically opposed interaction patterns – one cohesive and the other disparate – found that familial dynamics were reflected in, and reinforced by, the family members' joint and separate use of the material objects in the home (cf. Lunt and Livingstone, 1991).

Houses, flats or rooms are much more than shelter and places of security. They provide autonomy and a space to develop an identity (Saunders, 1990), and they are 'cultivators' (Kron, 1983) and symbols of the self (Cooper, 1976). Not only do they provide the arena for social activities and interactions, but the objects within them are often an illustrated history of the self, as well as an expression of current social standing, interests, religious and political beliefs, personal tastes and qualities. A fairly recent ethnographic study by Csikszentmihalyi and Rochberg-Halton (1981) investigated the meanings of personally cherished possessions as indications of the inhabitants' identities in over eighty Chicago family homes. Half the families were upper-middle-class and half lower-middle-class. Several members of each household were interviewed extensively and asked in an open-ended format which of the objects in the house were particularly important to them and the reasons why they treasured these possessions. The analysis of the resulting 315 interviews led to the conclusion that 'household objects constitute an ecology of signs that reflects as well as shapes the pattern of the owner's self' (1981, p. 17).

Their findings are wide-ranging, but will be summarized selectively here. Their generational analysis shows that young respondents described treasured possessions predominantly in terms of the active functions they fulfil for them as individuals, which the authors saw as an indication of adolescents' preoccupation with establishing an autonomous identity. In contrast, old people talked about their possessions as a record of their experiences and links to other people, signifying concerns with how one is related to others and with retrospectively evaluating one's life. Within this lifecycle change from action-related and functional purposes to contemplative and symbolic functions of possessions, they also describe gender-related differences. By comparison with women, men tended more towards action-related and self-referent descriptions of their personal possessions. These they saw as instruments for enjoyment and activity, and as symbols for achievement, physical prowess and general capabilities. In contrast, women showed a stronger tendency to emphasize personal possessions as symbols of interpersonal relationships, family continuity and involvement with a larger social network. To their own surprise, Csikszentmihalyi and Rochberg-Halton (1981) found virtually no class-related differences in response patterns, but this could be due to the fact that they compared upper-middle-class with lower-middle-class respondents, rather than people from very different social strata.

What is distinctive about this project is its concern with people's *own* accounts of what their household possessions mean to them, and its suggestive evidence that the meanings of treasured possessions can be viewed as reflections of social identity dimensions as well as identity development. However, the authors were concerned with the relation between 'people and things' in general and aimed at an initial, descriptive account of people's relations to their household possessions, rather than being concerned with explicitly formulated theories.

Favourite possessions as markers of age, sex and culture

The generational differences in favoured objects which emerged in the Chicago study just described imply that the meanings attached to possessions reflect different developmental stages of the self. However, the classification of respondents into three generations – children, parents, grandparents – means relatively loose age boundaries. For example, the youngest generation seems to have included 8-year-old children as well as 30-year-old adults. In order to study such developmental, or generational, changes in greater detail, Kamptner (1989, 1991a, b) carried out an extensive, open-ended questionnaire study with almost six hundred South Californian respondents in five tightly defined age groups: children of 10–11 years, adolescents of 14–18 years, young adults of 18–29 years, adults of 30–59 years, and senior citizens of over 60 years. Amongst various questions put to participants in this study, the one of most interest here concerns the possessions they most treasured, and the reasons for their attachments. For toddlers and very young children, their favourite cuddlies provide comfort and security, but are also involved in the beginning differentiation of self from the primary caretaker (see Chapter 3). The older children in Kamptner's research named stuffed animals, sports equipment and toys most often. The reasons given for their attachment by over two-thirds of the children were the enjoyment and activities afforded by these objects, and their physical properties. For the adolescents, possessions were more varied, but centred on music equipment, cars and jewellery. In addition to enjoyment, the social ties associated with these objects and the aspects of self they expressed emerged as the most common reasons.

Kamptner (1991b) draws on Erikson's (1980) model of identity development to explain this change. A sense of trust and security having been developed in early infancy, the central task of childhood is to build a sense of competence, mastery and independence, which is reflected in the children's focus on the opportunities for successful and pleasurable tactile experiences provided by their favoured objects. Erikson's (1980) main adolescent task, developing a sense of autonomous self-identity, is mirrored in the adolescents' activity-related and self-centred references to their possessions. Erikson's three adult identity phases – finding intimate relationships in early adulthood, establishing social links with different generations in middle adulthood, and engaging in a retrospective life review process in late adulthood – also appear reflected in how the adults studied described their attachments to their possessions. Young adults refer to the social ties that their cars, jewellery, photographs and general memorabilia symbolized, and the enjoyment they provided. As adults become older, photographs and jewellery take increasingly prominent places as favoured objects, with a growing emphasis on the social integration and networks they signify, on the positive emotions they afford and on the memories associated with them. The special significance of personal possessions for elderly people as a memory environment, a retrospective anchor of identity and an objectified history of the self has been described earlier.

The main five types of reason given – activity-related and pragmatic uses, emotional experiences, self-expression, symbols for interpersonal relationships, concretized personal history – correspond well with the symbolic-communicational model of the meanings of possessions for identity advanced in the previous chapter. In terms of overall development,

> the changes with age noted . . . in this study broadly suggest that with age there is a change in the 'referent' of treasured possessions from mother (in early life) to self (in middle childhood and adolescence) to others (in adulthood). (Kamptner, 1991b, p. 21)

This move from an activity-centred, pragmatic and self-concerned focus on possessions towards a greater emphasis on their symbolic features, particularly with respect to social relationships, is also reported by Myers (1985). In her investigation on special possessions, she found a change from treasured cuddlies, which heralded security and safety and augmented the nurturing person's comforting role, to a concern with objects as means for establishing autonomy, self-reliance and confidence in one's abilities in adolescence. Adults' attachments to their possessions were based on the symbolic expression of closeness, intimacy and relationships with others. Using a slightly different approach, Livingstone and Lunt (1991) categorized respondents according to their lifecycle stages and interviewed them at length about their consumer durables, finding age-related differences in object preferences similar to those already reported. These studies therefore strengthen and extend the findings and conclusions of the Chicago study a decade earlier. Kamptner (1989, 1991a, b) also describes gender differences which permeate all age groups. Girls preferred stuffed animals and dolls to the sports equipment named by boys, and from adolescence onwards women focus more on jewellery and photos than men, who, in turn, describe comparatively more active possessions (cars, sports equipment) or practical items. In terms of reasons given, men emphasized active and instrumental qualities, whereas women stressed their symbolic and expressive aspects, particularly in terms of social relationships. Again, these findings corroborate and extend Csikszentmihalyi's and Rochberg-Halton's (1981) results.

However, these findings do not necessarily imply that there is a quasi-universal pattern of either identity development or gender differences, mirrored in people's relationships with their favourite possessions. As a point in case, Kamptner (1991b) mentions the likelihood of social influences on these relationships and argues for the importance of studying SES or social class differences in people's object attachments, given that her sample, like that of the Chicago study, consisted entirely of middle-class respondents. Another way in which this issue of universality can be addressed is, of course, through cross-cultural comparisons.

Wallendorf and Arnould (1988) examined the meanings of individuals' favourite possessions in two quite dissimilar cultures. They used questionnaires, interviews and photographs to compare southwestern American city dwellers with village inhabitants in the African republic of Niger. Asked to talk about their single most favourite object, about half of the US sample named functional (e.g., clock, chair) and entertainment (e.g., stereo, TV) items, and the other half personal and decorative objects (e.g., photos, art and handicraft). About 60 per cent gave as reasons symbolic aspects and personal memories, attachments based on their being reminders of family, friends, past events and travels. A third of the women named functional and entertainment objects, and almost two-thirds referred to personal items. The pattern for men was exactly reversed. Men's comparatively more self-centred and pragmatic reasons contrasted with the women's emphasis on interpersonal ties and emotional attachments. In order to examine age-related changes, Wallendorf and Arnould (1988) split their adult respondents into six age groups. They noted that the younger people's concern with functional items and active pleasures was gradually replaced by more personal items, indicating an increasing concern with social networks and social history as represented in objects. So far, these results are entirely consistent with those of the studies reported earlier. On the basis of findings across different samples and a decade, it can therefore be concluded tentatively that at least for white American people, but probably for the industrialized West as a whole, the meanings of treasured possessions are not only gender-marked, they also undergo a definite developmental progression reflective of changing identity concerns.

However, a number of anthropologists, psychologists and other social scientists have argued that our prevailing concept of identity as autonomous individuality is a peculiarly Western construction, given that other cultures see the self as contextualized and inextricably embedded in social relationships (see Chapter 8). If the social constructionist view of possessions as symbols of identity is valid, one would expect that the rural African people studied by Wallendorf and Arnould (1988) would relate to their possessions rather differently. Indeed, not only did they have less possessive attitudes, they often had to be prompted to name a *material* object as their favourite possession, because they spontaneously referred to their fields, their children or their studies of the Koran. The objects they then talked about were virtually gender-segregated, with 85 per cent of the women naming marriage or domestic goods (e.g., silver jewellery, tapestries), whereas about half of the men named religious or magical items, such as the Koran or charms, with another 30 per cent choosing tools or livestock. Their reasons for treasuring these items were rather different from the American sample, with functional utility and sentimental, personal attachments featuring as minor factors. Instead, references to magical, spiritual efficacy, convertibility to cash, aesthetic value in achieving cultural ideals of beauty, and prestige comprised 60 per cent of responses. Thus it appears that the meanings of favourite possessions derive more from personal memories in America, where objects represent a person's unique, individual history. In Niger, meanings seem to refer to social status, and possessions are a reflection of social identity and of conforming to cultural, shared ideals. Wallendorf and Arnould (1988) note the cross-cultural similarity in gender differences, with women emphasizing social ties through favourite objects and men seeing their accomplishments and mastery represented, but warn against

> generalizing to a constant gender effect rather than a culture effect . . . [g]iven the patriarchal structure of both cultures studied . . . it would be necessary to compare these results with data collected in matrilineal or matriarchal societies. (p. 543).

As a further point relevant to gender, both this study and the research by Csikszentmihalyi and Rochberg-Halton (1981) or Kamptner (1989, 1991a, b) assessed differences in the kinds of possession women and men preferred *separately* from the reasons they gave for their attachments. This leaves it as an open question whether certain objects tend to be valued by most people for similar reasons, and gender differences in the values placed on possessions come about solely through different object preferences, or whether women and men actually relate to their possessions in different ways, so that even the same possession may well be treasured for different reasons.

Wallendorf and Arnould (1988) give an interesting non-Western illustration of possessions signifying developmental changes in the transition from one social identity to another at particular ages. For rites of passage into womanhood or manhood, initiates are often stripped of their possessions so that they can assume their new social identity in the community, which is symbolized by new special objects, whether they be a new robe, a spear or tribal body decorations. In terms of the findings on age-related differences in Niger, the younger generation appeared to be bent on obtaining Westernized goods to express their social differentiation from the formal strictures and conventions of their traditional roles, dependent on family authority until they establish their own households. In contrast, the older generations prefer objects long-established in their community. An example is that of younger men, who now prefer second-hand, locally reconditioned Western shirts and trousers, in contrast to the traditional long, loose shirt and baggy drawstring trousers worn by older men: 'This new dichotomy in rural clothing styles expresses the longstanding tension between fathers and sons' (p. 542).

In conclusion, the social embeddedness of identity in a rural community, such as these Niger villages, seems to find expression in the culturally specific meanings of possessions which emphasize social status and intergenerational connectedness. Joy and Dholakia (1991) emphasize that self-definition in India differs from Western conceptions, and illustrate that the acculturation of Indian professionals to Canada is reflected in changing meanings of home and possessions, particularly when first and second generation Indians are compared.

Conclusion

A *symbolic-communicational* model of possessions and identity was developed theoretically in the previous chapter, which asserted that a good part of the significance of material possessions stems from their symbolic meanings for identity. Its challenge of mainstream economic notions – that possessions serve mainly utilitarian functions and that purchasing material goods according to rational costs-and-benefits decisions is the main locus of our relations to them – is supported by various investigations, which illustrate that the social and psychological significance of material possessions stretches far beyond purchase and is inextricably involved in most aspects of everyday life and common knowledge.

Both this chapter and Chapters 2 and 3 were concerned with various bodies of literature connected with the psychological significance of material possessions. Early explanatory endeavours to reduce the relationship between people and their possessions to instinctual processes not only lack empirical support, but are also theoretically inadequate to deal with the social aspects of possessions. Later contributions attempted to follow a more constructive path by investigating the meanings of material possessions and the functions they fulfil. Virtually all of these contributions refer in some way to the important link between possessions and identity. Several empirical investigations of self-conceptions show that both adults and children regard possessions as an integral part of themselves. However, such a purely descriptive statement begs the question of the nature of this link. Drawing on a host of diverse developmental research, it appears that possessions play a decisive role in children's development of an identity because they constitute vehicles for drawing a boundary between what is self and what is other, at least in the Western world. This establishment of this boundary is obviously related to instrumental functions of material objects as control devices, but evidence suggests strongly that the development of this self–other distinction and children's knowledge about possession-related aspects are influenced by social factors. Similarly, Furby's (e.g., 1978a, 1980a) emphasis on the psychological significance of material possessions in terms of the quasi-physical control they afford has to be supplemented by different dimensions. We only need to examine the diverse bodies of research in abnormal psychology, sociology, consumer research and so on considered in this chapter, which persuasively illustrate the symbolic significance of material objects as parts of the extended self.

It can be concluded, therefore, that the main body of work discussed so far is at least consistent with, and in some parts provides direct support for, the *symbolic-communicational* account of the possessions–identity link. Such a social constructionist perspective seems to offer a clearer and more coherent formulation of the link between possessions and identity than the psychologically oriented literature has provided to date. The model put forward in Chapter 4 may therefore constitute a first step towards a much needed theoretical integration of this fragmentary and mainly descriptive area of research.

The following two chapters provide overviews and discussions of two series of studies which were directly developed from the social constructionist perspective outlined. They were designed to investigate two main issues. Firstly, a set of studies examines whether personal possessions can be meaningfully analysed as symbolic expressions of gender, social-material position and membership in different social groups. And, secondly, a set of investigations attempted to study the impact of material possessions and wealth on how we perceive the identities of others.

Notes

1. Richins's (1991) 18-item materialism scale consists of three subscales, but is internally consistent as a whole, with an overall Cronbach's alpha of 0.80 to 0.88. Drawing on samples of several hundred adults, scores on this scale appear to be normally distributed in the USA, with a mean of 46–7 and a standard deviation of 9.5.

6

Material possessions as reflections of identity:
Gender, social-material status and social groups

The social constructionist perspective on material possessions and identity, outlined in this book, highlights the intimate relationship between self-perception, other-perception and material symbols. Therefore it offers not a formulation of a *specific* theory about material possessions, but a *broader* framework within which different aspects of everyday understanding can be explored in their material context. In fact, throughout the previous chapters, particularly Chapter 4, topics were touched upon for which well-established social psychological theories exist, such as gender identity, stereotypes or person perception. The main aim of this and the subsequent chapter is to attempt an application of such theories to the subject of material possessions. No claim is made to provide comprehensive coverage of these complex and sprawling fields of investigation. Instead, contributions are selectively introduced and discussed as and when they are considered relevant for the argument put forward here. At the same time, empirical work carried out by the author is described in a summary fashion for illustrative purposes.[1] Adopting a social constructionist perspective does not prescribe any particular form of methodology. But its rejection of the 'objectivity' of empiricism suggests that the use of qualitative research techniques would be favoured. However, the virtually anti-empirical stance adopted by some social constructionists seems unnecessary, and the use of quantitative methods to complement qualitative ones appears a promising research strategy.

It was argued earlier that there are two major perspectives from which the significance of material possessions for identity can be examined. The following distinction is useful analytically, but cannot be clear cut as each of the two perspectives has implications for the other, and individuals adopt both simultaneously. The first is an *actor* perspective, in the sense that it investigates the role of material symbols from the viewpoint of individuals who are expressing something about themselves through their possessions. The second is an *observer* perspective, which is concerned with how inferences are made about other people's identities on the basis of their material possessions.

It appears useful to explore both perspectives, rather than focus on one to the exclusion of the other, in order to see how they may be related to each other. This chapter is mainly concerned with the actor perspective and explores personal possessions as symbolic expressions of gender, social-material position and membership in different social groups. The next chapter deals with the observer perspective by focusing on the impact of material possessions and wealth on how we perceive the identities of others. These two perspectives will be related to each other at a later stage.

Many aspects of self-definition become associated with people's possessions because they reflexively evaluate themselves on the basis of how others perceive them and respond to them in terms of material symbols. Or, put more simply, the judgments others (specific persons, social groups, society in general) are thought to make about us on the basis of our material possessions become an integral part of how we view ourselves. This argument contradicts the oft-made assumption that people's relationships with their most treasured personal possessions are highly idiosyncratic and private. On the contrary, the argument advanced here – that material objects come to symbolize cultural meanings which form part and parcel of our identity – would imply that the meanings of cherished possessions reflect major social dimensions of identity construction and maintenance. Gender and social-material location in society (a broad term to cover both socio-economic status, SES, and social class) are fundamental social dimensions on the basis of which others respond towards us. Consequently, it should be possible to use relevant social psychological work to investigate whether gender identity and identity dimensions related to socio-material position are reflected in the ways in which people relate to their personal possessions. For example, if female gender identity is characterized by an emphasis on interpersonal relationships, this should be reflected in the meanings women attach to their treasured personal possessions.

Furthermore, if possessions are viewed as symbolic manifestations of belonging to different social categories, it can be expected that consensual representations exist about different socio-economic groups in terms of the possessions group members would typically identify with and treasure. The social psychological literature on stereotyping is extensive and should therefore offer a reasonable basis from which to investigate whether such 'material stereotypes' exist. This assessment can be made by comparing the possessions that are thought to be 'typical' of different groups with the possessions members of these groups actually describe as important themselves. Is it really the case, as people seem to think, that business managers view their expensive cars, credit cards and filofaxes as their most treasured possessions? Not only is such research a fruitful way of investigating whether different socio-economic groups see different kinds of possessions as important, but it can also address the question of whether there is any 'truth' in material stereotypes. In that sense, this second area of investigation combines an actor perspective with elements of an observer perspective.

The account of how material objects may come to symbolize identity has stressed that the meaning of possessions cannot be understood adequately by investigating isolated objects which are supposed to signify different aspects of a person. Rather, identity was conceptualized as being affected by the total symbolic significance of a person's possessions. And, conversely, it would be expected that the meanings people attach to them as a whole, rather than single items, reflect broad dimensions of how their identity is structured. If this proposition is accepted for the moment, with the argument that both social-material position and gender are psychologically significant social categories, the following two questions can be asked. What general differences exist between women's and men's relationships to their personal possessions? And how do people from different social-material backgrounds differ in this respect?

In this form, the above questions are overinclusive and need further refinement. It would be extremely difficult to assess, for example, unconscious elements in that relationship. What can be studied empirically, though, is how people *themselves* describe what their possessions mean to them. What is proposed here is that the open-ended accounts people provide for why their personal possessions are important to them can be meaningfully related to gender and social-material background.

Identity-related meanings of possessions

Possessions and one's sense of identity are closely linked by way of consensually shared notions about material objects constituting symbols for a person's social position, conceptions, attitudes and personal qualities. The ways in which people relate to their possessions can be seen as reflections of how they view themselves and relate to their social and physical environment. Consequently, self-conceptions should be open to analysis through their material signs.

126 *Material possessions as reflections of identity*

It is often assumed that the meanings of one's most cherished personal possessions are unique and highly private: treasured items are thought to be associated with special memories and feelings, which cannot easily be appreciated by others. I certainly do not intend to suggest that there are hardly any differences between individuals, or that the nuances of such meanings cannot be idiosyncratic. But it is nevertheless proposed that these meanings are linked systematically to two broad social categories: gender and social-material position. Support for at least the gender argument comes from several recent studies, mainly carried out in the United States (see Chapter 5). However, given that the types of possession women and men prefer have been assessed separately from the reasons they give for their attachments, a clear-cut answer to the following question remains outstanding: do women and men simply prefer different objects (which everybody treasures for the same reasons) or is the actual *nature* of their object attachments different?

With respect to social-material position, hardly any research exists on the meanings different social strata attach to their material possessions. Csikszentmihalyi and Rochberg-Halton (1981) found virtually no class-related differences, but that may be due to their comparison of upper-middle- with lower-middle-class families, rather than people from more markedly different socio-economic strata.

The point of departure for my own research is that socially shared representations exist about gender, and also about people from opposite ends of the social-material spectrum. These representations can be viewed as organizing principles of identity, given that self-development involves reflexive internalization of social attitudes and standards. At the same time, both gender and socio-economic background are tied up with different social practices and social roles. With material possessions as symbolic embodiments of cultural meanings, it would be expected that their meanings reflect significant aspects of both gender identity and socio-economic position.

Personal possessions and gender identity

The term 'gender identity' is used here to refer not only to a person's cognitive awareness of being female or male, but also to the social psychological notion of individuals construing themselves and interacting with their social environment in terms of socially shared notions about gender and gender roles (e.g., Lloyd and Duveen, 1986). The notion of quite fundamental differences between male and female experience can be found, for example, in Parsons's well-known distinction between instrumental roles mostly fulfilled by men and expressive, caring roles more typical of women (e.g., Parsons and Bales, 1956), or in Bakan's 'duality of experience' (1966). The proliferating literature on gender-role stereotypes and attributes tends to echo these differences (for overviews see, e.g., Archer and Lloyd, 1985; Deaux, 1985; Wilkinson, 1986). Broadly speaking, this literature has continued to refer to a major difference between women and men: male achievement-oriented, individualistic self-assertion versus female nurturance, interpersonal warmth and emotional expressiveness. A host of empirical work, notably by Bem (e.g., 1974, 1978) and Broverman *et al.* (1970, 1972; Rosenkrantz *et al.*, 1968), identifies attributes such as being independent, forceful and self-sufficient as integral to our notion of *male* and characteristics such as being warm, understanding and sensitive to the needs of others as descriptive of our sense of *female*. But even if these attributes are part and parcel of gender stereotypes, and are the stuff of commonsense theories people hold about women and men, this does not of course mean that they provide a realistic description of actual sex differences, or that women and men think of themselves in such gender-loaded terms. Self-concepts of femaleness and maleness have received much less research attention than stereotypes, but some empirical work demonstrates that women and men do tend to describe themselves in the terms referred to above, although in a less clear-cut and exaggerated manner (e.g., Carlson, 1971; Rosenkrantz *et al.*, 1968; Siiter and Unger, 1978; Storms, 1979).

Several recent contributions have stressed that these 'male' and 'female' qualities should not be viewed as either *descriptive* or *prescriptive* personality attributes of individual women and men. In other words, they argue that these gender-role attributes do not actually describe what – in general – an individual woman is like compared to an individual man. Nor do or should they provide a blueprint for the personality characteristics of the *typical*, let alone the *ideal*, woman or man. Hare-Mustin and Marécek (1988), Morawski (1985) and Spence and Helmreich (1980), among others, criticize the social psychological literature on masculinity and femininity for lack of clarity with regard to this issue, and for unwittingly perpetuating rather traditional gender stereotypes as a consequence. Morawski (1985) accuses this work of potentially creating 'categorical realities' where, in fact, substantial overlap may exist between women and men in their personal qualities and self-conceptions.

However, other contributions maintain that women and men do undergo very different identity construction processes. For example, Williams (1984) argues that social identity theory (e.g., Tajfel, 1978a, 1982) postulates a universal, male-oriented mechanism of identity construction. According to social identity theory, an important part of self derives from processes of differentiation and comparison within an intergroup context. Individuals are motivated to achieve a positive social identity through favourable evaluation of their own group or social category in comparison with 'outgroups'. However, Williams maintains that identity is also constructed through affiliations with and attachments to others and other groups, particularly by women – a process of identity construction neglected by social identity theory. The rather complex issue of female social identity is further explored by Skevington and Baker (1989).

A similar notion is elaborated in feminist, psychoanalytically oriented contributions which argue that, because of our heavily gender-marked and gender-oriented society, girls tend to define themselves through, and in *unity* with, the still primarily female nurturer. In contrast, boys tend to define themselves in terms of being actively *different* from their primary caretakers (e.g., Chodorow, 1978; Eichenbaum and Orbach, 1983; Levenson, 1984; Sayers, 1986). Interview studies on gender also stress that women's descriptions of themselves are embedded in their connections to others and are presented in a 'relational mode of discourse' (e.g., Beckett, 1986). Work concerned with moral development also describes the relational way in which women talk about morality and about themselves (Gilligan, 1982; Gilligan and Attanucci, 1988; Lyons, 1983).

Drawing on these contributions in combination, the approach adopted here views the male *individualistic* and female *communal* qualities described above as *socially constituted representations of gender* or as *cultural assumptions about gender* (see also Billig *et al.*, 1988; Condor, 1987; Hare-Mustin and Marécek, 1988; Skevington and Baker, 1989). But these potentially stereotypical commonsense notions are an integral part of our shared beliefs, as well as of our social practices. They therefore act as organizing principles of identity construction and constitute the powerful frame of reference within which children are brought up, and within which women and men continue to define themselves. Or, as Lunt and Livingstone (in press) put it, 'ideology, culture and practical experiences of inequality combine to produce different "lenses" through which men and women view the world'.

The gender identity literature sketched above implies that women should show a greater tendency than men to describe personal possessions as important because they symbolize interpersonal integration, relatedness to others and emotional attachment. Men would be expected to make greater reference to instrumental, pragmatic, or action-related features of possessions, and to describe them as self-referent symbols of achievements. This means that their object attachments should differ in quality, over and above valuing different possessions.

As we saw in the previous chapter, various studies found that men focused more on practical and entertainment objects, whereas women seem more likely to choose items such as photos, textiles and mementos, although respondents would always talk about a fair variety of objects overall (Csikszentmihalyi and Rochberg-Halton, 1981; Kamptner, 1989, 1991a, b; Wallendorf and Arnould, 1988). In terms of reasons, women refer more to social ties with friends and family, whereas men argue that they treasure their possessions because they provide physical action, use and enjoyment. As none of these studies took gender as its main object of study, these differences are explained relatively curtly as the consequences of gender role divisions and socialization into male instrumental achievements and female familial, expressive concerns.

These considerations constitute the basis for a set of questionnaire studies I carried out. Over 160 respondents – business commuters, unemployed people and students – were asked to list five personal possessions they considered important and to describe in their own words, and in some detail, why each possession was important to them. Gender-relevant findings from two student samples are discussed here, whereas the following section considers both gender and social-material differences which emerged from the responses of business and unemployed people.

The objects listed as treasured possessions were sorted into the following typology:

1. Material possessions:
    (a) Assets (financial: bonds, credit cards, money; property: house, flat);
    (b) Transport (car, motorbike);
    (c) Basic utility (clothes, duvet, cooker);
    (d) Leisure (hi-fi, TV, camera, surfboard);
    (e) Extensions of self (trophies, special collections, religious or political symbols);
    (f) Sentimental (photo album, gifts, teddy bear);
    (g) Other (documents, plants).
2. Pets.
3. Non-material possessions (not relationships).
4. Relationships or people.

Only a small number of responses referred to non-material objects (such as pets, personal relationships, or physical and mental attributes). Material possessions were classified into seven main types, including 'basic utility', 'sentimental' or 'assets'.

The main runners in terms of special possessions were sentimental items (mostly photographs, gifts and jewellery, 20.2 per cent),[2] leisure objects (overwhelmingly music equipment, 22.6 per cent) and utility possession (mainly household equipment and appliances, 19.7 per cent). Gender differences in the types of possessions listed were not overly pronounced. The main exceptions were women listing more sentimental items (28.8 per cent compared to 11.5 per cent), whereas men showed a preference for action-oriented possessions, such as vehicles and leisure objects (40.6 per cent compared to 21.1 per cent).

The *accounts* of why possessions were considered special reveal a more strongly gender-differentiated picture, which implies that identical possessions may be treasured for very different reasons. The procedure for systematizing these reasons was more complex. Thirty-four finely-grained meaning categories were summarized into broader *super*-categories, as follows:

1. Qualities 'intrinsic' to object:
    (a) Durability, reliability, quality;
    (b) Economy;
    (c) Monetary value;
    (d) Uniqueness, rarity;
    (e) Aesthetics.
2. Instrumentality:
    (a) General utility of object;
    (b) Enables specific activity associated with object.
3. Other use-related features:
    (a) Enables social contact;
    (b) Provides enjoyment;
    (c) Provides entertainment or relaxation;
    (d) Enhances independence, autonomy, freedom;
    (e) Provides financial security;
    (f) Provides information or knowledge;
    (g) Provides privacy or solitude.
4. Effort expended in acquiring or maintaining possession.
5. Emotion-related features of possessions:
    (a) Emotional attachment;
    (b) Mood enhancer or regulator;
    (c) Escapism, switching off;
    (d) Emotional outlet/therapy;
    (e) Provides comfort or emotional security;
    (f) Enhances self-confidence.
6. Self-expression:
    (a) Self-expression *per se*;

    (b) Self-expression for others to see;
    (c) Individuality/differentiation from others;
    (d) Symbol for personal future goals;
    (e) Symbol for personal skills or capabilities.
7. Personal history:
    (a) Link to events or places;
    (b) Link to past or childhood;
    (c) General symbol of self-continuity;
    (d) Long-term association.
8. Symbolic interrelatedness:
    (a) Symbol for relationship with specific person(s);
    (b) Symbolic company;
    (c) Symbol of interrelatedness with particular group(s).
9. Non-codable statement.

The first reason category subsumes qualities intrinsic to an object, such as 'beautiful' or 'well made'. The next type of reason refers to an object's utility as directly related to its functional property (e.g., 'without my stereo I couldn't listen to my tapes'), and the third to other use-related features, such as 'gives me a sense of independence'. Further reasons refer to effort invested, or to emotional experiences (e.g., 'helps me to vent my frustration'). The last three kinds of reason are clearly of a symbolic nature: possessions described as expressive vehicles for self, such as 'tells others who I am', as signs of personal history (with no mention of other people) and, finally, as concrete reflections of interpersonal and social ties (e.g., 'my necklace means a lot to me because it was given to me by my grandmother'). The following explanation given by a 24-year-old male student gives a flavour of what respondents wrote, as well as how their reasons were analysed (*in brackets*):

> *Motorbike*. Most valuable thing I own (*monetary value*). Gives me a sense of independence (*enhances independence, autonomy, freedom*) and it's a means of transport (*enables specific activity associated with object*). I feel it says something about me (*self-expression for others to see*) and I want to be different (*individuality/differentiation from others*).

The reasons why women and men treasured their possessions differ quite substantially, and percentages[3] with respect to the main types of reasons are given in Figure 6.1.

Overall, the young adults studied referred prominently to *instrumental* and *use-related* reasons. This concern with activity-related, pragmatic aspects of personal possessions is not surprising, in the light of the developmental and generational changes in object attachments described in the previous chapter (see Csikszentmihalyi and Rochberg-

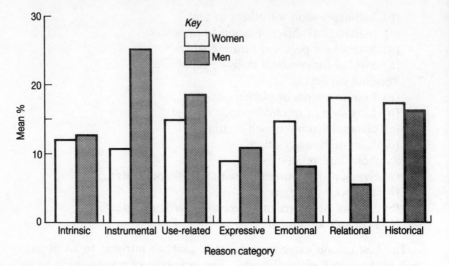

Figure 6.1 Reasons given by women and men for the importance of their material possessions

Halton, 1981; Kamptner, 1991a, b). Most of the students who took part in this study were in their early twenties and had left home recently, and their reasons reflect their self-oriented concern with establishing an independent, adult identity.

With respect to gender differences, men used the male instrumental, use-related and self-expressive reasons significantly more often than the female emotional and relational reasons, whereas the reverse was true for women. Women gave many more relational than instrumental reasons – in fact, *relational* reasons were the ones used most often by women, and least by men. Despite their common concern with functional and use-related features of possessions, men's responses refer *strongly* to instrumental and activity-related features, whereas women's reasons revolve *equally* around emotion-related features of possessions and their role as symbols for interpersonal relationships.

These findings provide information about *either* the kinds of possession women and men favour *or* about differences in the accounts they give of why these objects are important. As it stands, this leaves the possibility open that women simply prefer different possessions to those men prefer, but that both relate to particular objects in the same way – a question not as yet addressed empirically. Therefore correspondence analysis[4] was carried out, which allows for a visual, two-dimensional representation of the reasons frequently used in association with certain types of object, separately for women and men (see Figure 6.2).

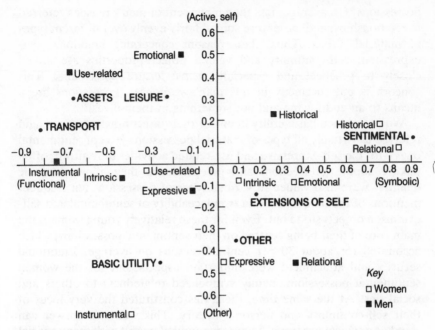

Figure 6.2 Women's and men's reasons for the importance of their material possessions: correspondence analysis

Figure 6.2 shows the kinds of reason women and men use when talking about particular types of possession. For example, instrumental reasons given by men are located in close proximity to transport (left-hand side). This means that they explained the personal importance of their cars or motorbikes almost exclusively by referring to their functional, practical use. Correspondence analysis only provides coordinates for the graphic display of such links between possessions and reasons, but meaningful interpretation of findings has to be provided by the investigator.

Men talked about their transport in mainly pragmatic terms, they treasured basic utility items for both their intrinsic qualities and the opportunities they provide for self-expression, and they valued assets for their use-related features. But by far the largest, and most varied chunk of reasons (on average 36 per cent) centred on their leisure possessions. Recreational items were used for self-expression and for emotional experiences – frequently 'switching off' or mood changes – and valued for their intrinsic quality, financial worth and the activities they make possible. Men even derived a greater sense of self-continuity and personal history from their leisure pursuits than from sentimental possessions. On average, less than 6 per cent of men's reasons referred to relationships, and these were spread fairly evenly over different types of material object. Thus, their reasons concerning emotions, self-expression, self-continuity and valued object properties are linked closely to practical and especially *active* leisure possessions. This concern is put succinctly in this man's response: 'Possessions are a means to an end for me and not something in themselves.'

Women valued basic utility items for their direct pragmatic uses, and referred to virtually all types of material possession – except sentimental ones – for the self-expressive and use-related activities they afford, often talking about the freedom and independence they allow. Intrinsic qualities were also valued in various types of possession, but frequent mentions of the uniqueness and irreplaceability of sentimental and self-extension objects stood out. Even for these relatively young women, the main core of their being centred on their sentimental possessions, which accounted for about 30 per cent of reasons on average. Emotional security and attachment were important aspects, but for the women sentimental possessions mainly symbolized relatedness to others and social ties. At the same time, these ties constituted the very locus of their self-continuity and personal history. This woman's answer can stand as a typical example: 'I have surrounded myself with many special friends and I love looking at them all about my room. I like to be reminded of their physical presence in the form of photos.'

Thus it appears that women's and men's preferred material possessions and reasons why these are meaningful range from functional to symbolic concerns. This is represented by the functional–symbolic horizontal axis of Figure 6.2, similar to the symbolic–functional dichotomy proposed by various researchers (e.g., Abelson and Prentice, 1989). By comparison, women's responses tend strongly towards the symbolic (right) pole and the men's towards the functional (left) pole. However, the findings of this study indicate that such a symbolic–functional dimension may usefully be supplemented by an active, self-oriented focus versus an other-oriented emphasis, which is explicitly postulated in the gender identity literature. With respect to Figure 6.2, it may be tentatively argued that the second dimension (represented by the vertical axis) can be interpreted as a reflection of active self-orientation at the top (particularly to the left), moving towards other-oriented concerns lower on the right, as indicated by women's and men's relational reasons, which combine a symbolic with an other-oriented perspective.

Taking these findings in combination, it does appear that not only do women and men prefer different objects, but they also relate to their personal possessions in fairly distinctive ways. Despite some overlap, it can be concluded that women tend to construe their relation to their favoured objects in a relational and symbolic manner, compared to men's activity-related, functional and self-oriented concerns. Moreover, if it is the case that traditional gender roles and gender stereotypes are criticized or even dissolved to some extent in student circles, it would be expected that these gender-distinctive features should be even more pronounced for people who are older and come from less homogeneous socio-economic backgrounds.

In short, the ways in which women and men relate to their personal possessions can be meaningfully interpreted as material reflections of gender identity. However, this conclusion carries two further implications. It can be argued that the meanings of material objects are inextricably involved in the *perpetuation* of sex-role definitions, and even of gender inequalities (see also Lunt and Livingstone, in press). This is because boys and girls are socialized with gender-typed role models, partly embodied in toys, and later come to relate to their possessions in ways which mirror gender identity. If one considers women's clothing in professional occupations as an example, their traditional style of dress (soft fabrics, flowing, elaborate and many-coloured) has symbolic connotations (delicate, whimsical, changeable, undisciplined) that seem in effect to disqualify them from active, equal participation in the workplace. In contrast, men's tailored, dark, plain outfits signify the 'male' attributes of reliability, strength and competence, which go hand in hand with success at work (cf. Douglas and Solomon, 1983; McCracken, 1990). In other words, '[i]t is partly because sexist distinctions between men and women are invested in the physical objects of our daily existence that new definitions of gender in this society have been so hard to establish' (McCracken, 1990, p. xv).

The second implication of the argument that material possessions are reflections of gender identity is that changes in concepts of maleness and femaleness should be reflected in changing material symbols. Relevant examples can, again, be found in the clothing and fashion literature. Cassell (1974) describes the link between the emerging women's movement in the 1960s and the concomitant invention of a radical feminist 'uniform'. Its practicality and starkness challenged supposed 'feminine' personal and physical qualities, and reflected a new sense of independence and strength through, for instance, making possible unhampered movement and sitting down without the obligatory crossed legs. McCracken (1990) observes that the emergence of a recent style of clothing reflects quite a different attempt to change concepts of femaleness. He refers to women professionals in North America whose suits and outfits are designed to convey a 'look of authority'. This is achieved by isolating some of the properties of male professional appearance and incorporating them into women's clothing. 'Power-dressing' thus captures broad-shouldered authority through thickly layered pads and supposed style through tailored suits with trousers. In a discussion on the creation and recreation of male gender identity in advertising, Wernick (1991) warns that men are now also increasingly goaded towards 'maximizing their value as circulating tokens of exchange' (p. 66), where material consumption is needed to prop up one's bodily and personal identity. Instead of a move towards gender equalization in terms of images which portray both women and men as developing towards becoming self-determined agents, the so-called equality in gender images in advertising is, according to Wernick, nothing more than the equality of 'self-absorbed, and emotionally anxious, personalities for sale' (p. 66).

Social-material status and possessions

In comparison to that in gender, psychological interest in social and economic stratification has been much less prominent (see e.g., Dickinson, 1986, 1990; Tizard and Hughes, 1984). Sampson (1981) poignantly criticizes the general neglect of material context in psychology in favour of 'over-individualized' models. This rings particularly true, given that work in other social scientific disciplines states, at least implicitly, that a person's social-material position in society is linked significantly to her or his values, self-conception and identity.

Much sociological and political thought is concerned with the economic-material basis of stratification in human societies, the carving up of individuals into fairly distinct social strata with different lifestyles, norms and behaviour. For example, Marxist analyses of Western industrialized society commonly argue that private ownership and/or control of the means of production are not only at the root of conflicts between those who have to sell their labour and those who own capital, but at the same time constitute an important determinant of social class. Considerations of space make it impossible to survey the theoretical disputes about the definition of social class here. But, although some Marxist authors tend to define class as a purely economic category which then unilaterally conditions individuals' thought and perception (e.g., Anderson, 1980; Cohen, 1978), other approaches see class as constituted by the dialectical interplay between productive relations and cultural determinants, such as traditions, value-systems and ideology. Thus they do not deny that people are influenced by their economic-material position, but argue that they actively make sense of it in social and cultural terms (e.g., Connell, 1977, 1983; Thompson, 1968, 1978). Arguments can also be found in Weber's writings (cf. Turner, 1985) that social stratification has both material and symbolic dimensions.

Given the continuing debate about an adequate definition of social class, it is argued here that an individual's social-material position is best viewed as a multidimensional interface of 'overlapping areas of inequality, particularly in power and authority, income and wealth, conditions of work, and lifestyles and culture' (Marwick, 1980, p. 172). Notwithstanding the fact that such a notion of social-material status has to be 'conceptually complicated, philosophically upsetting and methodologically challenging' (Coleman, 1983, p. 265), it can nevertheless be argued that people's social-material position is strongly implicated in each individual's psychological functioning and therefore continues to be a significant influence on their identity and consumption of material goods (cf. Coleman, 1983; Dickinson, 1986). Moreover, entertaining a broad notion of social-material position seems tenable, given the convergence of socio-economic status (SES) classifications derived from economic and socio-political theory on the one hand, and from more social psychological models, on the other, which have drawn on commonsense ideas and the social prestige accorded to different social classes (cf. Coleman, 1983).

However, social psychological work on how SES or social class may be related to identity is sparse. Bledsoe (1981) found that black adolescents could be reliably classified as coming from either a low or a high SES background on the basis of self-concept variables. Generally, low SES individuals tend to emphasize their concern with emotional relationships, whereas people from more affluent strata place more emphasis on autonomy and self-direction (Bieri and Lobeck, 1961; Klausner, 1953; McDonald, 1968). Similarly, high SES individuals tend to believe that they have more control over their lives (internal locus of control) than people from a more materially deprived background (cf. Lefcourt, 1966).

Investigations on social class differences lend further weight to the argument that people from high and low social-material backgrounds may differ in their future aspirations, their orientations towards self-development, and their outlook on economic security and personal independence. Generally, working-class people seem more concerned with economic security, whereas middle-class people value self-actualization and self-development more highly (see e.g., Agnew, 1983; Hyman, 1970; Strumpel, 1976). Basing his view on US interview studies with over seventy thousand respondents, Coleman (1983) concurs that social classes differ in self-concept, values and consumption goals. Working-class people emphasized family and regional ties, a short-term outlook on consumption concerned with instant gratification, and showed a preference for instrumental and recreational possessions to ease everyday life and fill their leisure time. In contrast, middle- and upper-class people wanted possessions which served prestige, status and self-expressive needs, emphasized 'doing one's own thing' in the true spirit of individualism and generally had a long-term, delayed gratification perspective, centred on self-development. Similarly, if one simply listens to the life histories of (European) working- and middle-class people, distinct relationships to material objects emerge, too. Whereas working-class people describe objects in concrete terms, without much nostalgia, middle-class accounts emphasize the abstract value of 'steering one's own life', and hardly refer to financial difficulties in obtaining possessions (cf. Lalive d'Épinay, 1986; Radley, 1990).

Reid's (1989) survey on social class differences in Britain indicates that unemployment appears to be an SES-related phenomenon, given that it is more prevalent and more likely to be long term among manual, partially skilled and unskilled workers. The literature on (un)employment generally points to the deleterious effects of being out of work on self-esteem, self-reported confidence and competence. Being unemployed means a low economic position combined with one of low social prestige and power. In comparison with employment, it is associated with loss of regular contacts beyond one's personal relationships, lack of goals transcending the private realm, loss of personal status and identity, and inactivity enforced by economic as well as psychological factors (e.g., Jahoda, 1981; Warr, 1983). In short, unemployment entails a loss of self-respect and long-term perspective, leading to a focus on the here and now. However, these 'latent' consequences of unemployment may not be linked to being out of work alone. Although the (un)employment literature has neglected social class, research by Payne *et al.* (1984) carried out in England indicates that the above consequences hold true for unemployed people from a working-class background (who constitute the majority of the unemployed, cf. Reid, 1989), whereas unemployed middle- or upper-class individuals suffer substantially less from financial strain and fill their time with activities and social contacts they enjoy, due to 'greater internal control and self-directedness among the middle-class sample' (Warr, 1983, p. 308).

It may be speculatively argued, then, that unemployment and a working-class background combine to a particularly disadvantaged social-material position, with the implication that middle-class people are concerned with their self-development in a long-term perspective in contrast to the unemployed's enforced concern with economic security and the pragmatic here and now. Given the research discussed up to now, it would clearly be expected that different social-material positions would lead to characteristic patterns of responses concerning personal possessions. The fact that Csikszentmihalyi and Rochberg-Halton (1981) failed to uncover such patterns may be explained by their restriction to upper-middle- and lower-middle-class comparisons. Due to material security and a highly individualized, long-term perspective, individuals from a middle-class background should describe personal possessions as important because they symbolize the self as a continuous, historical entity by being markers for their self-development over time. They may also refer to the uniqueness of possessions more than to their financial value. Conversely, due to economic as well as psychological insecurity, individuals from a deprived social-material background may tend to describe their special possessions as important because of their short-term rather than long-term aspects: their use-related and direct utilitarian features, the emotional experiences and reassurance they afford, and the money investment they represent.

Given that gender identity is reflected in the meanings of possessions, the question arises of how gender and social-material position may be related as organizing principles of self-conceptions. It is difficult to answer this question, since psychological research has neglected socio-economic stratification in much the same way as work on stratification (e.g., Abbott and Sapsford, 1987; Walby, 1986) or unemployment (cf. Bartell and Bartell, 1985) has overlooked gender. It seems that gender and social-material position can be viewed as two forms of stratification, both of which may be integral to lifestyle, outlook and probably identity, but whether they should be viewed as *independent* or *interrelated* remains an open question.

Unemployed people and business employees at managerial level differ radically in terms of their social-material position: in income, social prestige and social class background. The usual basis for social class classification is a major division between middle-class 'white collar' workers (classes 1, 2 and 3 non-manual) and working-class or manual workers (classes 3 manual, 4 and 5) (cf. Tizard and Hughes, 1984). Business occupations which involve managerial elements would usually be classified as belonging to classes 1 and 2, thus denoting an upper-middle to middle-class background. At least in the United Kingdom, the majority of unemployed people tend to be manual, partly skilled or unskilled workers, who would therefore be categorized as working- or lower-class. Comparing business commuters with working-class unemployed people constitutes a strong polarization in terms of both class and employment, and participants in my research were chosen in such a way that they differed not only in employment status, but also in terms of socio-economic status (Office of Population Censuses and Surveys,

140   *Material possessions as reflections of identity*

1980). The unemployed and business managers were given the same questionnaire used with the students, asking them to list their five most important possessions and to describe why they treasure them.

Maybe surprisingly, these two groups differed little in the *types* of material possession they listed, although business people were more likely to list 200-year-old grandfather clocks or antique sofas, compared to the unemployed's basic beds or cookers. The only exception was the slightly stronger emphasis on sentimental and 'other' possessions (often decorative nicknacks) by the business commuters (35.7 per cent as compared to 26.3 per cent). Again, leisure, utility and sentimental possessions were the main runners, accounting for 76 per cent of responses on average. However, gender differences were evident, much in line with the findings described for the students. Once more, women mainly listed a higher percentage of sentimental items (28.3 per cent) than men (15.4 per cent).

In terms of accounts of why these possessions were treasured, women differed from men in very similar ways as in the student groups, with women favouring *symbolic, relational* and *emotional* aspects of their objects compared to men's *instrumental* and *use-related* concerns (see Dittmar, 1991b, for details). Figure 6.3 gives an overview of the reasons given by business and unemployed people (without taking gender into account).

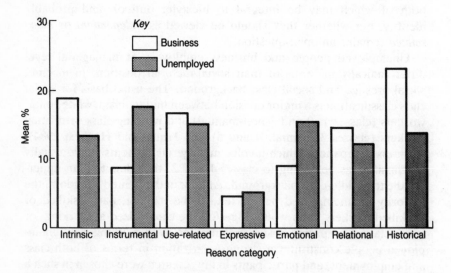

Figure 6.3   Reasons given by business people and unemployed people for the importance of their material possessions

The fact that possessions symbolize one's personal history was an important concern for everybody, which is to be expected of adults in their thirties and forties, who have established their independent homes and are more concerned with self-continuity and identity maintenance than younger adults. Social-material differences were evident in various ways. Business people referred to possessions as symbols of their personal history more often than to their instrumental and emotional features, whereas the exact opposite was true for the unemployed. In fact, the unemployed used instrumental and emotional reasons most prominently, whereas these were the least important concerns for the business managers. In terms of qualities intrinsic to objects, business commuters tended to refer to the unique and aesthetic aspects of their possessions (14.7 per cent) more than to their economic and monetary worth (4.0 per cent) – in contrast to the unemployed (5.4 per cent compared to 6.3 per cent).

Correspondence analysis was carried out to reveal the kinds of reason typically used by business and unemployed women and men for particular material possessions (for details, see Dittmar, 1991b). The gender-identity related meanings of possessions ranged from a rather prominent *male* activity-related, functional and self-oriented extreme to a *female* relational, symbolic pole, thus replicating the findings of the student studies but showing more pronounced differences. For the sake of simplicity, Figure 6.4 only displays social-material position, but not gender.

Both business commuters and unemployed people describe sentimental possessions in relational terms. But the business managers also saw them as intrinsically unique and beautiful, whereas the unemployed's intrinsic reasons refer more to economic or financial value and are tied up with assets (e.g., 'it's important because it cost a lot of money and I couldn't replace it'). Overall, the business managers' emphasis was on objects' intrinsic qualities and their value as symbols of personal history, mainly with respect to utility, leisure and sentimental possessions (35.2 per cent of reasons on average). In contrast, the unemployed focused on the directly functional, pragmatic and active emotional uses – 'switching off' and 'escaping' – of their leisure items and, to a somewhat lesser extent, of their utility objects (35.5 per cent). For the business people, emotional experiences were couched in terms of attachment or security, and seem closely related to their sense of personal history and self-continuity, which is derived not only from sentimental possessions, but also from other and recreational items. For the unemployed, personal history and relationships with others appear to be less prominent concerns, but they are more closely connected to each other and centre on their sentimental possessions.

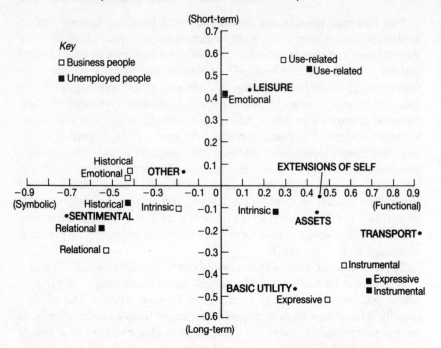

Figure 6.4 Business people's and unemployed people's reasons for the importance of their material possessions: correspondence analysis

Overall, business people are more concerned with the symbolic aspects of possessions, compared to the unemployed's emphasis on their material, utilitarian and instrumental features, and therefore their functional side (represented by the horizontal axis in Figure 6.4). Moreover, the second dimension (represented by the vertical axis) implies an activity-oriented, short-term perspective on possessions at the top pole, given the location of use-related and emotional features of leisure objects. The implied opposite extreme is more difficult to interpret, but it could be argued speculatively that it refers to more stable, long-term features of possessions, evidenced by the location of historical, relational and self-expressive reasons. Thus the meanings of personal possessions related to social-material position range from a symbolic, long-term extreme – more strongly endorsed by people from a high social-material position – to a functional, short-term perspective – predominantly used by people from a lower social-material position.

For people from radically different socio-economic strata, both gender and social-material position act as organizing principles of identity, which is reflected in the different meanings attached to personal possessions. In line with expectations derived from diverse sources on social class and (un)employment, business commuters were mostly concerned with possessions as unique symbols of their personal history, rather than with their material and pragmatic value. This supports the notion of a highly individualized, long-term perspective on self-development as a conscious project. In contrast, unemployed people focused on the instrumental and direct pragmatic aspects of possessions, their financial value and emotional features, such as mood adjustment and reassurance. These findings indicate a self-conception tied up with a short-term, functional perspective, at least in part arising from a constantly enforced concern with economic and emotional security. Moreover, based on statistical analyses, it can be argued tentatively that gender and social-material position are relatively *independent*, rather than *interrelated*, social identity dimensions. Both of them influence people's sense of identity and therefore, in turn, their relationship with their material possessions, but in separate ways.

This series of studies clearly illustrates that possessions can be meaningfully analysed as material signs of self-conceptions, as symbols of identity, which are systematically related to two broad social categories: gender and social-material position. This implies that analysis of the meanings of personal possessions constitutes an interesting methodological tool for studying personal and social identity, at least in our materialistic West. Moreover, the findings presented may not only be valid in the British context, given that they support and extend previous American research on gender. It could be argued that the Anglo-American and north-European Western world is characterized by similar systems of gender and economic stratification as well as by broadly similar forms of material symbolism. The suggestion that these findings may therefore be relevant for the industrialized West as a whole can only be assessed in future research.

Moving on to a different implication, material possessions are not simply an outer manifestation of identity as it exists *within* the person. Rather they are reciprocally and integrally involved in the *expression* and *reproduction* of self-definitions, value orientations and general outlook. If possessions play a crucial role in the development and maintenance of social aspects of our own identity, they may also be an important factor in how we structure, define and orient ourselves towards social reality. And if material context is as integral to social psychological functioning and everyday understanding as suggested here, it would follow that consensual *stereotypes* exist of different socioeconomic groups, not just in terms of the personal attributes and typical behaviours usually investigated in psychology, but in terms of material objects.

Material possessions as stereotypes

Despite the extensive work in social psychology on stereotypes and social categories, the relationship between group membership and material objects has not been examined at all. After briefly exploring some relevant theoretical issues, this section summarizes research by me which explores the images that different social groups have of each other in terms of material possessions.

The only directly relevant evidence concerning material stereotypes can be found in consumer research, which demonstrated that the consumer products white Americans use to describe themselves differ substantially from the products with which they describe black Americans in different income brackets (Sommers, 1964; Sommers and Bruce, 1969). In the research reported here, business managers, unemployed people and students listed the material possessions they themselves most treasured and, at the same time, they gave judgments about the possessions they thought a typical member of the other two groups would find important. The existence and extent of material stereotypes can be assessed by comparing the possessions described by a group with the objects others thought they would cherish (see also Jackman and Senter, 1980).

The social psychological literature concerned with stereotyping is extensive (see, e.g., Brown, 1988; Hamilton, 1981; Tajfel, 1981a, b). Rather than reviewing any of this work here, it seems more useful to discuss briefly those theoretical issues which offer some criteria for addressing the following question: are material images of different socio-economic groups similar to 'stereotypes' as described in the social psychological literature?

Consensus in stereotypes

There appears to be little agreement about the exact nature of stereotypes and, in particular, about whether they can be considered reasonable generalizations about groups or should be seen as irrational preconceptions (e.g., Brown, 1986; Campbell, 1967; Mackie, 1973). The three major conceptual orientations discernible now – socio-cultural, cognitive and psychodynamic – were anticipated by the journalist Lippmann in 1922 when he introduced the term 'stereotype' into the social scientific arena (cf. Ashmore and Del Boca, 1981). Psychoanalytically informed approaches usually explain prejudice against outgroups in terms of displaced aggression and view the content of stereotypes as ego-defensive projections (e.g., Adorno et al., 1950).

Socio-cultural approaches hold that stereotypical beliefs are socially shared and come to be internalized by individuals in their interactions with other people, and with societal institutions and conventions. However, the dominant perspectives in current social psychology are cognitive (e.g., Cantor, 1981; Hamilton, 1981) and social-cognitive (cf. Brown, 1988; Hogg and Abrams, 1988; Tajfel, 1969, 1978a, 1982). They focus on the perceptual-cognitive processes through which individuals structure and simplify information about their social environment.

The approach adopted here can be subsumed under the socio-cultural heading. It questions both the psychodynamic notion that stereotypes are nothing more than 'fallacious rationalizations for outgroup anti-pathy' (Mackie, 1973) and the cognitive assumption that stereotypes are inherently biased through human information-processing errors. As a consequence, a broad definition of a stereotype as a 'shared conception of the character of a group' (Brown, 1986) is used here, which emphasizes *consensus* as a major distinctive feature of stereotypes.

The mainly descriptive work on stereotypes inspired by the seminal Katz and Braly (1933) study took a rather rigid view of consensus (e.g., Brigham, 1971). Respondents (mostly college students) were asked to select a small number of adjectives which they thought were typical for different national and ethnic groups. Results appeared to illustrate graphically the flaw in stereotyped thinking – how could such large numbers of people endorse the view that there are generalizations true of *all* members of a group without exception? The prevalence of stereotyping does not seem to have diminished much over time (cf. Brown, 1986), but what has changed is the understanding of what people mean by 'typical' attribute. A series of studies demonstrated that stereotypes are not seen as descriptive of *all* members of a group by asking, firstly, what percentage of a national group possessed a stereo-typical quality and, secondly, what percentage of people in the world possessed that quality. *Typical* attributes mean qualities true of a higher percentage of the group in question than of people in general – *not* true of all group members and not even necessarily true of a majority (McCauley and Stitt, 1978; McCauley *et al.*, 1980). Basing their view on their research on race, gender and class stereotypes in America, Jackman and Senter (1980) argue that the much lamented rigidity and narrow-mindedness in stereotypes may be, at least in part, a methodological artefact. Supported empirically by Ehrlich and Rinehart (1965), they claim that the two predominant ways of studying stereo-types – asking people to pick out typical attributes or (dis)agree with categorical statements – have 'constrained respondents to express their beliefs about group traits in categorical terms, and [investigators] have then inferred that categorical thinking is endemic to intergroup perception' (p. 342).

With respect to material possessions, this implies that people may have fairly complex and qualified beliefs about distinctive objects treasured by different socio-economic groups. *Typical* possessions are those which are more closely, but not exclusively, associated with one particular group rather than another. Moreover, the focus on shared agreement raises the question of whether different social and economic groups hold the same, *consensual material image* about, for example, a business executive in middle management, or whether they have group-specific beliefs.

This notion of stereotypes as shared beliefs in tendencies is reminiscent in some ways of the literature on *prototypical* representations of natural (e.g., Mervis and Rosch, 1981; Rosch *et al.*, 1976) and social categories (e.g., Cantor, 1981; Cantor and Mischel, 1979). Object and person perception appear relatively similar from this perspective in the sense that both are organized in terms of fuzzy sets without exactly definable boundaries. An item becomes more prototypical the more attributes it shares with a *typical* category member. Object and person categories form hierarchical structures, and categories at particular levels of the hierarchy are more speedily processed, more easily retrieved from memory, and learned earlier on by children. Broadly speaking, this carries two implications. Firstly, the very structure and organization of categories reflect the level at which information processing can proceed best and, secondly, the fact that people agree on what belongs to a category derives from the actual co-occurrences of similar attributes in the natural and social environment. Put simply, birds, for instance, form a basic category because they actually possess similar attributes, such as having wings, laying eggs and so on.

However, the prototype approach to *social* categories can be criticized for both its realist and its innatist assumptions. Co-occurrences of similar attributes are not a decontextualized reflection of the world 'out there', for similarity is socially constructed. For example, a ragbag collection of 'bus', 'legs', 'rickshaw', 'aeroplane' and 'hovercraft' makes perfect sense under the heading 'means of transport', whereas a grouping of 'black cat', 'eightball at pool', 'black mass' and 'black civil rights campaigner' under the heading of perceptually 'black' objects appears absurd. And why do Asians constitute a meaningful social category while blue-eyed people do not? These examples suggest that what people perceive as belonging to a social category reflects social processes and conventions, rather than *intra-individual information-processing* principles (cf. Shweder and Miller, 1985).

Differences between groups and homogeneity within them

Following Bruner's (e.g., 1957) work on perception, Tajfel (e.g., 1959a, 1978a, 1981a, b) argued that social categories are useful and necessary because they help us order and simplify our world, which would otherwise be a set of chaotic and overwhelming stimulus configurations. Tajfel's work on social categorization followed from his research on judgments of physical stimuli. He proposed that if a discontinuous classificatory system, such as A and B, is imposed on a set of physical stimuli to be judged (e.g., length of lines), perceptual judgments will be modified in such a way that *differences between categories* and *similarities within categories* are accentuated (e.g., Tajfel, 1959a; Tajfel and Wilkes, 1963). In analogy with physical categorization, the function of social categories is seen as sharpening the distinctions between groups and minimizing differences within them, so that the recognition of members and non-members of those categories becomes easier. Despite the social elements in Tajfel's account, there remains an emphasis on perceptual factors when stereotypes are viewed as a direct offshoot of the categorical differentiation process, or, in Wilder's words (1981): 'Ingroup/outgroup bias may be a consequence of normal categorization processes' (p. 232). Categorical differentiation is a well-documented phenomenon in intergroup perception (e.g., Tajfel, 1984) and, if we leave the more tricky question of whether its origin may be social rather than primarily perceptual open for just a moment, it carries two implications for material possessions as stereotypes.

Categorical differentiation means that people exaggerate differences between groups, and minimize differences between individuals in the same group ('they're all the same'). Thus, for our three socio-economic groups, business commuters at managerial level are probably seen as radically different from the unemployed, but unemployed individuals may be viewed as very similar to one another. In that sense, stereotypes can be categorical, simplistic and quite narrow-minded.

A related phenomenon demonstrated by Wilder (1981), for example, is that people view individuals in an oversimplified, uniform and possibly rigid way only when those individuals belong to a group different from their own. When we think about our own groups, it seems clear that there are individual differences and variety in beliefs and characters, which cannot be reduced to two or three simple descriptive terms. Thus, people have more *complex* and *varied images* about themselves (ingroup), whereas stereotypes of groups they do not belong to (outgroup) tend to be *restricted* and *uniform*, a notion I will call *uniformity-variability of group images*.

Outgroup derogation

No matter what kinds of group in our society one thinks of, not only are intergroup differences and intragroup homogeneity exaggerated, but stereotypes are also often emotionally laden, so that *derogatory attributes* are applied to outgroups, and *flattering qualities* to the ingroup (e.g., Tajfel, 1982, 1984). In that way, stereotyping helps to preserve the individual's belief and value system. In publications following on from those of the early 1960s (e.g. 1981a), Tajfel argues that the *individual* functions of stereotypes – cognitive simplification of the social environment and value preservation – have to be complemented with considerations of their *social* functions, such as providing explanations of distressing large-scale social events, giving justifications of actions directed against outgroups and offering a source of positive social identification with one's own group as compared to other groups. Outgroup derogation thus bolsters one's self-image in the context of group comparisons. But even in Tajfel's *social* cognitive perspective, stereotyping is, in essence, still analysed in terms of universally applicable cognitive processes, and his emphasis remains on a model of stereotyping in which social content is grafted on to perceptually necessary categorization processes.

Critiques of perceptually based models of stereotyping contest that stereotypes are a natural by-product of human cognition, with prejudice becoming an inevitable feature of any kind of human society. First of all, categorization is only one process involved in human cognition, and it needs to be complemented by *particularization*, whereby individuals are distinguished from a general category and treated as a special case (cf. Billig, 1985). But more importantly, both these processes are *structured by the shared symbolic universe within which individuals and groups are embedded*. Such a social constructionist perspective problematizes the idea of 'perceptual bias' since there is no objective yardstick against which to measure stereotyped ideas. The 'stereotypy-as-error' position is not grounded empirically, nor can it be in principle:

the truth or falsity [of stereotypes] is never going to be known, because the research needed to find out will never be done. Is anyone interested in a project designed to find out whether approximately . . . 63.4 per cent of Germans are efficient (whatever efficient means)? (Brown, 1986, p. 594).

The present argument is by no means intended to imply that rigid, discriminatory stereotypes do not exist, but merely that stereotypical thinking has to be analysed not only in terms of *form and process*, but also in terms of *contents*. Moreover, such an approach allows for the possibility of sophisticated and complex shared beliefs about groups which might vary substantially socially and culturally (see also Mackie, 1973).

The 'kernel of truth' in stereotypes

Sociologists are likely to start from the position that groups and cultures do, in fact, differ and would therefore expect there to be a 'grain of truth' in stereotypes. In contrast, social psychology's emphasis on the falseness of stereotypes has at times almost become an implicit statement that all groups are on average identical (cf. Campbell, 1967). Given that the 'truth' of stereotypes cannot realistically be assessed, it is more informative and interesting to compare how members of a group view themselves with how they are viewed by others. Through delineating overlaps as well as differences in judgments, the relations between groups may be better understood through their reflection in group images. Thus, both self-description and descriptions by others can be viewed as 'real', and 'error' becomes a non-issue.

Considering just where the kernel of truth may lie, Campbell's (1967) contrast hypothesis about stereotypes suggests an important way in which real group differences enter into stereotypical descriptions:

> The greater the real differences between groups on any particular custom, detail of physical appearance, or *item of material culture*, the more likely it is that that feature will appear in the stereotyped imagery each group has of each other. (p. 358, emphasis added)

Thus, as a fifth criterion, stereotypes seem to have a kernel of truth, rather than being simply irrational. Differences between groups are no doubt exaggerated, but probably on those dimensions on which *real* inequalities exist (e.g., Campbell, 1967; Mackie, 1973). In the case of the present research, the three groups studied differ in terms of *relative wealth* and *employment status*. Thus objects indicating wealth and employment-related possessions should feature prominently in the material stereotypes held about students, business managers and unemployed people.

Respondents from these three groups listed their five most important possessions and, subsequently, wrote down those sets of five material objects they thought a *typical* member of each of the two other groups would list (i.e., unemployed participants were asked about a typical business commuter and a typical student; business commuters about a typical unemployed person and a typical student; and students about a typical business commuter and a typical unemployed person).

The possessions they listed were categorized into different types of material object, but actual individual items were also noted down for a qualitative analysis. Maybe surprisingly, business commuters, students and unemployed people overlapped considerably in the *types* of possession they described as most important to themselves. The only exception was in students listing more self-extension items, typically personal diaries and musical instruments, than the other two groups. If one looks at the actual *objects* listed, there remains some overlap in possessions referred to frequently (see Figure 6.5). Business commuters mentioned photos and sentimental mementos most often, whereas students and the unemployed referred prominently to their tapes, records and stereos. In addition, the unemployed were the only group concerned with basic items of furniture. However, the three groups differ more dramatically in idiosyncratic responses, mainly in terms of wealth. Only business commuters referred to such expensive items as antique furniture, collections of original artwork and video cameras. In contrast, unemployed people were more concerned with basic essentials, such as duvets, beds, cooking utensils, asthma inhalers or baby clothing.

When the *types* of possession listed by each group themselves (self-descriptions) were compared with the items listed for a *typical* member of that group by the other two groups (other-descriptions), two main findings emerged (see Dittmar, 1991a, for details). Firstly, types of possessions listed for self differed considerably from items listed by others for each of the three groups. And, secondly, the possessions listed by two groups for a typical member of the third did not differ from each other. This latter finding illustrates that material stereotypes were *consensual*. This means that even such economically different groups as business managers and unemployed people share a stereotype of the possessions of the typical student.

Considering each group in turn, the following picture emerges with respect to actual items listed (see Figure 6.5):

1. Business commuters: this group mentioned sentimental possessions such as photos and mementos most frequently, and much more prominently than the other two groups thought. Instead, the others added financial items, such as assets and credit cards, and employment-related objects, particularly a filofax and briefcase, business equipment and computers, as typical possessions of a business commuter. Cars were also described as typical treasured possessions, with examples like Porsche, Lamborghini and BMW.
2. Unemployed: the unemployed showed somewhat less variation in the possessions they listed themselves, with a good deal of emphasis on basic utility items, such as clothes and furniture. In essence, the possessions listed as typical for them amplify that trend, and – in comparison with the unemployed's actual possessions – reduce the

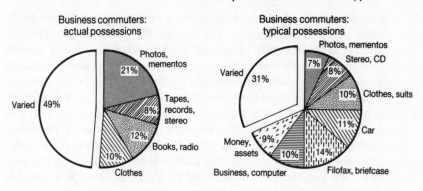

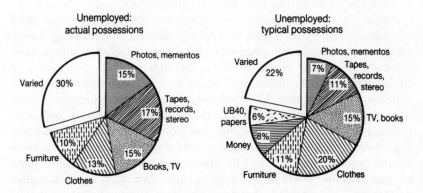

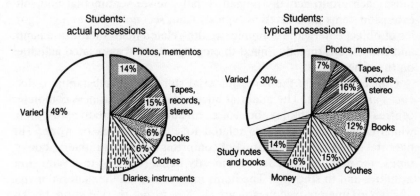

Figure 6.5 Actual and 'typical' possessions of three socio-economic groups

frequency with which music equipment and sentimental possessions were listed. Interestingly, and as for the business commuters, money as a financial item and (un)employment-related papers (benefit card, references) appeared as typical possessions, although hardly mentioned by the unemployed themselves.

3. Students: the findings for students follow the same general pattern, in the sense that fewer musical instruments and diaries, and also fewer sentimental possessions, were described as typical than students actually listed, and more books and clothes. And again, possessions related to financial concerns and main everyday activities, i.e., money, study notes and textbooks, emerge as typical, although hardly mentioned by the students.

Overall, typical possessions listed by others were less personalized than those each group actually named. Firstly, fewer sentimental and self-extension items were listed as typical. And, secondly, two new categories of object emerged: economic, wealth-related items on the one hand, and possessions directly linked to employment and associated activities on the other.

Concentrating on the three material stereotypes, substantial differences are apparent. The material image of a typical business commuter centres on clothes, filofax, briefcase, car, money and credit cards, all of which can be seen as items related to either finances or work. The material image of a typical student comprises clothes, stationery, books, tapes, records and stereos, i.e., mostly items referring to leisure time activities and to studying. The items most central to the material image of a typical unemployed person are clothes, furniture, television, books, photos and sentimental possessions. These seem to refer to basic essentials, passive entertainment and sentimentally charged objects.

Thus the consensually held material stereotypes differ substantially, whereas the possessions actually listed by the three groups show considerable overlap. In this way, group differences are exaggerated, particularly along socio-economic dimensions: relative wealth and employment-related features. These findings support the 'kernel of truth' notion, since it is the real inequalities between the three groups which are overemphasized in stereotypical images. Moreover, actual possessions listed were more *varied* and more *idiosyncratic*, whereas typical possessions were numerous, but more *homogeneous* overall (see Figure 6.5). Generally, variability in actual possessions is almost twice that of possessions described by others as typical. And, finally, some derogatory notes could be detected in such, admittedly rare, responses as 'Masonic membership card' or 'designer boxer shorts' as typical business possessions. And for the typical student, occasional references to 'drugs', 'homebrew kit', 'Mates condoms' and 'apple for the teacher' seem to express some doubt that serious study is the sole occupation of students.

Taking these findings in combination, it appears that material possessions are clearly used as stereotypical descriptors of different socio-economic groups, but in a relatively qualified fashion. They fulfil all of the five characteristics of stereotypes derived from the social psychological literature. Possessions actually described as important by self are more varied and heterogeneous than those possessions thought to be typical for a social group of which one is not a member. But stereotypes were fairly complex and sophisticated, drawing on a good number of typical material possessions to describe other groups. The material stereotype of each group was *consensual*, i.e. shared by two different socio-economic groups in each case. This result suggests that material group characteristics can be regarded as socially shared, societal representations. In other words, material symbols play an important role in structuring people's perception of different socio-economic groups. Real differences between the three groups were systematically exaggerated, and overlap underestimated. Both overlap and differences between actual and typical possessions give some insight into the relationships between these groups: relative wealth and employment status emerged as major themes. This would imply that sets of material possessions are used to *locate* other people in a social-material hierarchy. Placing and evaluating others in terms of their possessions fulfils an important function in orienting people in their social worlds, so that they can form impressions of others and anticipate the kinds of interaction that may take place with them.

The present study supports my notion that material possessions can function as stereotypes in social perception. The argument that such material stereotypes are representations which are shared and shaped socially and culturally would need to be addressed directly by cross-cultural research. This would be particularly effective in countries which differ from Western materialistic states, either in their economic organization or in the value placed upon acquiring material possessions. Of special interest would be *collectivist* cultures (cf. Hofstede, 1980), in which identity is thought to derive more from social relationships than from external, individualistic symbols.

Conclusion

In the first half of this chapter, the argument was put forward and illustrated empirically that major dimensions of identity, such as social-material position and gender, are reflected in the meanings possessions have for people. People thus express aspects of themselves and their identity through their possessions. The second half was concerned with the material possessions which are important to people from different social groups, and, at the same time, with the material images that exist of these groups: with how people *think* typical group members express their identity in terms of possessions. The three socio-economic groups studied overlap in the types of possession listed for themselves, but material stereotypes differ substantially along wealth and status dimensions. These results suggest that possessions are used as social-material *locators*, and may therefore constitute an important factor in how people structure their perception of social reality in materialistic cultures.

As a consequence of these latter findings, it would be expected that relative wealth plays an important role in the first impressions that are formed of other people. The notion that material possessions, and in particular assessments of relative wealth based on possessions, are used to make inferences about the identities of others is addressed in the following chapter.

Notes

1. Full methodological and statistical details of these studies are given in Dittmar (1990a). The main gist of the arguments presented here and relevant empirical details also appear in condensed and/or selective form in a series of articles and papers (Dittmar, 1989, 1991a, b).
2. Responses were converted into percentages so that each individual's response added up to 100 per cent. The figures given are average percentages for material possessions.
3. In order to even out the fact that some people had given few and some many reasons, the proportional frequency of responses in each reason subcategory was calculated for each individual and then converted into a percentage. For instance, if a person gave 12 reasons altogether and stated 'monetary value' three times, their score for this category would be $3/12 = 0.25$ or 25 per cent.
4. Correspondence analysis has only recently been acknowledged as a promising qualitative, factorial method for displaying associations and oppositions between two categorical variables in the same multidimensional space. Greenacre (1984) offers a good general discussion of this technique.

7

Fine feathers make fine birds:
The impact of material context on perceived identity

At this stage, it can be claimed with empirical backing that material objects play a profound role for their owner's identity. The studies reported in the previous chapter illustrate that broad social identity dimensions are reflected in, and probably in part maintained by, individuals' self-reported relationships with their personal possessions. Furthermore, material possessions are also manifest expressions of belonging to different socio-economic groups. But we do not only treat objects as symbols to remind *ourselves* of who we are, we also use them to display ourselves to *others*.

This chapter is concerned with the second major set of implications of the 'identity through possessions' model formulated in the introductory chapter. If a system of material symbols is part and parcel of how we perceive our social environment, it follows that the *placement* and *evaluation* of other people in terms of their possessions fulfils the important function of orienting us in our social worlds, so that we can form impressions of others and anticipate just how to interact with them. These kinds of concern make social psychological sense in a society that is characterized by heavy socio-economic stratification. Broadly speaking, this means that the *images* tied to *singular* possessions or *particular* brands of consumer durables may only be a minor contributor to evaluations of others, particularly in first encounters. Rather, it seems likely that *sets* of material possessions are used initially to locate another person in a social-material hierarchy, before considering their personal qualities and attitudes. In other words, *categorical judgments about relative wealth* should play a significant role in the first impressions we form about others.

By drawing on relevant evidence, mainly from consumer research, the initial question this chapter considers concerns the ways in which observers use others' possessions to make inferences about their identities. If it is true that first impressions involve locating others in terms of their social standing, so that we can judge their personal qualities, then socially shared representations should exist about what people from different material backgrounds *are like*. This issue is addressed by discussing attributional studies on poverty and wealth. Subsequently, the main bulk of this chapter attempts to apply different social psychological frameworks to the role of material context in forming impressions and gives an overview of some of my studies for illustrative purposes.[1]

Material objects and inferences about identity

The literature concerned with the social psychological significance of material possessions for identity from an *actor* perspective proved to be fairly sparse and fragmented. Even less systematic research has been carried out from an *observer* perspective: work which deals with how people make inferences about the identities of others on the basis of material objects. The symbolic-communicational model advanced in Chapter 4 draws an analytical distinction between material objects as symbols for the owner's unique personal qualities as an individual, and as symbols for group membership and social standing. Relevant research is therefore presented in terms of this distinction, at least initially. But an exploration of studies which investigate *configurations* of material possessions, rather than isolated items, soon makes it clear that these two kinds of evaluation are linked. The categorical location of individuals in terms of their social-material position seems to give rise to socially shared evaluations of their personal identity.

An early study by Thornton (1944) demonstrated that a difference as minor as whether a person wears glasses or not can lead to different evaluations: a person with glasses was seen as more industrious and intelligent than somebody without spectacles. However, such very first impressions may well change during social interaction (Argyle and McHenry, 1971). Similarly, women were viewed differently on five out of twenty-two personal attributes, depending on whether they wore lipstick or not (McKeachie, 1952). Wells *et al.* (1957) found that different representations existed about the personal characteristics of Ford, Buick and Chevrolet owners.

A particular consumer research methodology investigates the personal attributes projected on to buyers on the basis of the product brands they use: the 'shopping list experiment'. Typically, respondents are presented with a limited set of products bought by a fictitious person and then asked to evaluate that individual in terms of personal attributes. Differences in evaluations were demonstrated, for example, on the basis of real versus instant coffee (Haire, 1950), different beer brands (Woodside, 1972), cat food brands (Reid and Buchanan 1979), or soft versus alcoholic drinks (Woodside *et al.*, 1977). Other studies show that variations in clothing can also lead to the ascription of different personality traits (e.g., Douty, 1963; Hamid, 1968, 1969).

These kinds of investigation can serve as typical examples of a host of studies (see Holman, 1981, for a detailed review), which are interesting illustrations of the significance material objects have for perceived identity. But their focus on specific objects or brands, and isolated personal attributes, cannot offer any systematic insights into how material context influences impressions.

Other studies investigate inferences about group membership on the basis of material objects. For example, material goods symbolize social and political affiliations: they served as cultural signs for being part of the counterculture of the late 1960s and early 1970s (Buckley and Roach, 1974; Thomas, 1973), for the rejection of traditional values (e.g., Laumann and House, 1970), or the endorsement of radical feminism (e.g., Cassell, 1974). But, mostly, judgments about social identity on the basis of material factors seem concerned with status, social position and class. For example, Douty (1963) demonstrated that particular sets of clothes led to similar judgments about the owner's socio-economic status, regardless of the different targets who wore them. Social class ratings on the basis of photographs were also found to be consensual (e.g., Lasswell and Parshall, 1961). A recent study by Cherulnik and Bayless (1986) asked respondents to rate photographs of adults who were depicted in either an upper-middle-class or a lower-middle-class residential setting. The people in the more affluent setting received not only higher occupational ratings, but also consistently more favourable judgments about their personal qualities – despite arguments that symbols for social status are constantly changing (see Chapter 5).

Social status inferences affect more than impressions. An evaluation of people's social standing has direct consequences for how we behave towards them. For instance, Lefkowitz *et al.* (1955) found that pedestrians were more likely to cross a road against a red traffic light when somebody whose dress indicated high status took the lead than when that person was clad in inexpensive clothes. Strangers seem more honest in returning money apparently left in a phone booth when the caller's clothes suggest high rather than low status (cf. Bickman, 1971). It is interesting to note that a different group of respondents, who heard this situation described, predicted no difference in response (return of money) to the person dressed in a business executive suit as compared to somebody in a labourer's outfit. Either people were reluctant to admit that they would behave differently, or they were actually not aware how much such wealth and status information can influence their attitudes and actions. Doob's and Gross's (1968) much quoted 'horn-honking response' study showed that drivers were less likely to hoot at a car stationary in front of a green traffic light when the vehicle indicated that the driver had a high social position. Status of dress also influences the number of signatures collected for petitions (e.g., Darley and Cooper, 1972; Suedfeld *et al.*, 1971) or the perceived credibility of sales personnel (e.g., Leigh, 1981). Even this limited selection of examples suggests that social-material status inferences on the basis of material objects not only structure social reality to some extent, but they can also have profound implications for behaviour and interaction.

The investigation by Cherulnik and Bayless (1986) described above, as well as several more recent studies carried out by Belk and collaborators, present a considerable advance on the bulk of research described so far. They investigate the communicative properties of a *combination* of possessions rather than isolated items. Moreover, they examine inferences about *social standing* and *personal qualities* in conjunction.

Belk (1980) shows that the personal qualities projected on to others on the basis of material objects can be divided into two dimensions: affective (e.g., interesting, likeable, outgoing, kind) and dominant (e.g., successful, pushy, sophisticated). Having presented respondents with a description of a set of products, he asked them to evaluate the owner's personal qualities. Although the findings are not described in terms of status, but rather with respect to whether or not perceivers and targets used similar products, the results nevertheless indicate that affective qualities are thought to be more characteristic of a low-status student group and the dominance qualities more so of a higher-status student group.

People seemed to find it easy to come up with consensual judgments about the social position and personal attributes of house occupants after they had seen colour slides of different mobile and tract homes (Vershure *et al.*, 1977). Burroughs *et al.* (1991) take this kind of investigation one step further by addressing two main questions. The first concerns the extent of agreement of such observer-ratings with what owners think their possessions express about them, and the second deals with the relative usefulness of possession-information for making personality inferences. Women students were photographed in their favourite clothes and in the part of their room they felt best reflected their personality; they also provided lists of their most liked records, and their choice of study programmes. Observers rated a woman's personal qualities on the basis of only one of these four kinds of personal possession, but their judgments overall corresponded surprisingly well with her self-ratings. A second set of studies found that a person's possessions were seen as more informative about their personality than their typical behaviours and social activities. Moreover, using possessions, behaviours and social activities of actual students as stimulus materials, Burroughs *et al.* (1991) discovered not only that 84 per cent of observers preferred possessions over behavioural information in their first choice of cue, but also that those who made personality inferences on the basis of possessions were more accurate (i.e., agreed more with the owner's self-ratings) than observers who had chosen other information. This would suggest, then, that people are not only able to make personal identity inferences from material possessions, but also that they frequently make use of objects as a *particularly informative source* for impressions.

Stone (1962) argues from a Meadian perspective that appearance in general is used to *place* and identify a person, so that meaningful communication, discourse and interaction can take place. But he adds that a process of *personal evaluation* is inevitably also involved:

> The meaning of appearance . . . can be studied by examining the responses mobilized by clothes. Such responses take on at least four forms: identities are placed, values appraised, moods appreciated, and attitudes anticipated . . . By appearing the person *announces* his identity, *shows* his value, *expresses* his mood, or *proposes* his attitude. (p. 101, emphases in original)

Solomon (1986) similarly concludes in a review of relevant empirical work that the evidence confirms

> the belief that meanings transmitted by clothing affect the perception and thinking of both the viewer and the wearer. It is suggested that clothing provides information about social and occupational standing, sex-role identification, political orientation, ethnicity, and esthetic priorities. (p. 20)

Over thirty years ago, Goffman (1951) argued that the social status dimension of possessions and judgments about personal qualities are related, not independent. But rather than the symbolic dimensions of material possessions simply encompassing social as well as idiosyncratic information about others, he implied that categorical judgments of people lead to consensually shared evaluations of their personal qualities. As argued in Chapter 4, this suggests that the *locating* of others in a social-material hierarchy is of profound importance and that, therefore, judgments about relative wealth play a significant role for the impressions we form of others.

The notion that categorical judgments of social standing give rise to judgments of personal qualities is supported by the findings of Belk *et al.* (1982) that children and adolescents respond to photographs of cars and houses predominantly with status inferences (e.g., has money), but also with consensually shared personal evaluations of the owner (e.g., mean, successful). Maybe surprisingly, Driscoll *et al.* (1985) demonstrate in a comparable study that these 'stereotypical' impressions do not differ between children of different gender or class background. Belk (1978) used a 'lost property' paradigm, in which subjects had to reconstruct the owner's social and personal identity profile from the contents of allegedly found hand luggage. Its contents varied systematically (e.g., air ticket versus bus ticket, handstitched Moroccan leather versus imitation cowhide purse) and the sharpest differences in ratings were found for estimates of social background and income. However, these differences were accompanied by a variety of other judgments:

> Not only was the air traveler judged by relatively objective wealth-related criteria as being higher income, higher occupational status, more highly educated, and missing more money than the bus traveler, but he was judged by criteria objectively *unrelated* to wealth to be more likeable, successful, interesting, generous, responsible, attractive and aggressive!
> . . . [T]he more objective judgment of wealth creates a bias toward an array of other positive characteristics which bear no logical relationships to income. (pp. 45–6, emphasis in original)

Moreover, Belk's (1981) study of which characteristics of material goods are important in forming impressions about others clearly indicates that the actual cost of items is linked systematically to judgments not only about relative wealth, but also about personal qualities. It forms one of the most important cues for impressions, in addition to the personalizability and uniqueness of material possessions (see also Holman, 1981).

In conclusion, then, it may be argued that configurations of material possessions (rather than isolated items) serve to locate others in terms of class, status and social position, and that these categorical evaluations give rise to impressions of the owner's personal qualities and attributes. Some evidence tentatively suggests that these impressions based on relative wealth are consensual, i.e., widely shared. This would imply that socially shared representations exist of what relatively affluent people *are like* as compared to individuals from materially deprived backgrounds.

Perceived characteristics of 'wealthy' and 'poor' people

Research which may offer some indication about the characteristics that wealthy and poor people are thought to possess has mostly employed an attributional framework (cf. Heider, 1958; see Hewstone, 1989, for a general theoretical and empirical overview). Attribution theory is concerned with people's causal explanations for social events and has customarily employed a central (though not unproblematic) distinction between causes attributed to factors *internal* and *external* to a person. The particular studies of concern in this context asked respondents to provide causal explanations for wealth, poverty and material inequality. These kinds of investigation tend to demonstrate the importance of individualistic accounts – which explain why some people are rich and some are poor in terms of individual attributes – and their predominance over external explanations in terms of socio-economic structures or fate (e.g., Ashmore and McConahay, 1975; Baldus and Tribe, 1978; Feagin, 1972; Feather, 1974; Forgas *et al.* 1982; Furnham, 1982a, 1983; Furnham and Bond, 1986; Furnham and Lewis, 1986; Nilson, 1981). Although this literature is not concerned with the personal identities ascribed to others on the basis of relative wealth, a review of individualistic explanations for (non-)affluence may provide an initial insight into whether socially shared beliefs exist about the personal qualities of people from different material backgrounds.

Leahy's studies (1981, 1983a, b) on the development of notions about social inequality state that children soon develop a *psychological* model of wealthy and poor people in terms of different personal attributes, after having perceived them mainly in terms of *external* characteristics, such as possessions and clothes. He concurs with several other authors that there is a growing endorsement of the legitimacy of the distribution of wealth and poverty, which appears to be independent of the child's own relative socio-economic position (e.g., Connell, 1971, 1977; Crain and Crain, 1976; Cummings and Taebel, 1978; Dickinson, 1986; Emler and Dickinson, 1985). Furthermore, Baldus and Tribe (1978) showed that ideas about the characteristics of wealthy and poor people are consensually shared by 8- to 12-year-old children from different social class backgrounds. Their interviews illustrate that poor people were seen as tough, rough, lazy, inclined to drink, irresponsible and likely to have unlikeable and unsuccessful children. In contrast, rich people were seen as well-mannered, cheerful, nice, intelligent, happy and well-liked with successful and likeable children. Although the attributes given to wealthy people were mainly positive ones, the authors state that a small minority of their 12-year-olds saw rich people in a more ambivalent light, describing them as greedy and bossy.

Predominantly positive personal qualities for the affluent also appear in the individualistic attributions given by adolescents and adults for poverty, wealth and social inequality. However, these studies have tended to employ predetermined rating scales rather than more open-ended responses as Baldus and Tribe did (1978). Moreover, only a limited number of qualities was investigated, and studies have employed rather similar rating scales, which mainly derive from a study by Feagin (1972). This means that they can only present a narrow aspect of the characteristics of wealthy and poor people. But with these caveats in mind, these investigations in combination nevertheless suggest that wealthy people are seen as intelligent, responsible, hard-working, successful, skilful, physically attractive and resourceful. In contrast, poor people are viewed as lazy, unmotivated, lacking in abilities and skills, irresponsible, unattractive and lacking proper money management (e.g., Feagin, 1972; Feather, 1974; Forgas *et al.*, 1982; Furnham, 1982a, b, 1983; Furnham and Bond, 1986; Furnham and Lewis, 1986; Lewis, 1981; Nilson, 1981; Stacey and Singer, 1985).

Several authors describe differences in the degree to which such individualistic explanations are endorsed, depending on such factors as respondents' sex, level of education and religious affiliation (e.g., Feagin, 1972; Feather, 1974; Forgas *et al.*, 1982; Furnham, 1982a, b, 1983). But it nevertheless appears that these 'demographic variables . . . accounted for *small*, [although] significant proportions of variance in wealth attribution judgements' (Forgas *et al.*, 1982, p. 392, emphasis added). Although people may, and undoubtedly do, differ in terms of the extent to which they agree with explanations of relative wealth as a function of individuals' attributes, there is little indication that the actual *contents* of such representations differ much. The most consistent finding appears to be that a generally left-wing political outlook is associated with a somewhat stronger belief in structural and social causes of wealth and poverty than a right-wing outlook (e.g., Forgas *et al.*, 1982; Lewis, 1981; Pandey, *et al.*, 1982). But individualistic beliefs always seem to be endorsed to some extent (e.g., Nilson, 1981). Furnham (1983) argues that the attributes used to describe affluent people do not differ in *kind* for Labour and Conservative voters, but that their evaluative connotations were seen more positively by right-wingers (e.g., affluent individuals are 'hard-working' and 'thrifty') than by left-wingers (e.g., affluent individuals are 'ambitious' and 'ruthless').

For the concerns of this book, one of the most interesting questions is whether or not this individualistic model of personal qualities is endorsed equally by people from different socio-economic backgrounds, given that an individualistic outlook squarely lays the blame for poverty on the poor themselves (cf. Ryan, 1971). Some studies do report class and occupational differences (e.g., Feather, 1974; Furnham, 1982b), but there are also a good number of studies which do not (e.g., Feagin, 1972; Forgas *et al.*, 1982; Furnham and Bond, 1986). Particularly informative on this point is Nilson's (1981) analysis of over a thousand responses to an American National Election Survey. She failed to uncover differences in belief systems according to major social variables, such as income, occupational status or class. However, the situation may be different in a more openly class-conscious society like England.

In conclusion, it does appear that 'sociocultural stereotypes about "types of people" play a very important role in everyday explanations of wealth' (Forgas *et al.*, 1982, p. 390). Taken together, these studies would seem to indicate, at a general societal level, the existence of widely shared representations of the personal qualities of affluent and poor individuals. It is hardly surprising that, on the whole, the personal qualities of wealthy people are thought to be more positive than those seen as characteristic of poor people. But in the material discussed there were some indications that attitudes towards the affluent may not be free of ambiguity. A similar argument is put forward by Belk (1987) in his content analysis of material themes in American comics:

> These stories recognize that there is a temptation for the wealthy to use their wealth abusively and violate the rights of others while acquiring further wealth. However, the wealthy are generally regarded as sensitive to the rights of others and as having come by their wealth legitimately; we may be confident that they are entitled to it. The Protestant work ethic is still strong in these stories . . . The deserving poor are honest, intelligent and clean, lacking only the opportunity or circumstance to be wealthy. The undeserving poor are lazy or unintelligent, and are thus portrayed as lacking the internal motivation or ability to become wealthy. (p. 38)

A cross-cultural study on adolescents' self-conceptions (Tzeng and Everett, 1985) found that young British people view the wealthy both in a positive light as being independent and having a desirable social identity, and in a negative light as lacking warmth and cooperation.

Belk (1987) focuses on the mass media and mass communication as a source for encountering and internalizing socially shared representations of wealthy and poor people, and Nilson (1981) also raises the issue of ideological exposure: 'most Americans have heard the individualistic explanation of poverty and inequality more often and more favourably portrayed than they have the structural view. So the individualistic belief set should command more popular support' (Nilson, 1981, pp. 534-5). The arguments and evidence put forward by these authors would indeed imply that socially shared representations about the personal qualities of the wealthy and the poor are part and parcel of our symbolic universe. Beliefs about others on the basis of wealth may be more complex, diverse and ambiguous than revealed in the literature discussed. But, on the other hand, they may constitute dominant representations which have been incorporated, to some extent, in the belief systems of the vast majority of individuals, although there is some evidence to suggest that such belief systems may differ according to individuals' own relative socio-economic position, at least in some Western countries.

First impressions and material context

The marketing studies discussed at the beginning of this chapter highlight the significative role of consumer products. But they were carried out with an eye on advertising and purchase implications, rather than with the intention of accounting for the impact of actually owned possessions on first impressions. Some more broadly conceptualized research, which examined configurations of material possessions, suggests that assessments of a person's social-material standing give rise to socially shared evaluations of their personal identity. In a more indirect way, this particular point is echoed in attributional research on lay explanations for wealth, poverty and social inequality: on the whole, people tend to come up with quite individualistic theories for why some are rich and some are poor, which centre on the personal qualities and merits of the individuals concerned. Thus both sets of research suggest that material context should have a discernible influence on perceiving others' identities. So what theoretical frameworks are offered by psychology for an understanding of perceived identity, possessions and relative wealth?

The social psychological field traditionally concerned with how we view others is that of person perception, sometimes also referred to as impression formation. A literature search quickly reveals not only how extensive and varied this field is, but also that it shares a general concern with studying in detail the cognitive processes through which incoming information about others is analysed, integrated and combined to form an overall impression of a person. A few examples can illustrate this point. For instance, several developments have drawn on Asch's (1946) seminal work which deals with *central* personality traits. By presenting subjects with short attribute lists in which certain traits are systematically varied, he showed that certain personal attributes, such as 'warm' or 'cold', serve as central organizing qualities of the overall impression formed of the fictitious person's identity. Work on what has been termed *person memory* is concerned with the organization of such trait information in memory (e.g., Ebbesen, 1981; Hastie *et al.*, 1980) or with the processing and integration of information about several others (e.g., Pryor *et al.*, 1983). Other approaches have developed aspects of Asch's (1946) contention that the interpretation of single attributes is always influenced by other information also known about that person. Well-known examples are the meaning-change formulation (e.g., Hamilton and Zanna, 1974; Kaplan, 1971) or Anderson's weighted-average model (e.g., 1974), which aim at predicting the overall favourability of the impression people will form, given a set of attributes. Typically, and probably unavoidably, the stimulus materials used are quite sparse:

> In order to study very detailed cognitive processes, a certain *impoverishment* of stimulus materials seems inevitable, and so what we have [in impression formation] are mostly experiments on trait names (adjectives), verbal descriptions of action (sentences), occasionally still photos. (Brown, 1986, p. 378, emphasis in original)

Without questioning the importance and utility of this work, I would nevertheless argue that the overall emphasis on information processing tends to carry with it a neglect of the *social context* in which *real, everyday* impressions are invariably formed. This point is underpinned empirically, for example, by studies on situational (e.g., Forgas *et al.*, 1979) or other contextual factors in social information processing (e.g., Higgins and McCann, 1984; Swann, 1984). The need for more person perception research in 'environmental', i.e., broader social and material, context has been stressed (e.g., Cherulnik and Bayless, 1986).

However, even if this literature does not provide many relevant research findings for the question addressed here, the traditional impression formation paradigm does offer an interesting research methodology. People are not asked *directly* about their beliefs of what individuals from different wealth backgrounds *are like*. Rather, the question addressed is: if the *same* person is portrayed in relatively wealthy or relatively poor material circumstances, does that material context give rise to systematically different impressions and evaluations?

Despite a similarity in method, the present aim of tapping socially shared representations about material identity through an impression formation paradigm differs radically from the traditional concerns of person perception work. One of my studies which used such an impression formation approach starts from the proposition that material possessions give rise to a categorical judgment of relative wealth which, in turn, leads to expressive evaluations of an individual's personal qualities. In analogy with the literary movement of *chosisme* (e.g. Barbu, 1963; Perec, 1965), which aims at portraying an actor's identity, intentions and characteristics solely by reference to material objects, one way of accessing socially shared notions about material identity is to present respondents with a written description of a person, which includes a variety of material possessions, and to ask them to evaluate this person in terms of personal qualities.

At the University of Sussex, 120 students read a one-page description of a person, allegedly extracted from a novel. Given that the possessions–identity link appears gender-marked (see Chapter 6), this person was described as either female or male. Such an extract constitutes the kind of stimulus material which actually occurs in everyday life in the sense that people form impressions of the novel characters they read about. The material possessions in this vignette varied systematically, so that it portrayed the central character in either fairly affluent, average or quite poor material circumstances, including dress, room interior, transport and work equipment. For example, the affluent person possessed an expensive wardrobe, whereas the poor person had an old, narrow wardrobe. Respondents then evaluated the person they had read about in terms of various personal qualities. These personal qualities represent five identity dimensions as follows:

1. Autonomy (e.g., autonomous, self-reliant).
2. Direct control (e.g., in control of her or his environment).
3. Forcefulness (e.g., dynamic, assertive, dominant).
4. Warmth (e.g., friendly, warm, unselfish).
5. Individuality (e.g., unique, believes in self-expression).

Drawing on a variety of contributions, it could be expected that the identity projected on to a person on the basis of her or his material circumstances would vary along these identity dimensions. The *direct control* that possessions afford their owners has been emphasized (Furby, 1978a, 1980a), their role as regulators of interpersonal encounters (*forcefulness, warmth*) has been commented on (Isaacs, 1935), they have been viewed as means for expressing *individuality* (e.g., Holman, 1983), and examinations of Western conceptions of identity stress that *autonomy* is one of its main defining characteristics (see Chapter 8).

The findings showed, firstly, that consensual judgments were made about the described person's relative wealth on the basis of her or his material possessions and, secondly, that all five identity dimensions were affected by material context. The level of control people can exert

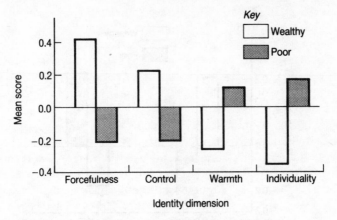

Figure 7.1 Relative wealth and perceived identity

over their environments and lives was thought to be greater with increasing wealth, as well as their forcefulness. In contrast, both interpersonal warmth and expressive individuality were viewed as less prominent the more affluent a person is (see Figure 7.1).[2] These findings were the same for female and male respondents, and irrespective of whether they had read about a man or a woman. They therefore suggest the existence of *consensual* representations of a person's identity, based on relative wealth. It is interesting to note that they echo research discussed in Chapter 6, which indicates that middle-class individuals stress the importance of self-direction and control as values for themselves, whereas working-class people describe themselves as more concerned with interpersonal relationships. On the whole, we find that the wealthy are seen in a somewhat ambivalent, rather than completely positive light, given that they are thought to lack warmth and expressiveness.

In contrast to these gender-independent evaluations, the identity dimension referring to autonomy and self-reliance differed with material circumstances according to whether the 'novel' character had been a woman or man. The female person was seen as having more autonomy when wealthy, whereas the male character – somewhat counterintuitively – was viewed as less autonomous when affluent (see Figure 7.2). These findings can be explained tentatively by drawing on Deschamps's (1982) analysis of socially shared representations as reflections of societal power relations. One of his main points is that the *dominant* are seen as autonomous and self-governing agents, whereas the *dominated* are viewed as an undifferentiated 'other'. The present

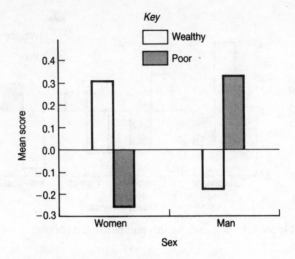

Figure 7.2 Autonomy ratings according to
material setting and target sex

findings support the idea that economic freedom through material
wealth is seen as an important means for women to attain autonomy: to
be able to decide about their lives and to gain bargaining power. For
men, relative wealth is not seen to make such a dramatic difference for
their autonomy, but the decrease with wealth may mean that the
possessions and wealth of men are thought to derive mainly from their
active efforts at procuring them in their role of *male breadwinner*. This
role may well be seen as one that leads to increasingly stressful and
complex work situations – curtailing personal freedom – the higher
earnings become.

Overall, this study offers illustrative support for the notion that
widely shared representations exist about possessions and identity,
which act as a strong influence on first impressions. The argument that
such representations are socially constructed is supported by the entirely
different findings of an identical study carried out with 240 Italian
students at the University of Rome (cf. Dittmar *et al.*, 1989). But this
type of research is fairly limited in several respects. Because it uses
written materials and students as respondents, it leaves open two
important questions. What happens when people form *actual* impressions of people they see, rather than read about? And, more importantly, if one wants to advance the position that first impressions are
influenced by societally shared representations with more certainty,
what exactly are the processes by which material context enters into the
perception of other people?

In search of theoretical frameworks

The search for relevant theoretical frameworks has to begin with some general considerations of different social psychological perspectives which may be relevant to material possessions and perceived identity. The *similarity-attraction paradigm* (e.g., Byrne, 1971) asserts in a general way that we like those who hold similar attitudes to our own, by implication including attitudes towards material possessions. But it could be argued that specific material possessions are less important for how we view other people than assessments about their relative wealth. Work on *intergroup relations* inspired by Tajfel (e.g., 1978a), one of the major research areas in social psychology during the last decade, implies that our own material location relative to that of the person we are evaluating should strongly affect the kinds of impression we would form of her or him. In contrast, a social constructionist emphasis on *dominant representations* suggests that people from different wealth backgrounds may form similar materially based impressions, relatively independently of their own material position.

The interindividual approach: attitude similarity

The idea that attraction and similarity are linked is hardly a recent recognition, given Aristotle's assertion that 'We like those who resemble us, and are engaged in the same pursuits . . . We like those who desire the same things as we' (as quoted in Byrne, 1971, p. 24). The main assertion of the classic similarity-attraction paradigm, that we are attracted to those we think hold similar attitudes to our own, was investigated with the 'bogus stranger' method. First, respondents' attitudes towards a number of issues are ascertained and later they are given information about another (fictitious) person's opinion on these issues. In various studies (reported in Byrne, 1969, 1971) it was found that, with increasing attitudinal similarity, the 'bogus stranger' was increasingly liked, but also viewed as more intelligent, better informed and well adjusted. In fact, Byrne claims that this relationship can be stated in terms of an empirical law, whereby attraction towards a stranger is a linear function of the proportion of similar attitudes the stranger is thought to hold (Byrne and Nelson, 1965).

Given that material possessions can be viewed as self-extensions and symbols of beliefs and attitudes, it might be argued that similar attitudes towards specific material possessions influence our liking and evaluation of other people. If others agree with our attitudes, it confirms our view of the world and facilitates social interaction (e.g., Gonzales *et al.*, 1983). In fact, similar economic attitudes appear to generate attraction

(Byrne *et al.*, 1966), and attitude similarity affects our evaluation of others' personal attributes (Byrne *et al.*, 1986).

The categorical approach: intergroup relations

Many social psychologists, notably proponents of intergroup perspectives, have attacked the predominantly individualistic focus of the discipline (e.g., Turner and Oakes, 1986), including such formulations as the attitude similarity paradigm (e.g., Brown, 1984). Instead of interpersonal processes, they stress the behavioural, cognitive and evaluative implications of belonging to social groups for self-perception, other-perception and behaviour in general (e.g., Tajfel, 1978a, b, 1984; Turner and Oakes, 1986). Much of the research carried out on intergroup relations has focused on membership in small, clearly circumscribed groups. But the proponents of a Tajfellian approach emphasize that belonging to broad social categories – such as race, gender or class – influences social evaluation and interaction despite the absence of small group characteristics: cohesive interpersonal relationships, consensual systems of norms and face-to-face interaction. These significant social category memberships are mainly characterized by a sense of belonging to them, an identity criterion (e.g., Turner, 1984).

As mentioned in Chapter 6, the basis of Tajfel's work on social categorization is to be found in his research on the influence of categories on quantitative judgments about physical stimuli (e.g., Tajfel, 1959a; Tajfel and Wilkes, 1963). Physical and social categorization are analogous in at least one way: stereotypic judgments of people in terms of their group membership also involve accentuation of intragroup similarity and intergroup differences (Tajfel, 1959a; Tajfel *et al.*, 1964). This cognitive accentuation rule is complemented with a social one, which states that accentuation increases further when intergroup comparisons are particularly value-laden or important to the individuals concerned (Tajfel, 1959a, b, 1978a). However, this perceptually based model of social categorization is insufficient in itself to explain why individuals may see those groups and social categories they belong to in a more favourable light than those they do not belong to. In order to account for such discrimination, Tajfel complements categorization with his concept of *social identity*.

During a series of experiments aimed at pinpointing which group characteristics need to be present for intergroup discrimination to occur, Tajfel *et al.* (1971) made the unexpected discovery that mere categorization into different groups (originally thought of as a control condition) led to discriminatory behaviour. Dividing school boys into two groups on the basis of preferences for abstract paintings was sufficient to make them systematically favour ingroup over outgroup members. But given that categorization into such *minimal* groups and attitude similarity (preference for artist) were confounded, Billig and Tajfel (1973) separated them experimentally and concluded that mere categorization is the more salient, and therefore critical, elicitor of ingroup favouritism.

In order to account for such findings, Tajfel (e.g., 1978a) proposed an extension of Festinger's social comparison theory (1954), now commonly referred to as *social identity theory*, or SIT for short. It makes two main, important assumptions. Firstly, it stipulates that a significant component of people's identities derives from their group memberships and, secondly, it maintains that individuals evaluate their beliefs and activities by comparing them to those of others. Social identity refers to those aspects of self-concept which are based upon group memberships and their emotional, evaluative and other psychological correlates. SIT's main underlying motivational hypothesis is that individuals seek to maintain a positively valued social identity by comparing ingroups favourably with outgroups. A further corollary, elaborated in particular by Turner (e.g., 1987), concerns differences between interpersonal and intergroup behaviour. *Interpersonal* behaviour means that 'the interaction between two or more individuals . . . is *fully* determined by their interpersonal relationships and individual characteristics', whereas *intergroup* behaviour is characterized by 'interactions between two or more individuals . . . *fully* determined by their respective memberships of various social groups or categories' (Tajfel and Turner, 1979, p. 34, emphases in original). But Tajfel (1978a) asserts emphatically that

> at least one of these extremes – the interpersonal one – is *absurd*, in the sense that no instances of it can conceivably be found in 'real life'. It is *impossible* to imagine a social encounter between two people which will not be affected . . . by their mutual assignments of one another to a variety of social categories about which some general expectations concerning their *characteristics* and behaviour exist in the minds of the interactants. (p. 41, emphases added)

In terms of possessions and identity, SIT would therefore lead to the expectation that a wealthy individual should evaluate somebody who is also affluent more favourably than somebody who is less well off. At the same time, less affluent people should prefer those from a similar background to their own. But given the negative image of poor individuals, would it really be the case that a person from a deprived material background views a fellow poor individual in a more positive light than somebody who has 'made it' materially?

Ingroup favouritism and outgroup discrimination seem very robust and symmetrical phenomena in artificially created laboratory groups (see Tajfel, 1982; Wetherell, 1982). But studies of actual groups in the 'real world' highlight that we live in a society where group relations invariably involve unequal status, and where ingroup favouritism is often limited, particularly for people who belong to underprivileged groups (e.g., Brown, 1978; Doise and Sinclair, 1973; Skevington, 1980, 1981; Van Knippenberg and Van Oers, 1984). Ng (1982) illustrates that the usual pattern of favouring the ingroup and discriminating against the outgroup is changed radically, even within the laboratory minimal group paradigm, as soon as one group is given more power than the other.

Social categories which are viewed negatively cannot easily provide their members with a positive social identity. Minority group members may internalize the negative representations held about them and come to identify with majority evaluations; for example, black children preferring white dolls (Clark and Clark, 1947). Tajfel (1978b) outlines a number of strategies members of disadvantaged groups can adopt to achieve some positive identity. But when status differences are stable, disadvantaged groups are often left with having to create, or single out, particular dimensions of comparison on which they can view themselves as positively distinct from high-status groups (see also Lemaine, 1974).

Various ethnolinguistic studies carried out during the 1960s examined how members of different ethnic groups (and invariably different socio-economic status) evaluate themselves and each other. They typically found that high-status listeners rated their own (tape-recorded) speakers more positively on various social and personal qualities. In contrast, low-status listeners would evaluate not their own, but the *high-status* speakers more favourably on a *majority* of attributes. So they accentuated group differences in favour of the outgroup (e.g., Anisfeld *et al.*, 1962; Cheyne, 1970; Lambert *et al.*, 1960). Tajfel (1959b) fore-shadows later SIT-derived work on intergroup perceptions and status, because he describes the exaggerated negative self-evaluation of the disadvantaged group as a reflection of existing differences in socio-economic status between the two linguistic communities.

More recently, Van Knippenberg (1978, 1984; Van Knippenberg and Wilke, 1979) has argued that social identity theory can indeed be extended to intergroup perceptions and evaluations, including those of unequal status groups. First, it is necessary to distinguish between consensual and competitive characteristics. *Consensual* characteristics are qualities where both groups agree as to which is superior, often status-related attributes which stem from a socially shared appraisal of the relative social standings of both groups. In contrast, *competitive* characteristics are qualities on which the two groups disagree about the direction of the difference, usually attributes not related to status. In a stable situation, high-status individuals can rest comfortably on their established, already positive social identity and, as a consequence, are not particularly worried about marked intergroup differences or ingroup superiority. The situation is very different for low-status individuals. Assuming that they cannot leave their group easily, the awareness that they are relatively disadvantaged should make comparisons with high-status group members salient and worrying. They would therefore exaggerate intergroup differences on consensual characteristics because they are related to status. Competitive, status-unrelated qualities should be both accentuated and evaluated in favour of the ingroup, so that low-status individuals can claim for themselves at least some comparison dimensions which contribute to a positive social identity.

Students who attended either high- or low-status technical colleges were asked to evaluate both their own and the other group on various status and human relations attributes. Part of the findings were in line with SIT-derived predictions about consensual and competitive qualities, but while the low-status students accentuated group differences on status (income, leadership, socio-economic status or SES, success) in favour of the outgroup as expected, they thought these dimensions more important and valuable than did the high-status group. Moreover, for the human relations dimension (warm, friendly), which would appear a good candidate for competitive evaluations, both groups rated the lower-status students more positively. In order to explain these anomalies, Van Knippenberg puts forward two propositions which go beyond social identity conceptualizations. Firstly, he argues that group descriptions do not simply reflect individuals' desire to depict their own group favourably *vis-à-vis* outgroups, but that they constitute *strategic comments* about intergroup relations:

> It is in the interest of the lower status group to emphasize the value of status. It is their way of saying . . . that the existing status differential is highly important to them. I assume that, if they were given the opportunity, they would qualify the superior status of the other group as illegitimate. The higher status group does not boast of its superior status. Its members seem to indicate that the status difference is quite unimportant, i.e. no reason for other groups to be concerned about. The higher status group's evaluation of status is interpreted as a strategic measure to secure its privileged position. It can be argued that group ascriptions and evaluations of characteristics serve to express the subject's view with regard to the *legitimacy* of the status relationship. (1984, p. 572, emphasis in original)

Secondly, he suggests that group comparisons can be seen as acts of *mutual validation*, which essentially preserve existing status differences. The high-status students are quite happy to rate the low-status group as superior on human relations (friendly, cooperative). This provides them with some form of positive social identity, but – through its harmless nature – does not threaten the privileged position of the high-status group. Low-status groups adopt evaluations which are essentially in agreement with those of the high-status group because that is all they can do in order to maintain some form of positive image.

Van Knippenberg (1978, 1984) describes his model as an extension of SIT, but I would propose that his two notions of strategic comments and mutual validation sit uneasily with both the perceptual and motivational underpinnings of social identity theory.

The role of social categorization in intergroup behaviour is viewed by SIT, at least in part, in terms of *perceptual processes* where within-group similarities and intergroup differences are exaggerated as a means for clearly distinguishing between category members and non-members. However, Van Knippenberg's strategic comment formulation suggests that the degree of accentuation in evaluating members of one's own group compared to members of other groups is a function of a person's *relative status position*, rather than constituting a perceptual process which takes place independently of social context. As a second point, SIT can provide an elegant explanation of the processes underlying competitive group descriptions through the motivation towards positive distinctiveness. But there is no comparable explanation with respect to consensual descriptions, which appear to be taken for granted rather than as requiring theoretical analysis. This neglect seems all the more glaring in the light of the many SIT studies which find a good number of consensual descriptions for and by high- and low-status members, but few competitive ones. Both concepts advanced by Van Knippenberg try to account for the relative or complete absence of ingroup favouritism – particularly for low-status individuals – by stressing the necessity to extend one's analytic focus from the two groups investigated to viewing them as embedded in a *wider structure of social relations*. This implies that it is important to conceptualize group descriptions in terms of *generally shared representations* about the characteristics of high- and low-status individuals. By analysing such group descriptions as comments about existing status relations and in terms of their role in the maintenance of existing status differentials, van Knippenberg takes some important steps away from SIT towards viewing intergroup perceptions as socially constituted representations, which are shared to a significant extent *across* category boundaries.

A social construction approach: dominant representations

Individuals perceive reality within the context of socially shared meaning systems (see Chapter 4), and a good portion of social knowledge is available to us in the form of 'information which is free-floating, available to all regardless of their position in a structure of social relationships' (Connell, 1977, p. 150). Such information is presented and represented, for example, in the mass media, but also in everyday conversation and communication. For instance, Adoni and Mane (1984) review the role of the mass media in shaping both collective and individual consciousness: they organize the knowledge people have of their everyday lives and other, more remote, contexts, and they present that knowledge with greater or lesser prominence. In that sense, socially shared beliefs can be regarded as a quasi-autonomous environment which forms part of the very structure of society itself (e.g., Farr and Moscovici, 1984; Moscovici, 1984, 1988). The argument that widely shared notions exist about people from different material backgrounds is supported by evidence from economic and political socialization, which indicates that children possess an understanding of the distribution of wealth and societal status relations long before they enter into the economic environment, where they can gain direct experience themselves (see Chapter 3). Given that representations about people from different wealth categories seem to favour the wealthy rather than the poor, it may be argued that the symbolic environment we share contains not simply socially shared beliefs, but *dominant representations*, which are related to the distribution of power and status in society.

The argument that among a variety of possible representations some are more prevalent and dominant than others is usually encountered in the sociological and political literature concerned with ideology. Generally, such contributions agree that dominant meaning systems reflect the social composition of society (e.g., Adorno, 1967, 1968; Goff, 1980; Hall, 1986; Sampson, 1983). This literature is far too complex and diverse to be discussed here, but a few comments may be useful nevertheless.

What is described as the *dominant ideology thesis* by Abercrombie *et al.* (1980) is encapsulated in the often-quoted statement by Marx and Engels (1965) that 'the ideas of the ruling class are in every epoch the ruling ideas: i.e., the class which is the ruling material force of society is at the same time its ruling intellectual force' (p. 61). But beyond agreement on such a shorthand definition, ideology has been conceptualized in a variety of ways. Painting with a broad brush, two usages can be distinguished (see also Billig *et al.*, 1988; Sampson, 1983). Firstly, ideology has been defined as particular sets of internally consistent ideas (such as Marxism, fascism, communism). In this context, 'capitalist' ideology has been described as a set of ideas which serve those in power to conceal their real interests and to manipulate the beliefs of the disadvantaged into a 'false consciousness' to get them to accept the status quo. This usage will not concern us here. Secondly, and less prominently, ideology has been viewed more broadly as the ideas and values held by people, which reflect their particular socio-cultural context. Such a perspective makes ideology virtually coterminous with common culture or common sense (e.g., Geertz, 1964; Thompson, 1986). So, beliefs, values, and social practices can be understood as part of 'lived ideology', which epitomizes the 'social patterning of everyday thinking' (Billig *et al.*, 1988, p. 28). Stressing the similarity between the notions of common culture and ideology need not imply, however, that shared representations do not reflect the power structure of a given society (see also Spears, 1989). In order to emphasize this point, the term *dominant representations* is used throughout the remainder of this book.

As Connell (1983) states, 'dominant groups shape the words we have to talk with, the concepts we have to think with' (p. vii). He provides a striking example of how dominant representations may enter into self-definition. Attributional research on the characteristics of wealthy and poor people noted the repeated references to intelligence. Connell (1971) asked adolescents from relatively deprived backgrounds about their choice of future occupation and was given explanations such as the following (described in Connell, 1977, pp. 152–3):

> I'd like to do something with science . . . [but] I'm not brainy enough (Girl, 12).
>
> I don't think I've got the brains really, the intelligence
> [to become a kindergarten teacher], you know you've got to go all through school and then university . . . I'd go in for a factory (Girl, 13).
>
> I want to join the Air Force and be an electrical engineer, but . . .
> I haven't got the intelligence (Boy, 15).

Connell (1977) stresses that these adolescents are of normal intelligence and concludes that the 'trouble with them is not that they are subnormal, simply that they are working-class . . . [they] are convinced, before they have really begun, that they are not able' (p. 153).

One of the rare social psychological treatments of power relations and shared representations can be found in Deschamps (1982). This contribution emphasizes the importance of asymmetrical power relations between social categories, which manifest themselves not only at a concrete but also at a symbolic level:

> the world order, created and conceptually constructed, as it is, by those who dominate it, implies the fact that membership of groups is not equally salient for all. Its salience varies for individuals considered as social actors depending upon their possession of power or lack of it; and upon their

distance from a point of reference in relation to which everyone is *supposed* to be able to define himself . . . but which, in reality, only tends to define those who are the owners of material or symbolic capital. (p. 88, emphasis in original)

This implies that dominant representations should exist about what individuals from high and low socio-economic status backgrounds are like. However, such a shared frame of reference does not mean that people simply internalize such representations, only that there is a socially given *framework*, with respect to which everybody has to define herself or himself and others. As a consequence, the outlooks of the *dominant* and the *dominated* differ, since both groups necessarily define themselves in relation to the same societal norms: the *dominant*, as individual subjects, are always included in the context which provides the general point of reference and therefore experience a *congruent social identity*; for the dominated, however, the *object* identity attributed to them in and through their social relations is inherently contradictory and lacks congruence with the general norm defining all human beings.

Although Deschamps (1982) is mainly concerned with the social identity implications of such dominant representations, his arguments are also relevant for intergroup perception and evaluation. The dominant representations perspective advanced here provides an explanation for the existence of consensual group descriptions, which is not given by social identity theory. Moreover, with respect to impression formation and relative wealth, it would lead to the expectation that people would form essentially similar first impressions of others on the basis of their relative wealth, quite irrespective of their own material background.

Material impressions and different socio-economic backgrounds

In order to address the guiding theoretical question of whether *general* representations of identity exist as a function of material context, or whether such representations are *specific*, either with respect to material background or with respect to attitudes towards particular possessions, two groups of adolescents were studied – one from a fairly affluent, middle-class background and the other from a less well-off, working-class background. If perception is guided by *interindividual* considerations as suggested by the similarity-attraction paradigm, it would be expected that these adolescents form favourable impressions of somebody who they think has attitudes similar to their own towards particular possessions. The *intergroup relations* approach highlights the importance of social category membership and suggests that impressions are shaped by our motivation to see somebody from a similar material background in a more favourable light than people from different backgrounds. Notwithstanding the theoretical refinements introduced in recent extensions of social identity theory, this approach suggests that people feel some affinity towards others with similar financial and material resources and therefore view them in a favourable light. It would therefore predict an *interaction effect*: perceptions of a wealthy and a less well-off person should be very different for the working-class as compared to the middle-class adolescents. This expectation is based on the assumption that the two groups from different socio-economic background identify with their own social category to some extent.

On the other hand, adolescents may not have such a *politicized* awareness of socio-economic stratification, and therefore do not construe their social environment in terms of social class identification. This could mean that they are very much aware of wealth differentials – and would therefore focus on a person's material standing – but that their impressions are not influenced by interpersonal or intergroup concerns: their impressions may reflect in quite a passive way *dominant representations* about the characteristics of wealthy and poor people. This would mean that impressions should be consensual, quite irrespective of perceivers' material backgrounds and attitudes.

These three approaches have been separated analytically, but it is not necessarily true that they are mutually exclusive, or unrelated. They may form a kind of hierarchy: the attitude similarity framework focuses on very particular features between two persons; the intergroup relations model deals with broader issues involving the social groups and categories individuals belong to; and the dominant representations perspective is concerned with general, societal influences on how people perceive others. Most probably, perceiving others' identities in a material context has general as well as particularistic aspects. However, the question of interest here concerns the relative influence of material attitude similarity, category membership and dominant representations when people form first impressions about the identities of other people.

For this more extensive study with adolescents from different socio-economic backgrounds, it was decided to use short videos as stimulus material, which show a person in her or his 'home'. Videos offer a rich and naturalistic depiction of a person in comparison with written descriptions. Two young people (one female, one male) were filmed in either relatively wealthy or relatively impoverished surroundings (e.g., kitchen, living-room, car), resulting in four short videos. Differences in material circumstances were not overly extreme, but reflected those between a well-to-do middle-class context and a less affluent context, which included clean but rather basic essentials and commodities. Over a hundred 16–18-year-old adolescents took part in this study, who came either from a public school, fairly affluent, middle-class background or from a working-class background. Small groups of these adolescents were shown *one* of the videos, and were then asked to describe the person they had seen in terms of various personal qualities. They also judged whether they shared similar attitudes to specific material possessions with that person and indicated how much they liked her or him. Finally, they described how similar the material circumstances displayed in the video were to their home environment.

Similar attitudes to material possessions: Overall attitude similarity combined respondents' ratings of how important various objects *displayed in the video* would be to them personally with ratings of how important they thought they were to the person in the video. The higher the perceived attitude similarity between adolescents and video character with regard to material possessions, the more personal liking they expressed for the person shown. However, impressions formed of the video person's identity were *not* systematically related to attitude similarity (see Dittmar, 1990b).

Similarity in perceived wealth between video and parental home: Both groups of adolescents agreed that one video setting displayed significantly more wealth than the other. As expected, the adolescents from a middle-class background saw the *wealthy* video setting as more similar to their parental homes than the *poor* video in terms of the level of material wealth displayed. The reverse effect emerged for the working-class adolescents (see Figure 7.3).

Social identity processes have been shown to occur as soon as the most minimal of category-related cues are given (e.g., see Brown, 1988, for an overview of the minimal group paradigm). This was certainly the case with respect to the videos presented, which portrayed different, consensually recognized levels of wealth. There is also evidence that such processes operate even if a person is not directly perceived as an ingroup or outgroup member, as long as that person is seen as belonging to a similar or dissimilar social category (Brown, 1984) – which was the case in the present study. But the expectation derived from social identity theory of an *interaction* between adolescents' background and the material setting in the video in terms of the impressions they formed was not confirmed.

Dominant representations: Instead of differences between the middle-class and working-class adolescents, it was found that impressions differed only on the basis of the material circumstances portrayed

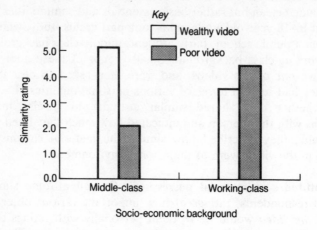

Figure 7.3 Material similarity between video and home environment

in the video. This implies that representations about the identity of wealthy as compared to less affluent individuals are *shared across* different socio-economic groups. Impressions were summarized into the five identity dimensions described earlier – autonomy, direct control, forcefulness, warmth, individuality – and a sixth dimension was added concerning abilities and resources (e.g., intelligent, educated, success-ful). Both working-class and middle-class adolescents agreed that the wealthy person was more intelligent, successful and educated, as well as more in control of her or his life and environment, than the poor character. A similar, but less pronounced, trend emerged also for forcefulness. In contrast, the person in the poor video was seen as warmer, friendlier and more self-expressive (see Figure 7.4).

The findings for the identity dimension of autonomy are more complex. The middle-class adolescents saw the video person as moder-ately autonomous, regardless of whether that person was rich or poor, a man or a woman. In contrast, the working-class adolescents saw autonomy as strongly related to both gender and wealth. The female video character was viewed as less autonomous and self-reliant when poor than when wealthy, whereas the reverse was found for the male character (see Figure 7.5).

Taken together, these findings indicate that neither assumed similar attitudes towards specific material possessions nor similarity in socio-

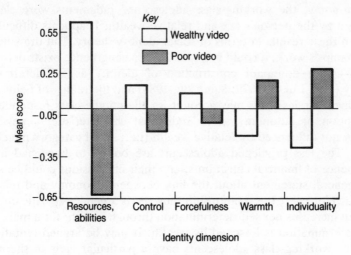

Figure 7.4 Perceived identity and relative wealth (video)

economic standing exerted much influence on the impressions adolescents formed about the personal identity of an individual shown on video. Differences between the working-class and middle-class adolescents were only found with respect to evaluating the autonomy and self-reliance of the video character. Whereas the middle-class adolescents always saw the person depicted as somebody with a moderate amount

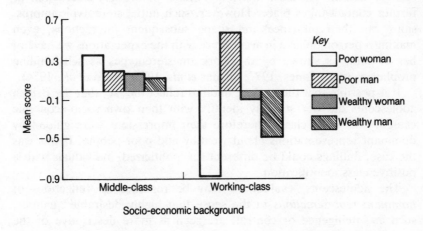

Figure 7.5 Autonomy ratings by two groups of adolescents

of autonomy, the working-class adolescents' judgments were clearly affected by the person's sex and relative wealth. It appears difficult to explain these results in terms of social identity theory. But drawing on Deschamps's work, it could be argued that a congruence exists between the Western dominant construction of identity as self-determined agency (e.g., Lukes, 1979; Sampson, 1988) and the reality of belonging to affluent circles. This may account for the middle-class respondents' perception of autonomy as an individual characteristic: a personal quality not influenced by relative wealth (i.e., social category membership). The less privileged adolescents are bound to have had more experience of financial constraints, and their impressions could be seen as a general statement about the link between autonomy and relative wealth. However, the relationship they see is a gender-specific one. A woman increases her self-determination through wealth; for a man, this self-determination is lessened by wealth. It may be argued tentatively that the working-class adolescents have a particular view of the male breadwinner, whereby earning a lot of money means having to enter into increasingly high-powered jobs which leave less space for a personal life. This might indicate that they view certain aspects of wealth in a negative light, at least as they apply to men.

The findings that both groups of adolescents agree in their impressions for all other identity aspects lends support to the notion that widely shared representations exist about what wealthy and less affluent people *are like*. This argument is strengthened further by the striking similarities in findings with the earlier vignette study with young adults. These representations influence impressions on the basis of a person's relative wealth – at least first impressions, before any interaction or further contact takes place. However, such initial stereotypic impressions can then influence and shape subsequent interactions, even making a person behave in accordance with the expectations we have of her or him, as shown by the work on stereotypes as self-fulfilling prophecies (e.g., Jones, 1977; Snyder *et al.*, 1977; Word *et al.*, 1974).

It is possible that the present findings reflect the fact that the British adolescents did not strongly identify with their own socio-economic category or social class. Therefore their impressions were guided by dominant representations about wealthy and poor people. If this was the case, findings could be different for 'politicized' individuals with a positive class identification.

The adolescents' evaluations may be regarded as reflections of *dominant representations* in the sense that highly desirable qualities, such as intelligence or control, are seen as more descriptive of the wealthy. But it appears that these representations contain ambivalent elements, given that impressions of warmth and expressiveness favour the less affluent. The dominant Western conception of identity (see Chapter 8) emphasizes the importance attached to the cultural values of control, assertion and self-direction. Therefore such qualities as being friendly and emotionally expressive may be regarded as desirable, but somehow less important, qualities. Drawing on Van Knippenberg's (1984) notion of *mutual validation*, it is maybe not surprising that such attributes are accorded to less affluent strata of society, which may at the same time play a role in the maintenance and positive evaluation of wealth differentials.

Conclusion

When the last two chapters are considered together, they do seem to illustrate that social psychological theories can be applied successfully to studying and conceptualizing the role of material possessions in everyday social life. Given that social psychology offers a good number of established frameworks for understanding the perception and representation of social phenomena (e.g., social identity theory, social representations, etc.), it certainly has the potential to provide fertile ground for attempting to gain a better understanding of the ramifications of materialism for day-to-day living and our relationships with others.

Moreover, although the studies reviewed cannot offer any conclusive evidence for the symbolic-communicational model of material possessions advanced in Chapter 4, they nevertheless provide illustrative support for the propositions that the meanings of possessions as symbols of identity are socially constituted, that our own identity is expressed and reinforced by what we have, and that we evaluate others in the context of their material things by drawing on socially shared representations.

The previous chapter was mainly concerned with an *actor* perspective, with how identity is symbolically expressed from the viewpoint of the owner, whereas this chapter has dealt with the *observer* perspective and focused on the impact of material possessions and wealth on perceived identity. Although they examine different specific topics and therefore cannot be compared in any direct sense, a brief consideration of how these perspectives relate to each other nevertheless reveals several common themes. First of all, the model of the meanings and functions of possessions described in Chapter 4 can be applied to both an actor and an observer point of view, given that both used distinctions between functional and symbolic aspects of possessions and, within the symbolic range, the distinction between social standing and personal qualities. Secondly, in Chapter 6, people from fairly affluent backgrounds referred to self-directedness and self-development, whereas participants from less privileged socio-economic categories were more concerned with the practical and emotional functions of possessions. Broadly speaking, these dimensions are also reflected in the perception of others: the wealthy are seen as forceful and in control, and the less affluent as warm and cooperative. Furthermore, women and men described fairly distinctive relationships with their possessions, which centred on an autonomy-relatedness dimension. The theme of autonomy also emerges in the gender-specific representations people hold about the link between this aspect of identity and relative wealth.

The presence of such broad, overarching themes in both the expression and perception of identity with respect to possessions and wealth may well indicate a cultural *thinking environment* which is characterized by two main features. Firstly, Western culture seems to endorse a particular conception of identity, which is not shared by the non-Western world. And, secondly and more speculatively, it appears that socio-cultural notions about the *link* between identity and material social reality are somewhat ambiguous, potentially ideological in nature and articulated only implicitly. The concluding chapter addresses these issues.

Notes

1. Full methodological and statistical details of the studies described can be found in Dittmar (1990a). The main gist of the arguments presented here and selected empirical details also appear in a series of articles and papers (Dittmar, 1990b, 1991c; Dittmar et al., 1989).
2. For the sake of simplicity, only findings for the affluent and poor material circumstances are displayed in Figures 7.1 and 7.2. The means reported throughout this chapter refer to factor scores (for each identity dimension), which constitute standardized combinations of the original variables. Further empirical details can be found in Dittmar et al. (1989).

8

The current Western conception of identity:
The materialism–idealism paradox

The symbolic meanings of material possessions are integral to expressing our own identity and perceiving the identity of others. Yet this symbolic-communicational role played by material objects has several peculiar features, which have little in common with the more traditionally recognized communication system *par excellence*: language. These peculiar features of material symbols were touched upon in Chapter 4 and can now be reviewed with the hindsight and back-up of empirical research. They raise questions about the implications of the link between material objects and identity for everyday social life and, in particular, they highlight the significance of the ways in which this link is recognized – or, as the case may be, *not* recognized – in socially shared representations.

When compared to the elaborate communication system of language, material possessions are more restricted in the number and range of things they can express as symbols of identity. Particularly when used to perceive others, material possessions convey first of all *social* categories, *types* of person, or *stereotypes* of different social groups. We use material objects to *locate* others in a social-material hierarchy, before the more subtle and varied meanings of their possessions tell us about more individual, personal aspects of the owners' identities. This book has not been concerned with specific single possessions or particular types of possession as expressions of very personal, idiosyncratic or even unconscious aspects of identity. Rather, it has focused on the relationship between possessions and broader social identity dimensions; the emerging importance of social and material placement has to be understood in the context of the increasingly finely graded socio-economic stratification which permeates social and private life in Western societies.

It also seems that many of the representations people hold about the identity aspects which go with different material circumstances are shared across different socio-economic groups, maybe even shared at a societal level. At least in terms of first impressions, we may draw on such socially shared notions, rather than be guided by the motivation to perceive people from a socio-economic background similar to our own in a category-defensive, positive light. The fact that, of course, our own relative material location nevertheless enters into such impressions is documented by the different ways in which working-class and middle-class adolescents described the link between autonomy and relative wealth (see Chapter 7).

Moreover, the messages given and received via material symbols may not always be overt, and their interpretation not always conscious and deliberate. O'Guinn's and Shrum's (1991) study concerned with the mass-mediated construction of subjective economic norms gives some suggestion of the possible extent to which the mass media messages we are continuously bombarded with are unthoughtfully reproduced in social perception and social explanation (see Chapter 4). Or, to give another example, consider Bickman's (1971) contradictory findings of the *different* rates at which people returned money allegedly left in a public phone booth to a stranger who wore either a business suit or a labourer's overall on the one hand, and the *equal* return rates predicted by people who simply heard the situation described to them on the other. A possible explanation is that people are loath to admit that they would be more honest towards an individual from a higher social-material background than towards a builder, but it seems equally – if not more – likely that people are not directly aware of the extent to which material context influences their perception and impressions.

Looked at slightly differently, material possessions may constitute particularly powerful symbols precisely because they circumvent explicit messages about status, wealth and power differences, while depicting and thus reinforcing these differences in a visible and compelling way. However, while material symbols allow for the *representation* of social structures, social categories and social processes, their subtle symbolic elusiveness makes them difficult to manipulate for innovation and social change. As suggested in Chapter 5, the endless pursuit of 'displaced ideals' through acquiring increasingly more expensive material goods is not conducted in such a way that the 'ideals' are amenable to change, only the alleged means (possessions) for achieving them. Cushman (1990) even talks of an 'empty self' which, we have learned throughout socialization, requires us to fill it up continuously with material goods and consumption experiences, in order to reconstitute and recreate our identity – with advertising as one of the main professions to provide the meanings of material symbols. Thus, material symbols display social information that is not easily transformed, and in that sense they form a conservative code (see also McCracken, 1990). If they help to maintain the status quo and the social composition of society, they can be considered *ideological* in a broad sense. McCracken observes in this context that

[t]he study of the expressive properties of material culture must reckon with a paradox. Material culture is . . . extremely limited in its expressive range . . . it is a relatively impoverished means of communication. It stands as a kind of mystery, then, why culture should utilize it for any communicative purpose . . . The answer to this paradox must be that material culture . . . has certain virtues not shared by language. (p. 69)

Some of the virtues – and vices – which constitute peculiar features of material possessions as a communicative, symbolic system have been touched upon above. What needs and deserves further consideration is what I have termed the *materialism–idealism paradox* in our current Western conception of identity, particularly the nature of the link between material possessions and identity, and the shared conceptions of that link.

Of course, this chapter cannot even begin a thorough examination of these issues, given their breadth and complexity, and the selective comments it offers turn it inevitably into both a speculative and a cursory appraisal. However, its main aim is not to provide solutions to the difficulties posed by the combination of our material, consumption orientation and increasingly fluid, yet fragmented, sense of identity. Rather it is to pose broad questions about material symbols of identity, which have wide-ranging social and scientific ramifications. This is done, initially, by considering our contemporary, dominant notion of identity and the relative importance within it accorded to material context and material reality. This link between material possessions and identity turns out to be problematic, even paradoxical. Moreover, it can be argued that, for this very reason, dominant representations about material identity have ideological dimensions and connotations. Whether or not one agrees with these more tentative interpretations of the research discussed throughout the book, it seems clear that material social reality constitutes a powerful and pervasive context which is reflected in the ways in which our own identities and our impressions of others are constructed.

The dominant Western conception of identity

Identity can be considered from a world-view perspective (cf. Robbins, 1973), whereby it can be interpreted as the shared understandings within a society or culture of what it means to be a person. Thus identity becomes a social product, which clearly implies that conceptions of self or personhood are socio-culturally and historically relative. Or, as Sampson (1983) puts it: 'Personhood . . . is a sociocultural product, mediated by the underlying principles and structures of a particular social system that define what it means (the concept) and what it is (the actuality) to be a person' (p. 136). Our current concept of identity seems a peculiarly Western notion, although both laypeople and psychologists tend to treat it as a universally and transhistorically valid perspective (e.g., Cushman, 1990; Sampson, 1983, 1988). Its main distinctive feature is the notion of an *independent self*, which contrasts with the *interdependent self* of many non-Western cultures (e.g., Kon, 1984; Markus and Kitayama, 1991) and of our very own history (e.g., Cherry, 1967; Cushman, 1990; Weintraub, 1978). And these are the two angles, *synchronic* cultural differences and *diachronic* historical development, from which our dominant Western conception of identity can be looked at.

Identity in cross-cultural perspective

Baumeister (1987) offers a conceptual scheme of four dimensions along which differences or changes in conceptualizations of identity can be analysed. These are knowledge of the self, definition and creation of identity, human potential and fulfilment and, finally, the nature of the individual–society relationship. I am particularly concerned here with the definition of identity, and the opposition between a self that is *independent* from its social context and a self that is completely *embedded* within social relationships (cf. Markus and Kitayama, 1991). It seems that most non-Western cultures recognize explicitly that identity derives from people's enmeshment in social relations and the concomitant rules and duties conferred on them by their social roles in the community.

Lee (1950) describes the Wintu Indian culture of northern California as one in which the self is not viewed as the pivotal, clearly circumscribed centre of an individual's subjective world, but as a relational entity that fuzzily blends with the environment and other people. Major aspects of contemporary African identities are described in similar terms by Nobles (1976). Kon (1984) contrasts European with Japanese conceptions of personhood. Instead of viewing human behaviour as the consequence of personal motives, the Japanese see identity as the 'sum total of several autonomous "areas of duty" to one's family and community' (p. 41). Shweder and Bourne (1982) asked Indian Hindu and American adults to describe somebody they knew well and found that Indians saw personhood as located in time, place and specific relationships. When they explained somebody's behaviour, they referred to social roles and particular circumstances. In contrast, the Americans decontextualized identity by viewing it as a composite of abstract, situation-free personality traits: people behave the way they do because they *are* honest, or conniving, or bad-tempered. Miller (1984) traced the development of conceptions of the person in these two cultures and, although she found little differences in young children's explanations of social behaviour,

> over development, Americans gave increasing weight to general
> dispositions of the agent . . . [whereas] Hindus gave greater weight to
> contextual factors . . . Evidence suggested that the observed trends
> reflected individuals' acquisition of *conceptions of the person emphasized in*
> *their culture*, rather than *differences in . . . cognitive capacities*. (Shweder
> and Miller, 1985, p. 54, emphases added)

Shweder and Miller (1985) describe in some detail the duty-based and role-centred character of Hindu identity, which differs radically from the Anglo-American rights-based and person-centred notion of self. Harrison's (1985) anthropological account of the dualistic conception of selfhood in a Melanesian society shows how a relational notion of identity can exist alongside an individualistic one, albeit in different spheres of societal organization. In this community, everyday sociality is governed by *understanding*, mutual identification and traditional rules, whereas religious rituals are under the influence of *spirit* which furthers self-assertion, personal autonomy and independence from social relations. Semin and Rubini (1990) document through an analysis of types of verbal abuse that southern Italians, whose life is characterized by strong familial ties, have a more socio-centred relational identity than northern Italians, who tend to live in a less traditional, more urban environment.

In a recent review on *Culture and the Self*, Markus and Kitayama (1991) argue that different cultural constructions of self and identity exert a profound influence on individuals' cognition, emotion and motivation. In particular, they contrast the Anglo-American, Western conception of identity as a set of context-independent, enduring personality traits with a notion of an *interdependent* identity in Asian, African, Latin American and Southern European cultures. They describe the white, middle-class Western developmental imperative as becoming independent of others, and as discovering and expressing one's unique attributes, which are significant in regulating behaviour. In contrast, an interdependent identity means that behaviour is seen as context-bound and aimed towards a harmonious fit with the expectations and evaluations of others, who are continuously involved in one's definition of self. The idea of personality attributes only makes sense in specific social domains, such as the family or work:

> The interdependent self also possesses and expresses a set of internal attributes such as abilities, opinions, judgments and personality characteristics. But these internal attributes themselves are understood as situation-specific, and thus as sometimes elusive and unreliable. (p. 11)

For example, in a cross-cultural study comparing Japan with the USA, Cousins (1989) used the Twenty Statements Test, which asks respondents to answer the question 'Who am I?' twenty times. She employed two different forms: the first consisted of the traditional format just described, and the second required that the question 'Who am I?' be answered repeatedly in specific contexts, such as family, home or work. The Americans used more generalized personality attributes when describing themselves abstractly, whereas the Japanese used stable, internal characteristics more when talking about themselves in particular social roles.

From his analysis of the cultural foundations of personhood in Bali, Java and Morocco, Geertz (1979) concludes with this – still succinct and valid – encapsulation of contemporary Western identity:

> The Western conception of the person as a bounded, unique, more or less integrated motivational and cognitive universe, a dynamic center of awareness, emotion, judgment, and action organized into a distinctive whole and set contrastively both against other such wholes and against a social and natural background is, however incorrigible it may seem to us, a rather peculiar idea within the context of the world's cultures. (p. 229)

Yet, despite the clear evidence that even these brief examples provide for the socio-cultural relativity of conceptions of identity, self-contained individualism as an unchangeable, transhistorical entity is generally accepted as the current concept of self (cf. Cushman, 1990). This seems even more peculiar when it is considered that the bounded self emerged slowly and unevenly in Western history:

> The individual, bounded, communally isolated self is a modern phenomenon . . . roughly parallelling the development of industrialization and the rise of the modern state. (Cushman, 1990, p. 601)

The rise of autonomous individuality

It appears that in contemporary Western cultures, people think of themselves as isolated, separated individuals. They see themselves as people with *frontiers*, divided from each other as visibly as their bodies are by an inner being which is their very own (e.g., Bellah *et al.*, 1985; Carrithers *et al.*, 1985; Cherry, 1967; Dumont, 1965; Geertz, 1979; Mauss, 1985; Morris, 1972; Sampson, 1977, 1981; Semin, 1986, 1987; Tuan, 1982). At least in part, this notion arose in conjunction with the increasing differentiation and specialization of both the division of labour and social systems (e.g., Hirschman, 1977; Kon, 1984; Lukes, 1979; McCracken, 1985; Weintraub, 1978; Wikse, 1977). In Marx's words: 'the further back into the depths of history we penetrate, the more an individual . . . appears as being dependent on and belonging to a larger whole' (as quoted in Kon, 1984, p. 36).

The last section reviewed evidence for the socio-cultural relativity of conceptions of personhood and identity. Such conceptions can be analysed in terms of two main dimensions along which they differ. Firstly, the degree to which the self–other distinction is rigid or fluid varies. And, secondly, the extent to which control and power are seen as residing in the person on the one hand, or in the surrounding physical and social context on the other, can change. It is argued here that the contemporary Western notion of identity combines a sharp distinction of self from others and environment with an emphasis on the autonomy and self-determination of the individual (see also MacIntyre, 1988; Sampson, 1977, 1988, 1989).

Bellah *et al.* (1985) use the terms *expressive* and *utilitarian individualism* to describe two strands in current conceptions of identity. Other authors refer to the expressive component as *individuality* and the utilitarian one as *individualism* (e.g., Lukes, 1979; Morris, 1972; Weintraub, 1978). I propose that the contemporary Western conception of identity is best viewed as a composite notion in which elements of both individuality and individualism are merged into what I would term *autonomous individuality*.

Expressive elements include the supreme and intrinsic value attached to each single human being. Every person possesses a qualitative uniqueness which is developed and cultivated as an end in itself. Rogers's (e.g., 1961) concept of becoming a person through *self-actualization* captures the essence of this idea. The historical emergence of individuality as a concept can be traced through autobiographical writings (e.g., Weintraub, 1978), analyses of art and literature (e.g., Morris, 1972; Tuan, 1982), philosophical developments (e.g., Carrithers *et al.*, 1985; Lukes, 1979) or cultural anthropology (e.g., Belk, 1984b; Bellah *et al.*, 1985).

Concomitant with an emphasis on uniqueness and self-development are notions of personal autonomy and self-control. These components of our contemporary notion of identity are dealt with prominently in writings which deal with the development of industrialization and capitalism (e.g., Dumont, 1965; Hirschman, 1977). Several contributions trace the transition from viewing the individual as embedded in a religious moral context to conceiving of personality as an expression of self-governed and self-assertive agency in an increasingly differentiated commercial system (e.g., Kon, 1984; Weintraub, 1978). This transition is evidenced by the rise of the doctrine of utilitarianism or the protestant work ethic (e.g., Weber, 1958). This notion of autonomy views the individual as independent of socio-cultural context, as a self-contained motivational centre of thought and action. These various elements are synthesized into the Western conception of autonomous individuality, which views the individual as an entity whose essence is constituted by an abstract set of unique personality attributes, which are independent of social and material context (e.g., Miller, 1984; Shweder and Bourne, 1982; Shweder and Miller, 1985).

Weintraub (1978) traces historical changes in conceptions of self by analysing autobiographical writings. He describes personhood in antiquity and the Middle Ages as a derivative from strong kinship ties and each person's enmeshment in social relations. Conduct and evaluation of self and others drew meaning from socially sanctioned rules and models, not from any individually held standards. Drawing on a variety of sources, Baumeister (1987) and Cushman (1990) also trace the historical emergence of our current notion of identity as autonomous individuality. Baumeister (1987) argues that the late medieval period witnessed the arrival of a crystallized concept of the single human life, rather than human life as a collectivity. For example, Aries (1981) illustrates that during the twelfth century the early Christian belief that salvation occurred to a collectivity was replaced by a concept of the last judgment evaluating 'individual' souls. Cherry (1967) traces this development through etymological shifts in the meaning of 'individual'. The word used to refer to an inseparable part of a whole, before it acquired its current meaning of isolated, self-contained atom. Not until the sixteenth century did people think of an *actual self*: the individual as a basic unit of consideration.

This shift from a communal to an individual subject went hand in hand with the change from a religious to a scientific frame of reference, the switch from rural to urban settings, and the gradual replacement of agricultural by industrial social organization (cf. Cushman, 1990). A comparison of population figures between the late eighteenth century and the 1970s – in both Britain and America – shows that the percentage of people living in an urban setting increased more than eightfold, and that the percentage of people living in households of seven or more members dropped from over a third to under 7 per cent (cf. Cushman, 1990; Mitchell, 1984; Office of Population Censuses and Surveys, 1974). In short, ascribed identity derived from fixed social roles, community and shared meaning has given way to a personally achieved identity with specific psychological boundaries, internal control and the motivation to manipulate the external world for one's own personal good.

So far, I have referred to the *Western* notion of identity. But several authors provide empirical evidence that the notion of the autonomous individual is particularly prevalent in the United States, Australia and Great Britain (e.g., Hofstede, 1980; Triandis *et al.*, 1988; see Segall, 1986, for a brief overview). So the conception of identity I have described in this section is found in its purest form in the *Anglo-American* countries and cultures.

The cultural conception of autonomous individuality is at odds with the social constructionist assertion that self and society are crucially interdependent. This is particularly true in modern and postmodern society, where individuals are inextricably immersed in society, due to such large-scale factors as ever-growing economic interdependence, mass-produced goods, or the influence of the mass media, experts and science. Cherry (1967) similarly argues that our predominant construction of '[t]he "individual", isolated person is a [cultural] invention' (p. 472). In particular Sampson (1977, 1981, 1983, 1985, 1988, 1989) has criticized the mainstream of psychological theorizing for uncritically taking on board this cultural conception of personhood and, as a consequence, neglecting the social and material contexts in which human social psychological functioning is embedded. Interestingly enough, most non-Western conceptions of what it means to be a person explicitly acknowledge the interrelationship between society and individual. Our contemporary Western notion of the decontextualized, autonomous and unique person, which does not acknowledge material context, seems to be the exception rather than the rule.

However, a very different picture of current identity has emerged throughout this book. Materialism in general, and the emphasis on material possessions in particular, have to be seen as crucial elements of Western social systems and appear to be reflected in what was termed the *identity through possessions* model. The theoretical framework advanced in Chapter 4 suggests that a particularly important factor in drawing materially based inferences is *locating* others in terms of their social standing and status, which then gives rise to judgments about their personal qualities. This suggests that socially shared representations exist about what people from different material backgrounds *are like*. Both arguments are supported by research (see Chapters 6 and 7). But such an idea clashes with the contemporary Western conception of identity as autonomous individuality, which implies that personal characteristics have nothing to do with a person's possessions and wealth.

Wealth-unrelated aspects of identity

The conclusion to be drawn from what has been discussed throughout this book is that *we are what we have*. In contrast, the dominant Western view described above implies that identity is seen as unique and autonomous, uninfluenced by other people and socio-cultural surroundings. Thus, identity should be independent of material context in the sense that *we are who we are no matter what we possess*. These two notions are obviously contradictory, and any investigation of the link between perceived identity and material possessions should therefore study carefully how the personal attributes of others are viewed with respect to material context.

The impression formation paradigm used in Chapter 7, in which the same person was presented in different material contexts, does not raise the issue of material possessions explicitly. Rather, respondents are asked about the impressions they have formed of a person depicted in one particular type of context. Such an examination focuses on the *actual* perception of identity aspects in a material context. But in order to investigate the extent to which such personal qualities are believed to be intrinsic features of a person's identity independent of material possessions, one needs to ask respondents directly whether these qualities are in any way related to, or affected by, what a person possesses. Such an examination focuses on people's *beliefs* about the link between identity and material context.

The studies reported in Chapter 7 illustrate the impact of material possessions on perceived identity, but this demonstration becomes even more powerful if it can be shown that those qualities which were *perceived* differently (on the basis of material surroundings) are *normally believed to be* essential, intrinsic and context-free aspects of identity. Students were asked to judge those attributes. For each quality, they indicated on 7-point scales the extent to which having the quality in question is intrinsic to a person (1) or in any way *related to*, or *affected by*, such factors as what a person owns, how they dress, which type of car they drive and so on (7).

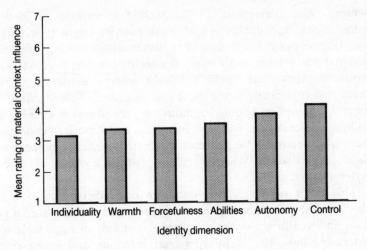

Figure 8.1   Wealth-unrelated dimensions of identity

The findings show (see Fig. 8.1) that the identity dimensions examined in Chapter 7 – individuality, warmth, forcefulness, abilities, autonomy and control – are seen as aspects of a person's identity which, overall, are *not* influenced by material context: they are *wealth-unrelated* attributes. Control was the only dimension which was judged even near neutral with respect to material circumstances; all others were seen as intrinsic personal qualities (i.e. mean ratings were lower than 4.5). So, in conclusion, we find that aspects of identity are judged to be independent of material context when people are asked directly about the link between possessions and identity. However, this professed belief is clearly contradicted by the *actual* perception of others' identity, which is significantly influenced by their possessions and wealth. Taken in combination, these findings indicate a contradiction, or paradox, in socially shared representations about the link between identity and material possessions.

The materialism–idealism paradox

An examination of commonsense as well as scientific notions of personhood in terms of the relationship between *what one has* and *who one is*, i.e., between material possessions and identity, reveals a dominant message that each of us has a unique individuality and personality which are our very own, untouched by and independent of material circumstances (cf. Cherry, 1967; Geertz, 1979; Sampson, 1985;

Semin, 1986; Weintraub, 1978). Such a conception of identity as autonomous individuality would mean that we ought to evaluate the *true*, unique personality of another person without being influenced by material possessions and wealth. It also implies that personal qualities should be viewed as wealth-unrelated aspects of identity. This was illustrated empirically in the study just described. This *idealistic* or lay-innatist assumption about the nature of personhood is a highly valued notion, particularly in northern European and American countries, but there also seems to be full cognizance that material possessions are highly regarded in Western culture, which consists of essentially materialistic societies.

This latter notion, which stands in contradictory relation to the idealist assumption about personhood, recognizes that material possessions and wealth are central regulators, not only of large-scale societal processes, but also of interpersonal relations and impressions. In Chapter 6 we saw that material images of groups differ predominantly in the wealth conveyed by different possessions. The introduction noted, furthermore, that, at least in the Western industrial world, material possessions have become increasingly important for assessing *who somebody is* since earlier forms of identity construction through membership in tightly knit small groups have been gradually superseded (see Barley, 1989; Belk, 1982, 1984b; Fromm, 1976). This would imply that the impressions people form of others' personal identities are strongly influenced by material possessions, and particularly by relative wealth. Moreover, in conjunction with the idealist perspective on personhood, it may well be the case that assessing who somebody is by their material possessions is seen as a negative way of judging others, since it violates the idea of the 'ineffable self' (Weintraub, 1978). Consequently, people may not admit easily to forming impressions about others on a material basis.

Here, then, we find two contradictory assumptions about who somebody is in commonsense notions of identity. The idea that such an *idealism–materialism paradox* may exist in individuals' ideas about others' identities becomes less strange when related to recent arguments that commonsense is complex and frequently contains such 'ideological dilemmas' (cf. Billig *et al.*, 1988).

An anecdotal illustration of this idealism–materialism paradox can be found in the feature film *Trading Places*. Here, two influential political figures enter into a bet for £1 about whether or not swapping a wealthy, reputable and up-and-coming member of Parliament and stockbroker with an uneducated street beggar would lead them to grow into the new, totally incongruous roles thrust upon them, and thus alter their outlook and personal characteristics – in short, their identity as people. To cut a long, amusing story short, the reputable member of Parliament is slung out into the street with not a penny to his name and the street beggar is given the clothes, large estate house, bank accounts, servants, etc. of the member of Parliament. In a remarkably short time, the former street beggar becomes a successful and respected business man with polished social manners and commendable moral code, whereas we encounter the former member of Parliament as a drunken and dishevelled man in a Santa Claus outfit stealing food at a Christmas party. Whether or not one sees this turn of events as realistic, which wins the bet for the political figure who believes that material possessions and wealth determine the identity and character of a person, it is clear that the comic aspect of the film can only come about because contradictory sets of beliefs exist about the link between a person's material position and who s/he is as a person.

In a more serious vein, such a materialism–idealism paradox should reveal itself in an empirical investigation on material possessions and identity in two ways. Firstly, if this paradox exists, people should describe personal qualities as wealth-unrelated aspects of a person's identity, which then are nevertheless shown to vary systematically with a person's possessions and wealth when people form impressions. Taking the findings of the study described earlier and of Chapter 7 together, this was indeed the case. And, secondly, this paradox would also be illustrated if it turns out that respondents acknowledge that *other* people's impressions may well be influenced by material possessions, while they consistently maintain that their *own* perceptions of others are unaffected by such considerations.

Over two hundred students estimated both the extent to which they thought that their own first impressions are influenced by a person's material possessions, and the extent to which they thought people in general are so influenced. As Figure 8.2 shows, these respondents maintained that they are relatively uninfluenced in their impressions by material factors, a judgment which is clearly questionable in the light of the research described in Chapter 7. The recognition that possessions and wealth do have an impact on impressions appears only in a general form – with respect to other people. These findings imply that people seem aware of the link between possessions and identity, but are less happy to admit to it – particularly with respect to themselves.

The materialism–idealism paradox comes about from contradictory assumptions about identity. The *idealistic* assumption holds that each individual has a unique and material-free identity, but there is also an apparently less comfortable awareness that material context is integral to *who somebody is*, which presents a *materialistic* acknowledgement of

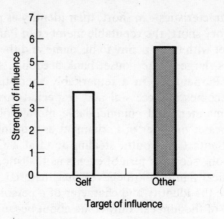

Figure 8.2 Estimated influence of
material possessions on impressions

the relation between possessions and identity. The earlier reference to
this materialism–idealism paradox as a potential 'ideological dilemma'
was not accidental, and the next section explores whether dominant
representations about the link between possessions and identity can be
said to have ideological elements.

Dominant representations and ideology

The notion that ideology can be understood as socially shared representations, which dominate the symbolic universe we live in, has been
mentioned already. 'Ideology' has been conceptualized in a variety of
ways, sometimes more broadly as the ideas and beliefs groups of people
hold, reflecting their particular socio-historical context (see also Billig
et al., 1988; Sampson, 1981; Thompson, 1986). But mostly it has been
interpreted in a more narrow fashion as those self-contained, internally
consistent sets of ruling ideas which serve the interests of economically
dominant groups, prominently by Marx and Engels (e.g., 1965) and
members of the Frankfurt school (e.g., Adorno, 1967, 1968; Marcuse,
1968). Billig *et al.* (1988) favour the broader conception of ideology, but
criticize both types of approach for their underlying assumption that
ideology is inherently *consistent* and *coherent*. They argue that, on the
contrary, dominant representations are complex and frequently contain
contradictory notions – ideological dilemmas – which enable us to think

and argue. Billig's contribution thus points to an important neglect in the literature on ideology, yet it de-emphasizes other crucial aspects of commonsense belief systems. Firstly, it neglects the fact that at least part of commonsense is constituted by dominant representations, which reflect societal power relations (e.g., Deschamps, 1982). And, secondly, it ignores the possibility that these dominant representations may play a role in the legitimization and maintenance of the status quo, thus – however indirectly – serving the interests of the already powerful (see also Spears, 1989).

It may be argued tentatively that the contents of the impressions people form of others in different material circumstances and the contradictory beliefs about the link between possessions and identity can be viewed as a reflection of dominant representations. Moreover, these socially shared notions appear to have ideological components because they appear related to societal power relations. There are three aspects to this argument.

Firstly, dominant representations about what wealthy and less affluent people *are like* not only influence first impressions, but they depict wealthy individuals in a more flattering and positive light – as more intelligent, assertive and in control – than less privileged people. But, secondly, it also emerged that representations about the wealthy contain ambivalent elements: impressions of interpersonal warmth and expressiveness favour less affluent individuals. However, these can be fitted into an ideological interpretation of impressions and wealth with the help of Van Knippenberg's (e.g., 1984) *mutual validation* model, which may turn out to be more unilateral than reciprocal. The dominant Western conception of personhood exemplifies the importance that is accorded to autonomy, control and self-reliance, and such attributes as 'warm' and 'friendly' may well be seen as pleasant, but somehow less important, aspects of identity. Being granted such attributes certainly does not threaten the privileged position and positive identity of the economically advantaged, and may make the unequal distribution of wealth appear less unpalatable. It is therefore not surprising that such attributes are accorded to the less affluent strata of society, and may simultaneously play a role in the maintenance and positive evaluation of wealth differentials. Henley's analysis (1977) of power as symbolically expressed in interaction and non-verbal communication makes an additional interesting point. She argues that qualities referred to as 'human relations' by Van Knippenberg (1984), which are valued positively and seen as more descriptive of lower status groups, are, in fact, power-related and status-related characteristics. She argues that the powerless are the ones who relieve tension, agree with, understand and disclose personal emotions and ideas to the powerful, in a way which both expresses and maintains power differentials. But whereas Van Knippenberg sees these attributes as status-unrelated qualities which are somehow 'given' to the low-status group, Henley's argument stresses both the reality of these human relations characteristics and the fact that the link between them and status would, of course, be reflected in our symbolic universe.

And, finally, the materialism–idealism paradox may well be an *ideological dilemma*. It is a dilemma because the assumptions that *we are what we have* and *who we are has nothing to do with what we possess* stand in a contradictory relationship, but appear side by side in the representations of individuals. However, the notion of autonomous individuality as the culturally valued form of identity is endowed with positive meanings. On the other hand, the recognition that material possessions and wealth are crucially involved in the identities of self and others is viewed in a negative light, i.e., we do not do justice to somebody's *true* identity if we judge them by their material context. With respect to dominant representations and ideology, this lay idealist view of the person may be seen as helping to gloss over the fact that Western societies are divided and stratified by wealth, and that the wealthy are in a much better position to choose and determine their lifestyles and thus be in control. Even the materialism–idealism paradox can be viewed speculatively as playing a role in the maintenance of the distribution of wealth, in the sense that locating and evaluating others in terms of their material position is of functional value in orienting people in their social environment, but the simultaneous idea that we are all self-determining and self-contained agents underplays the prominent role of material context for *who we are*.

In short, the materialism–idealism paradox in socially shared representations of identity may be involved in the reproduction of our social and cultural order. Cushman (1990) also talks about a paradox in current conceptualizations of self, but takes a slightly different approach. He agrees that the way in which identity is predominantly construed in a particular era is by no means accidental: 'Culminating with the Victorian era, the [then] concept of the deep, secret, instinct-driven, potentially dangerous self was used by the state to justify its role as official controller of selves' (p. 600). Without sliding into any form of conspiracy theory, it can be asserted nevertheless that power, social process and belief systems are inextricably intertwined. Similarly, our current dominant notion of autonomous individuality has a role to play in our increasingly consumption-driven Western societies.

To the idea of individualism, Cushman (1990) adds further features of a particularly *postmodern* identity, for which he coins the term *empty self*. Maintaining a coherent biographical sense of identity has become an increasingly arduous task, because it has to transcend the diverse and shifting kaleidoscope of roles, contexts and places between which we constantly move (see also Giddens, 1990). In part at least, the abstract, unique and stable personal attributes which are supposed to form the core of our identity have to be made concrete, reproduced and recreated in and through material goods. Thus the clash between the subtle, yet powerful, symbolism of material possessions and our supposedly context-free identity fits into a consumption society. As Cushman (1990) puts it: 'I believe that the construction of the post-World War II middle-class American self is a good illustration of how the economy and the power structure impact on personality' (p. 600); yet a lifestyle solution, which takes the place of necessary political change, provides a merely illusory cure of the *empty self* through 'substituting one identity, one life, for another . . . accomplished by purchasing and "ingesting" . . . [products] which will magically transfer the life-style of the model to the consumer' (p. 605). Again, we find the argument that material goods and the social construction of their symbolic dimensions help to reproduce the status quo, rather than change it.

What has been argued so far casts the pursuit of identity through consumption and material goods in a fairly negative light, as a pursuit which has to be understood in the context of ideology and power. But there are also positive angles to it. Recently, the long overdue shift from analysing material reality in terms of production of goods to a consideration of consumption has made it clear that causal models based on a starkly class-segregated society are outmoded (e.g., McCracken, 1990; Lunt and Livingstone, in press). The possibility of *acquiring* an identity through external signs, such as possessions and lifestyle, has meant a blurring of traditional class boundaries. But, put in an exaggerated way, the argument that all are much freer to acquire the lifestyle – and thus identity – of their choice (e.g., Askegaard, 1991) runs the risk of slipping into an imaginary world of equal opportunities, and thus of becoming a rhetoric that all are equal, even if some remain more equal than others. For example, Douglas and Isherwood (1979) provide an illuminating, and in my opinion still poignant, analysis of class-related consumption patterns in England. Whereas the middle-class use their possessions for long-term self-development, the working-class engage in repetitive short-term uses. This conclusion is echoed to some extent in the meanings currently attached to personal possessions by people from different social-material strata (see Chapter 6). Therefore, the *identity through possessions model* advanced here can be seen as part and parcel of a society marked by unequal power relationships, despite the increasing complexity of socio-economic stratification and the limited mobility afforded by it.

Conclusion

This chapter has attempted to interpret the research findings discussed throughout the book in a broader, if more speculative, framework. What remains to be done is to draw together the various strands of research and discussion in the form of an overall conclusion and possible avenues for future work.

Social and scientific implications

The discussion of literature which was considered relevant to the concerns of this book revealed a relatively fragmented and disparate picture. The bulk of psychologically oriented contributions tended to be descriptive, were concerned with very specific material aspects and lacked overall theoretical integration. Much of the emphasis of this work can be described as intra-individual and, at best, interpersonal. The symbolic-communicational account of the link between material possessions and identity developed in Chapter 4 provides a conceptual framework which, it is hoped, constitutes a step towards a much-needed theoretical integration. One of its main implications – which is supported by the research reported – is to question the potential utility, or even the possibility, of developing a domain-specific theory concerned with material possessions *per se*. On the contrary, the social psychological significance of possessions and wealth has been demonstrated with respect to various areas of social cognition which are traditionally dealt with separately, such as gender identity, stereotyping, impressions and person perception. In conjunction with reporting research, this book has also attempted to apply such theories to the present concern with material context. On the whole the theoretical frameworks referred to offered a fruitful starting point for exploring various aspects of the link between possessions and identity. For instance, not only does gender identity shape people's construction of social reality, but it is also reflected in their relations to their possessions.

Yet these frameworks have been found wanting in some of their inherent assumptions about social psychological functioning. With respect to stereotyping, it appears that material group images are exaggerated, but they nevertheless constitute reflections of *real* status and wealth differences. At least in this respect, this finding questions the notion that stereotypes are best viewed as the outcome of information-processing biases. Furthermore, the research on possessions and impressions raises questions for the perceptual (categorical accentuation) and motivational (ingroup favouritism) underpinnings of social identity theory with respect to broad social categories. Social identity theory may provide an elegant and comprehensive analysis of inter-group relations between clearly defined, small-scale social groups. But it seems that an understanding of the meaning and implications of membership in broad social categories could benefit from investigations of the influence of generally shared representations – and particularly ideologically loaded ones – on the definition and perception of such broad categories (see also Rabbie's and Horwitz's (1988) call for a conceptual distinction between social groups and social categories in social identity theory).

In general, then, it may be argued that, despite their undisputed merits, the cognitive and social-cognitive formulations which have dominated work on social cognition for the last decade have paid too little attention to the social, and particularly the material, context in which people express themselves and perceive others.

I would like to emphasize at this point that the social constructionist perspective advanced in this book has to be critical, by default, of the more traditional psychological work on social cognition discussed throughout, on at least two counts. Firstly, social constructionism makes distinctive assumptions about the nature of social cognition – particularly in terms of the origins of knowledge and the individual-social interface – which are not shared by these earlier perspectives. And, secondly, precisely because of its distinctive conceptualization of social cognition, does it raise research questions which would not have been posed from these other perspectives. Only if identity and the meanings of material possessions are seen as socially constituted, can the notion of material symbols of identity as partially establishing, maintaining and reproducing gender identity, for example, be formulated and examined. However, I would like to stress even more forcefully that the social constructionist approach towards the psychology of material possessions adopted here is not antagonistic to, but is rather intended to interact beneficially with, mainstream social psychological work. For this reason, social constructionism has been used as an integrative framework for seemingly disparate and partially contradictory findings in various research fields.

With respect to the three-fold classification proposed in Chapter 4 which (somewhat crudely) categorized approaches to social cognition into *innatist*, *realist* and *social constructionist* ones, it is argued here that the findings reported in this book lend support to the argument that socially constituted representations about the link between material possessions and identity significantly inform the ways in which people construe themselves and others in a material context.

This social constructionist viewpoint on material possessions could potentially open up many avenues for future research. For example, it may well be the case that *ideological* representations about wealthy and poor people play a less prominent role for the perception of others when individuals have had the chance to engage in social interaction with people they meet, or when they have a more pronounced, politicized and positive identification with their own social class and socio-economic category. Further research along those lines may suggest limits to the argument that stereotypic beliefs about the personal characteristics of the wealthy and the poor are accepted and reproduced in a fairly passive and unquestioning way. The issue of socially shared representations, and their potentially ideological contents with respect to material possessions, is in line with recent contributions, which propose that ideology as it is represented in commonsense should constitute an important social psychological concern (e.g., Billig *et al.*, 1988; Bouton, 1984). This argument could be investigated further through an examination of how the link between possessions and identity is portrayed in the mass media. One possibility would be to study the messages conveyed in TV or newspaper advertisements for consumer durables. Another would be an investigation of soap operas or other television series. The way the contents of such media representations relate to the findings presented here could then be examined. Another interesting aspect of representations about identity and possessions is their potentially paradoxical nature, which could be analysed further through studying naturally occurring discourse, such as groups of people discussing whether *to have* and *to be* amount to the same thing.

A further implication raised by a social constructionist approach concerns potential cross-cultural differences in the role that possessions and wealth play in social life. The notion of an *inter*dependent, rather than *in*dependent, identity may suggest that material possessions are seen as expressions of social, rather than personal, identity in non-Western cultures (see also Wallendorf and Arnould, 1988). Alternatively, identity may be constructed predominantly through social relations, so that possessions play a subordinate or even negligible role as symbols for identity.

The pervasiveness of material social reality

This book proposes that material possessions have socially constituted meanings, over and above instrumental utility. It argues further that this symbolic dimension of material objects plays an important role for the owner's identity. The introductory and final chapters placed this role of possessions in a broader historical and cultural context. Diverging approaches argue that Western societies are characterized by the strongly rooted belief that *to have is to be*. This notion is a relatively recent development, tied up with the rise of individualism and mass consumer society, which have increasingly led people to define themselves and others through what they possess. This assertion – that the symbolic meanings of possessions and wealth are an integral feature of expressing one's own identity and perceiving the identity of others – has to lead to the proposition that material possessions have profound significance for the social psychological reality of everyday life. And, given that this significance has been documented empirically throughout, this book may make a contribution towards the 'important and overdue . . . investigation of the significance of things and their ownership' (Csikszentmihalyi, 1991, comment on *To Have Possessions: A handbook of ownership and property*), which has suffered neglect to date.

If this argument does pinpoint an important feature of everyday social life – at least in Western materialistic societies – it is one that would, and does, manifest itself in several ways. As illustrated throughout, an individual's identity is influenced by the symbolic meanings of her or his own material possessions, and the way in which s/he relates to those possessions. Material possessions also serve as expressions of group membership and as means for locating others in the social-material environment. Moreover, material possessions provide people with information about other people's identities. In fact, one may therefore talk about a *folk* psychology of possessions and identity. This folk psychology is characterized by contradictory representations, given that the dominant Western conception of *autonomous individuality* implies an *idealist* view of identity, which contrasts with the *materialist* notion demonstrated in this book. Furthermore, people's beliefs about possessions and identity can be interpreted as reflections of *ideological* representations. Cushman (1990) suggests a similar social constructionist approach to identity in a brief but rather eloquent passage:

> Culture is not indigenous clothing that covers the universal human, it *infuses* individuals, *fundamentally shaping and forming them* and how they conceive of themselves and the world . . . instructing and forbidding them to think and act in certain ways . . . The *material objects* we create, . . . are not only the expression of an era. They are also the immediate 'stuff' of daily life, and as such they *shape and mould the community's generalized reality orientation* in subtle and unseen ways. Consequently, they *inevitably reinforce and reproduce the constellations of power, wealth and influence* within their respective societies. (p. 601, emphases added)

This suggests that material social reality is an integral, pervasive aspect of everyday social life, of construing ourselves and others. Therefore it needs to be investigated in its broad implications for self-definition, other-perception and interactions with the physical and social environment. These are concerns not only for psychologists, but also for sociologists, anthropologists, economists and other social scientists. Only a truly interdisciplinary perspective can hope eventually to contextualize the *individual* in material terms, and thus move closer to a comprehensive understanding of the implications the materialistic orientation of Western culture has for everyday social reality.

Bibliography

Abbott, P. and Sapsford, R. (1987) *Women and Social Class*. London: Tavistock.

Abelson, R. P. (1986) Beliefs are like possessions. *Journal for the Theory of Social Behaviour*, *16* (3), 223–50.

Abelson, R. P. and Prentice, D. A. (1989) Beliefs as possessions: a functional perspective. In A. R. Pratkanis, S. J. Breckler and A. G. Greenwald (eds.), *Attitude Structure and Function*, pp. 361–81. Hillsdale, NJ: Erlbaum.

Abercrombie, N., Hill, S. and Turner, B. S. (1980) *The Dominant Ideology Thesis*. London: Allen and Unwin.

Adoni, H. and Mane, S. (1984) Media and the social construction of reality: toward an integration of theory and research. *Communication Research*, *11* (3), 323–40.

Adorno, T. W. (1967) Sociology and psychology. *New Left Review*, *46*, 67–80.

Adorno, T. W. (1968) Sociology and psychology II. *New Left Review*, *47*, 79–96.

Adorno, T. W., Frenkel-Brunswick, E., Levinson, D. J. and Sanford, R. N. (1950) *The Authoritarian Personality: Studies in prejudice*. New York: Harper and Row.

Agnew, R. S. (1983) Social class and success goals: an examination of relative and absolute aspirations. *Sociological Quarterly*, *24* (3), 435–52.

Allport, G. W. (1949) *Personality: A psychological interpretation*. London: Constable.

Anderson, N. H. (1974) Cognitive algebra: integration theory applied to social attribution. In L. Berkowitz (ed.), *Advances in Experimental Social Psychology*, Vol. 7, pp. 1–101. New York: Academic Press.

Anderson, P. (1980) *Arguments within English Marxism*. London: NLB.

Anisfeld, M., Bogo, N. and Lambert, W. E. (1962) Evaluation reactions to accented English speech. *Journal of Abnormal and Social Psychology*, *65*, 223–31.

Appadurai, A. (1986) *The Social Life of Things: Commodities in cultural perspective*. Cambridge: Cambridge University Press.

Archer, J. and Lloyd, B. B. (1985) *Sex and Gender*. Cambridge: Cambridge University Press.

Argyle, M. (1986) Preface in A. Furnham and A. Lewis, *The Economic Mind: The social psychology of economic behaviour*. Brighton: Wheatsheaf.

Argyle, M. and McHenry, R. (1971) Do spectacles really affect judgements of intelligence? *British Journal of Social and Clinical Psychology, 10* (1), 27–9.

Aries, P. (1981) *The Hour of our Death*. New York: Knopf.

Armon-Jones, C. (1986) The thesis of constructionism. In R. Harré (ed.), *The Social Construction of Emotions*, pp. 32–56. Oxford: Blackwell.

Asch, S. E. (1946) Forming impressions of personality. *Journal of Abnormal and Social Psychology, 41*, 258–90.

Ashmore, R. D. and McConahay, J. B. (1975) The problems of too little. In *Psychology and America's Urban Dilemmas*, pp. 32–55. New York: McGraw-Hill.

Ashmore, R. S. and Del Boca, F. K. (1981) Conceptual approaches to stereotypes and stereotyping. In D. L. Hamilton (ed.), *Cognitive Processes in Stereotyping and Intergroup Relations*, pp. 1–35. Hillsdale, NJ: Erlbaum.

Askegaard, S. (1991) How people change life styles. Paper presented at the Joint Conference of the Society for the Advancement of Socio-Economics and the International Association for Research in Economic Psychology on 'Interdisciplinary Approaches to Economic Problems', 16–19 June, Stockholm, Sweden.

Averill, J. R. (1982) *Anger and Aggression: An essay on emotion*. New York: Springer.

Avineri, S. (1968) Homo Faber. In *The Social and Political Thought of Karl Marx*, pp. 65–95. Cambridge: Cambridge University Press.

Bakan, P. (1966) *The Duality of Experience*. Chicago: Rand McNally.

Bakeman, R. and Brownlee, J. R. (1982) Social rules governing object conflicts in toddlers and preschoolers. In K. H. Rubin and H. S. Ross (eds.), *Peer Relationships and Social Skills in Childhood*, pp. 99–111. New York: Springer.

Baldus, B. and Tribe, V. (1978) The development of perceptions and evaluations of social inequality among public school children. *Canadian Review of Sociology and Anthropology, 15* (1), 50–60.

Barbu, Z. (1963) *Chosisme: A socio-psychological interpretation*. Paris: Plon.

Barley, N. (1989) *Native Land*. Harmondsworth: Penguin.

Bartell, M. and Bartell, R. (1985) An integrative perspective on the psychological response of women and men to unemployment. *Journal of Economic Psychology, 6* (1), 27–49.

Barthes, R. (1983) *The Fashion System*. New York: Hill and Wang.

Baumeister, R. (1987) How the self became a problem: a psychological review of historical research. *Journal of Personality and Social Psychology, 52* (1), 163–76.

Beaglehole, E. (1931) *Property: A study in social psychology*. London: Allen and Unwin.

Beckett, H. (1986) Cognitive developmental theory in the study of adolescent identity development. In S. Wilkinson (ed.), *Feminist Social Psychology: Developing theory and practice*, pp. 39–56. Milton Keynes: Open University Press.

Beggan, J. K. (1991a) Possessions as instruments of psychological compensation. Paper presented at the Joint Conference of the Society for the

Advancement of Socio-Economics and the International Association for Research in Economic Psychology on 'Interdisciplinary Approaches to Economic Problems', 16–19 June, Stockholm, Sweden.

Beggan, J. K. (1991b) Using what you own to get what you need: the role of possessions in satisfying control motivation. In F. W. Rudmin (ed.), *To Have Possessions: A handbook on ownership and property*. Special issue of *Journal of Social Behavior and Personality*, 6 (6), 129–46.

Belch, G. E. and Landon, E. L. (1977) Discriminant validity of a product-anchored self-concept measure. *Journal of Marketing Research*, *14* (2), 252–6.

Belk, R. W. (1978) Assessing the effects of visible consumption on impression formation. In *Advances in Consumer Research, Vol. 5*, pp. 39–47.

Belk, R. W. (1979) Gift–giving behaviour. In J. N. Sheth (ed.), *Research in Marketing, Vol. 2*, pp. 95–126. Greenwich, CT: JAI Press.

Belk, R. W. (1980) Effects of consistency of visible consumption patterns on impression formation. In J. C. Olson (ed.), *Advances in Consumer Research*, *Vol. 7*, pp. 365–71. Ann Arbor, MI: Association for Consumer Research.

Belk, R. W. (1981) Determinants of consumption cue utilization in impression formation: an association derivation and experimental verification. In *Advances in Consumer Research, Vol. 8*, pp. 170–5. Ann Arbor, MI: Association for Consumer Research.

Belk, R. W. (1982) Acquiring, possessing, and collecting: fundamental processes in consumer behavior. In R. F. Bush and S. D. Hunt (eds.), *Marketing Theory: Philosophy of science perspectives*, pp. 185–90. Chicago: American Marketing Association.

Belk, R. W. (1983) Worldly possessions: issues and criticisms. In R. P. Bagozzi and A. M. Tybout (eds.), *Advances in Consumer Research, Vol. 10*, pp. 514–19. Ann Arbor, MI: Association for Consumer Research.

Belk, R. W. (1984a) Three scales to measure constructs related to materialism: reliability, validity, and relationships to measures of happiness. In T. C. Kinnear (ed.), *Advances in Consumer Research, Vol. 11*, pp. 291–7. Provo, UT: Association for Consumer Research.

Belk, R. W. (1984b) Cultural and historical differences in concepts of self and their effects on attitudes toward having and giving. In T. C. Kinnear (ed.), *Advances in Consumer Research, Vol. 11*, pp. 753–60. Provo, UT: Association for Consumer Research.

Belk, R. W. (1985) Materialism: trait aspects of living in the material world. *Journal of Consumer Research*, *12* (3), 265–80.

Belk, R. W. (1987) Material values in the comics: a content analysis of comic books featuring themes of wealth. *Journal of Consumer Research, 14* (1), 26–42.

Belk, R. W. (1988) Possessions and the extended self. *Journal of Consumer Research, 15* (2), 139–68.

Belk, R. W. (1991) The ineluctable mysteries of possessions. In F. W. Rudmin (ed.), *To Have Possessions: A handbook on ownership and property*. Special issue of *Journal of Social Behavior and Personality*, 6 (6), 17–55.

Belk, R. W., Bahn, K. D. and Mayer, R. N. (1982) Developmental recognition of consumption symbolism. *Journal of Consumer Research, 9*, 4–17.

Bellah, R. N., Madsen, R., Sullivan, W. M., Swidler, A. and Tipton, S. M. (1985) *Habits of the Heart: Individualism and commitment in American life*. Berkeley, CA: University of California Press.

Beloff, H. (1957) The structure and the origin of the anal character. *General Psychology Monographs*, *55*, 145–72.

Bem, S. L. (1974) The measurement of psychological androgyny. *Journal of Consulting and Clinical Psychology*, *42* (2), 155–62.

Bem, S. L. (1978) Beyond androgyny: some presumptuous prescriptions for a liberated sexual identity. In J. Sherman and F. L. Denmark (eds.), *Psychology of Women: Future directions of research*, pp. 1–23. New York: Psychological Dimensions.

Bentham, J. (1931/1894) *The Theory of Legislation* (edited by C. K. Ogden) London: Routledge and Kegan Paul.

Berger, P. (1966) Identity as a problem in the sociology of knowledge. *Archives Européenes de Sociologie: European Journal of Sociology*, *7*, 105–15.

Berger, P. and Luckmann, T. (1967) *The Social Construction of Reality: A treatise in the sociology of knowledge*. Published in 1967 by Harmondsworth: Penguin.

Bernard, L. (1924) *Instinct: A study in social psychology*. New York: Holt.

Berti, A. E., Bombi, A. S. and Lis, A. (1982) The child's conceptions about means of production and their owners. *European Journal of Social Psychology*, *12* (3), 221–39.

Bhaskar, R. (1979) On the possibility of social scientific knowledge and the limits of naturalism. In J. Mepham and D.-H. Ruben (eds.), *Issues in Marxist Philosophy*, *Vol. 3*, pp. 107–39. Brighton: Harvester.

Bhaskar, R. (1989) *Reclaiming Reality: A critical introduction to contemporary philosophy*. London: Verso.

Bickman, L. (1971) The effect of social status on the honesty of others. *Journal of Social Psychology*, *85*, 87–92.

Bieri, J. and Lobeck, R. (1961) Self-concept differences in relation to identification, religion, and social class. *Journal of Abnormal and Social Psychology*, *62* (1), 94–8.

Billig, M. (1985) Prejudice, categorization and particularization: from a perceptual to a rhetorical approach. *European Journal of Social Psychology*, *15* (1), 79–103.

Billig, M. (1988) Social representation, objectification and anchoring: a rhetorical analysis. *Social Behaviour*, *3*, 1–16.

Billig, M., Condor, S., Edwards, D., Gane, M., Middleton, D. and Radley, A. (1988) *Ideological Dilemmas: A social psychology of everyday thinking*. London: Sage.

Billig, M. G. and Tajfel, H. (1973) Social categorization and similarity in intergroup behaviour. *European Journal of Social Psychology*, *3* (1), 27–52.

Birdwell, A. E. (1968) A study of the influence of image congruence on consumer choice. *Journal of Business*, *41*, 76–88.

Blayney, M. and Dittmar, H. (1991) Women's self-reported eating behaviour and the evaluation of television advertisements. Unpublished manuscript, University of Sussex, England.

Bledsoe, J. C. (1981) Is self-concept a reliable predictor of economic status? *Psychological Reports*, *49* (3), 883–6.

Bloom, L. (1991) People and property: a psychoanalytic view. In F. W. Rudmin (ed.), *To Have Possessions: A handbook on ownership and property*. Special issue of *Journal of Social Behavior and Personality*, *6* (6), 427–43.

Blumberg, P. (1974) The decline and fall of the status symbol: some thoughts on status in a post–industrial society. *Social Problems*, *21* (4), 490–8.

Blumer, H. (1966) Sociological implications of the thought of George Herbert Mead. *American Journal of Sociology*, 71, 535–44.

Blumer, H. (1969) *Symbolic Interactionism: Perspective and method*. Englewood Cliffs, NJ: Prentice-Hall.

Bogatyrev, P. (1971) *The Functions of the Folk Costume in Moravian Slovakia*. The Hague: Mouton.

Bourdieu, P. (1973) The Berber house. In M. Douglas (ed.), *Rules and Meanings: The anthropology of everyday knowledge*, pp. 98–110. Harmondsworth: Penguin.

Bourdieu, P. (1979) *La distinction*. Paris: Editions de minuit.

Bouton, C. (1984) Self and society: a critique of symbolic interactionism. *Papers in the Social Sciences*, 4, 107–17.

Brashear, D. B. and Willis, K. (1976) Claiming our own: a model for women's growth. *Journal of Marriage and Family Counseling*, 2 (3), 251–8.

Braun, O. L. and Wicklund, R. A. (1989) Psychological antecedents of conspicuous consumption. *Journal of Economic Psychology*, 10, 161–87.

Brigham, J. C. (1971) Ethnic stereotypes. *Psychological Bulletin*, 76 (1), 15–38.

Bronson, W. C. (1975) Developments in behavior with age-mates during the second year of life. In M. Lewis and L. A. Rosenblum (eds.), *Friendship and Peer Relations*, pp. 131–52. New York: Wiley.

Broverman, I. K., Broverman, D. M., Clarkson, F. E., Rosenkrantz, P. S. and Vogel, S. R. (1970) Sex-role stereotypes and judgments of mental health. *Journal of Consulting and Clinical Psychology*, 34 (1), 1–7.

Broverman, I. K., Vogel, S. R., Broverman, D. M., Clarkson, F. E. and Rosenkrantz, P. S. (1972) Sex-role stereotypes: a current appraisal. *Journal of Social Issues*, 28 (2), 59–78.

Brown, B. B. and Harris, P. B. (1989) Residential burglary victimisation: reactions to the invasion of a primary territory. *Journal of Environmental Psychology*, 9 (2), 119–32.

Brown, R. (1986) *Social Psychology: The second edition*. New York: Free Press.

Brown, R. J. (1978) Divided we fall: An analysis of relations between sections of a factory work force. In H. Tajfel (ed.), *Differentiation Between Social Groups*, pp. 395–429. London: Academic Press.

Brown, R. J. (1984) The role of similarity in intergroup relations. In H. Tajfel (ed), *The Social Dimension*, Vol. 2, pp. 604–23. Cambridge: Cambridge University Press.

Brown, R. J. (1988) *Group Processes: Dynamics within and between groups*. Oxford: Blackwell

Brown, R. J. and Turner, J. C. (1981) Interpersonal and intergroup behaviour. In J. C. Turner and H. Giles (eds.), *Intergroup Behaviour*, pp. 33–65. Oxford: Basil Blackwell.

Bruner, J. S. (1957) On perceptual readiness. *Psychological Review*, 64 (2), 123–52.

Buckley, H. M. and Roach, M. E. (1974) Clothing as a nonverbal communicator of social and political attitudes. *Home Economics Research Journal*, 3, 98–102.

Burk, C. (1900) The collecting instinct. *Pedogogical Seminary*, 7, 179–207.

Burris, V. (1983) Stages in the development of economic concepts. *Human Relations*, 36 (9), 791–812.

Burroughs, W. J., Drews, D. R. and Hallman, W. K. (1991) Predicting personality from personal possessions: a self-presentational analysis. In F.

212 Bibliography

W. Rudmin (ed.), *To Have Possessions: A handbook on ownership and property*. Special issue of *Journal of Social Behavior and Personality*, 6 (6), 147–64.

Buss, D. M. (1989) Sex differences in human mate preferences: evolutionary hypotheses tested in 37 cultures. *Behavioral and Brain Sciences*, 12, 1–49.

Buss, D. M., Abbott, M., Angleitner, A., Asherian, A. *et al.* (1990) International preferences in selecting mates: a study of 37 cultures. *Journal of Cross-Cultural Psychology*, 21 (1), 5–47.

Byrne, D. (1969) Attitudes and attraction. In L. Berkowitz (ed.), *Advances in Experimental Social Psychology*, Vol. 4, pp. 36–89. London: Academic Press.

Byrne, D. (1971) *The Attraction Paradigm*. New York: Academic Press.

Byrne, D., Clore, G. L. and Smeaton, G. (1986) The attraction hypothesis: do similar attitudes affect anything? *Journal of Personality and Social Psychology*, 51 (6), 1167–70.

Byrne, D., Clore, G. L. and Worchel, P. (1966) Effect of economic similarity–dissimilarity on interpersonal attraction. *Journal of Personality and Social Psychology*, 4 (2), 220–4.

Byrne, D. and Nelson, D. (1965) Attraction as a linear function of proportion of positive reinforcements. *Journal of Personality and Social Psychology*, 1 (6), 659–63.

Cameron, P., Conrad, C., Kirkpatrick, D. D. and Bateen, R. J. (1966) Pet ownership and sex as determinants of stated affect toward others and estimates of others' regard of self. *Psychological Reports*, 19, 884–6.

Cameron, P. and Mattson, M. (1972) Psychological correlates of pet ownership. *Psychological Reports*, 30, 286.

Campbell, C. (1991) Consumption: the new wave of research in the humanities and social sciences. In F. W. Rudmin (ed.), *To Have Possessions: A handbook on ownership and property*. Special issue of *Journal of Social Behavior and Personality*, 6 (6), 57–74.

Campbell, D. T. (1967) Stereotypes and the perception of group differences. Article excerpted from *American Psychologist*, 22, 817–29, and reprinted in E. P. Hollander and R. G. Hunt (eds.) (1976), *Current Perspectives in Social Psychology*, 4th Edition, pp. 358–63. New York: Oxford University Press.

Camras, L. A. (1984) Children's verbal and nonverbal communication in a conflict situation. *Ethology and Sociobiology*, 5 (4), 257–68.

Cantor, N. (1981) A cognitive–social approach to personality. In N. Cantor and J. F. Kihlstrom (eds.), *Personality, Cognition and Social Interaction*, pp. 23–44. Hillsdale, NJ: Erlbaum.

Cantor, N. and Mischel, W. (1979) Prototypes in person perception. In L. Berkowitz (ed.), *Advances in Experimental Social Psychology*, Vol. 12, pp. 3–52. London: Academic Press.

Caplan, A. L. (ed.) (1978) *The Sociobiology Debate*. New York: Harper and Row.

Carlson, R. (1971) Sex differences in ego functioning: exploratory studies of agency and communion. *Journal of Consulting and Clinical Psychology*, 37 (2), 267–77.

Carrithers, M., Collins, S. and Lukes, S. (eds) (1985) *The Category of the Person*. Cambridge: Cambridge University Press.

Carroll, M. N. (1968) 'Junk' collections among mentally retarded patients. *Journal of Mental Deficiency*, 73, 308–14.

Carter, A. (1988) *The Philosophical Foundations of Property Rights.* Brighton: Harvester.

Cassell, J. (1974) Externalities of change: deference and demeanor in contemporary feminism. *Human Organization, 33*, 85–94.

Chapin, F. S. (1928) A quantitative scale for rating the home and social environment of middle class families in an urban community. *Journal of Educational Psychology, 19* (2), 99–111.

Chapin, F. S. (1959/1935) *Contemporary American Institutions: A sociological analysis.* New York: Harper.

Charlesworth, W. R. and le Frenière, P. (1983) Dominance, friendship, and resource utilization in preschool children's groups. *Ethology and Sociobiology, 4* (3), 175–86.

Charney, R. (1980) Speech roles and the development of personal pronouns. *Journal of Child Language, 7* (3), 509–28.

Cherry, C. (1967) 'But there is nothing I have is essential to me' (or 'the human race is not a club') In *To Honour Roman Jakobson, Vol. 1*, pp. 462–74. The Hague: Mouton.

Cherulnik, P. D. and Bayless, J. K. (1986) Person perception in environmental context: the influence of residential settings on impressions of their occupants. *Journal of Social Psychology, 126* (5), 667–73.

Cheyne, W. M. (1970) Stereotyped reactions to speakers with Scottish and English regional accents. *British Journal of Social and Clinical Psychology, 9*, 77–9.

Chiat, S. (1981) Context-specificity and generalization in the acquisition of pronominal distinctions. *Journal of Child Language, 8* (1), 75–91.

Chodorow, N. (1978) *The Reproduction of Mothering.* Berkeley, CA: University of California Press.

Clark, K. B. and Clark, M. P. (1947) Racial identification and preference in Negro children. In T. Newcomb and E. L. Hartley (eds.) *Readings in Social Psychology*, pp. 169–78. New York: Holt.

Cocanougher, A. B. and Bruce, G. D. (1971) Socially distant reference groups and consumer aspirations. *Journal of Marketing Research, 8*, 379–81.

Cohen, F. S. (1954) Dialogue on private property. *Rutgers Law Review*, Winter Issue.

Cohen, G. A. (1978) *Karl Marx's Theory of History: A defence.* London: Clarendon Press.

Coleman, R. P. (1983) The continuing significance of social class to marketing. *Journal of Consumer Research, 10*, 265–80.

Condor, S. (1987) From sex categories to gender boundaries. *Newsletter of the Social Psychology Section of the British Psychological Society, 17*, 48–71.

Connell, R. W. (1971) *The Child's Construction of Politics.* Melbourne: Melbourne University Press.

Connell, R. W. (1977) *Ruling Class, Ruling Culture: Studies of conflict, power and hegemony in Australian life.* Cambridge: Cambridge University Press.

Connell, R. W. (1983) *Which Way is Up? Essays on sex, class and culture.* Sidney: Allen and Unwin.

Connor, S. (1989) *Postmodern Culture: An Introduction to Theories of the Contemporary.* Oxford: Blackwell.

Cooley, C. (1902) The social self – 1. The meaning of 'I'. In *Human Values and Social Order*, Chapter 5. New York : Charles Scribner's Sons.

Cooley, C. (1908) A study of the early use of self-words by a child. *Psychological Review*, *15*, 339–57.

Cooper, C. (1976) The house as a symbol of the self. In H. M. Proshansky, W. H. Ittelson and L. G. Rivlin (eds.), *Environmental Psychology*, pp. 453–48. New York: Holt, Rinehart and Winston.

Cottrell, L. S. (1978) George Herbert Mead and Harry Stack Sullivan: an unfinished synthesis. *Psychiatry*, *41* (2), 151–62.

Cousins, S. (1989) Culture and selfhood in Japan and the US. *Journal of Personality and Social Psychology*, *56*, 124–31.

Covert, A. M., Whiren, A. P., Keith, J. and Nelson, C. (1985) Pets, early adolescents, and families. *Marriage and Family Review*, *8* (3–4), 95–108.

Crain, W. C. and Crain, E. F. (1976) Age trends in political thinking: dissent, voting, and the distribution of wealth. *Journal of Psychology*, *92* (2), 179–90.

Cronk, G. F. (1973) Symbolic interactionism: a 'left-Meadian' interpretation. *Social Theory and Practice*, *2*, 313–34.

Crosby, F. (1976) A model of egotistical relative deprivation. *Psychological Review*, *83* (2), 85–113.

Crosby, F. (1982) *Relative Deprivation and Working Women*. Oxford: Oxford University Press.

Csikszentmihalyi, M. (1991) Comment on cover of F. W. Rudmin (ed.), *To Have Possessions: A handbook on ownership and property*. Special issue of *Journal of Social Behavior and Personality*, *6* (6).

Csikszentmihalyi, M. and Rochberg-Halton, E. (1981) *The Meaning of Things: Domestic symbols and the self*. Cambridge: Cambridge University Press.

Cummings, S. and Taebel, D. (1978) The economic socialization of children: a neo-Marxist analysis. *Social Problems*, *26* (2), 198–210.

Cushman, P. (1990) Why the self is empty: toward a historically situated psychology. *American Psychologist*, *45* (5), 599–611.

Danziger, K. (1958) Children's earliest conceptions of economic relationships. *Journal of Social Psychology*, *47*, 231–40.

Darley, J. M. and Cooper, J. (1972) The 'clean for gene' phenomenon: the effect of student's appearance on political campaigning. *Journal of Applied Social Psychology*, *2*, 24–33.

Davis, J. H. (1987) Preadolescent self-concept development and pet ownership. *Anthrozoos*, *1* (2), 90–4.

Davis, K. (1949) Jealousy and sexual property. In *Human Society*, pp. 175–94. New York: Macmillan.

Dawe, H. C. (1934) An analysis of two hundred quarrels of preschool children. *Child Development*, *4*, 139–57.

Dawkins, R. (1976) *The Selfish Gene*. New York: Oxford University Press.

Deaux, K. (1985) Sex and gender. *Annual Review of Psychology*, *36*, 49–81.

Dellinger, R. W. (1977) Keeping tabs on the Joneses. *Human Behaviour*, November, 20–30.

Derdeyn, A. P. (1979) Adoption and the ownership of children. *Child Psychiatry and Human Development*, *9* (4), 215–26.

Deschamps, J.-C. (1982) Social identity and relations of power between groups. In H. Tajfel (ed.), *Social Identity and Intergroup Relations*, pp. 85–98. Cambridge: Cambridge University Press.

Deschamps, J.-C. (1984) The social psychology of intergroup relations and categorical differentiation. In H. Tajfel (ed.), *The Social Dimension, Vol. 2*, pp. 541–59. Cambridge: Cambridge University Press.

Deutsch, W. (1984) Besitz und Eigentum im Spiegel der Sprechentwicklung. In C. Eggers (ed.), *Bindungen und Besitzdenken beim Kleinkind*, pp. 255–76. Munich: Urban and Schwarzenberg.

Deutsch, W. and Budwig, N. (1983) Form and function in the development of possessives. *Papers and Reports on Child Language Development*, *22*, 36–42.

Dickinson, J. (1986) The development of representations of social inequality. Unpublished doctoral thesis, University of Dundee, Scotland.

Dickinson, J. (1990) Adolescent representations of socio-economic status. *British Journal of Developmental Psychology*, *8* (4), 351–71.

Dittmar, H. (1986) Exploration of the meaning of possessions in three subject groups. Unpublished manuscript, University of Sussex, England.

Dittmar, H. (1988) Commonsense beliefs concerning the functions and meanings of material possessions. Unpublished manuscript, University of Sussex, England.

Dittmar, H. (1989) Gender identity-related meanings of personal possessions. *British Journal of Social Psychology*, *28*, 159–71.

Dittmar, H. (1990a) Material possessions and identity. Unpublished doctoral thesis, University of Sussex, England.

Dittmar, H. (1990b) Material wealth and perceived identity: impressions of adolescents from different socio-economic backgrounds. Paper presented at the XVth Colloquium of the International Association for Research in Economic Psychology, University of Exeter. Published in S. E. A. Lea, P. Webley and B. Young (eds.), *Advances in Economic Psychology*, *Vol. 2*, pp. 805–12. Exeter: Washington Singer.

Dittmar, H. (1991a) Material images of different socio-economic groups: material possessions as 'stereotypes'. Paper presented at the Joint Conference of the Society for the Advancement of Socio-Economics and the International Association for Research in Economic Psychology on 'Interdisciplinary Approaches to Economic Problems', 16–19 June, Stockholm.

Dittmar, H. (1991b) Meanings of material possessions as reflections of identity: gender and social-material position in society. In F. W. Rudmin (ed.), *To Have Possessions: A handbook on ownership and property*. Special issue of *Journal of Social Behavior and Personality*, *6* (6), 165–86.

Dittmar, H. (1991c) Perceived identities of the 'poor' and the 'affluent': are impressions based on social category membership or 'ideological' representations? Paper presented at the British Psychological Society's Social Psychology Section Annual Conference, University of Surrey, England, 20–2 September.

Dittmar, H. and Bates, B. (1987) Humanistic approaches to the understanding and treatment of anorexia nervosa. *Journal of Adolescence*, *10*, 57–69.

Dittmar, H., Mannetti, L. and Semin, G. (1989) Fine feathers make fine birds: a comparative study of the impact of material wealth on perceived identities in England and Italy. *Social Behaviour*, *4* (3), 195–200.

Dixon, J. C. and Street, J. W. (1975) The distinction between self and not–self in children and adolescents. *Journal of Genetic Psychology*, *127*, 157–62.

Doise, W. and Sinclair, A. (1973) The categorization process in intergroup relations. *European Journal of Social Psychology*, *3* (2), 145–57.

Dolich, I. J. (1969) Congruence relationships between self-images and product brands. *Journal of Marketing Research*, *6*, 80–4.

Donner, D. (1981) Bike thieves take more than just metal: they steal a big part of someone's life. *Daily Utah Chronicle*, *94*, 30 October, 11.

Doob, A. N. and Gross, A. E. (1968) Status of frustrator as an inhibitor of horn-honking responses. *Journal of Social Psychology*, 76, 213–18.
Douglas, M. and Isherwood, B. (1979) *The World of Goods: Towards an anthropology of consumption*. London: Allen Lane.
Douglas, S. E. and Solomon, M. R. (1983) Clothing the female executive: fashion or fortune? In P. E. Murphy *et al.* (eds.), *1983 AMA Winter Educators' Conference: Proceedings*, series no. 49. Chicago: American Marketing Association.
Douty, H. I. (1963) Influence of clothing on perception of persons. *Journal of Home Economics*, 55 (3), 197–202.
Dreman, S. B. and Greenbaum, C. W. (1973) Altruism or reciprocity: sharing behavior in Israeli kindergarten children. *Child Development*, 44, 61–8.
Drever, J. (1917) *Instinct in Man*. Cambridge: Cambridge University Press.
Driscoll, A. M., Mayer, R. N. and Belk, R. W. (1985) The young child's recognition of consumption symbols and their social implications. *Child Study Journal*, 15 (2), 117–30.
Dumont, L. (1965) The modern conception of the individual. *Contributions to Indian Sociology*, 8, 13–61.
Dupré, J. (1987) Sociobiology and the problem of culture. *Behavioral and Brain Sciences*, 10 (1), 75–6.
Dürkheim, E. (1957) *Professional Ethics and Civic Morals* (translated by C. Brookfield) London: Routledge and Kegan Paul.
Ebbesen, E. B. (1981) Cognitive processes in inferences about a person's personality. In E. T. Higgins, C. P. Herman and M. P. Zanna (eds.), *Social Cognition, Vol. 1*, pp. 247–76. Hillsdale, NJ: Erlbaum.
Eggers, C. (1983) Bericht über das Eröffnungssymposium der Klinik für Kinder– und Jugendpsychiatrie zum Thema: Kind und Besitz – Zur Ontogenese the kindlichen Bindungs– und Besitzverhaltens. *Acta Paedopsychiatrica*, 49, 271–2.
Eggers, C. (ed.) (1984) *Bindungen und Besitzdenken beim Kleinkind*. Munich: Urban and Schwarzenberg.
Ehrlich, H. J. and Rinehart, J. W. (1965) A brief report on the methodology of stereotype research. *Social Forces*, 43, 564–75.
Eichenbaum, L. and Orbach, S. (1983) *Understanding Women*. New York: Basic Books.
Eisenberg-Berg, N., Haake, R. J. and Bartlett, K. (1981) The effects of possession and ownership on the sharing and proprietary behaviors of preschool children. *Merrill-Palmer Quarterly*, 27 (1), 61–8.
Ellis, L. (1985) On the rudiments of possessions and property. *Social Science Information*, 24 (1), 113–43.
Ellwood, C. (1927) *Cultural Evolution: A study of social origins and development*. New York: Century.
Emler, N. and Dickinson, J. (1985) Children's representation of economic inequalities: the effects of social class. *British Journal of Developmental Psychology*, 3 (2), 191–8.
Engel, J. F. (1985) Toward the contextualization of consumer behavior. In C. T. Tan and J. N. Sheth (eds.), *Historical Perspective in Consumer Research*, pp. 1–5. National University of Singapore: School of Management.
Erikson, E. (1980) *Identity and the Life-cycle: A re-issue*. New York: Norton.

Ertel, S., Wechsung, S. and Ardelt, S. (1971) Wertvoller Besitz, Selbstbereicherung und Selbstwertgefühl. *Zeitschrift für Sozialpsychologie*, 2 (3), 295–307.

Evans, F. B. (1959) Psychological and objective factors in the prediction of brand choice. *Journal of Business*, 32, 340–69.

Faigin, H. (1958) Case report: social behavior of young children in the kibbutz. *Journal of Abnormal and Social Psychology*, 56, 117–29.

Farr, R. (1987) Social representations: A French tradition of research. Special Issue: Social representations. *Journal for the Theory of Social Behaviour*, 17 (4), 343–69.

Farr, R. and Moscovici, S. (1984) *Social Representations*. Cambridge: Cambridge University Press.

Feagin, J. R. (1972) Poverty: we still believe that God helps those who help themselves. *Psychology Today*, 6, 101–29.

Feather, N. T. (1974) Explanations of poverty in Australian and American samples: the person, society or fate? *Australian Journal of Psychology*, 26 (3), 199–216.

Featherstone, M. (1991) *Consumer Culture and Postmodernism*. London: Sage.

Felson, M. (1978) Invidious distinctions among cars, clothes and suburbs. *Public Opinion Quarterly*, 42 (1), 49–58.

Festinger, L. (1954) A theory of social comparison processes. *Human Relations*, 7, 117–40.

Feyerabend, P. (1975) How to defend society: against science. *Radical Philosophy*, 11, 3–8.

Forgas, J. P., Argyle, M. and Ginsburg, G. P. (1979) Social episodes and person perception: the fluctuating structure of an academic group. *Journal of Social Psychology*, 109 (2), 207–22.

Forgas, J. P., Morris, S. L. and Furnham, A. (1982) Lay explanations of wealth: attributions for economic success. *Journal of Applied Social Psychology*, 12 (5), 381–97.

Formanek, R. (1991) Why they collect: collectors reveal their motivations. In F. W. Rudmin (ed.), *To Have Possessions: A handbook on ownership and property*. Special issue of *Journal of Social Behavior and Personality*, 6 (6), 275–86.

Fournier, S. and Richins, M. (1991) Some theoretical and popular notions concerning materialism. In F. W. Rudmin (ed.), *To Have Possessions: A handbook on ownership and property*. Special issue of *Journal of Social Behavior and Personality*, 6 (6), 403–14.

Franks, D. (1985) The self in evolutionary perspective. In H. A. Farberman and R. S. Perinbanayagam (eds.), *Studies in Symbolic Interaction, Supplement 1. Foundations of Interpretive Sociology: Original essays in symbolic interaction*, pp. 29–61. Greenwich, Connecticut: JAI Press.

Freud, S. (1908) Character and anal eroticism. In A. Richards (ed.) (1977), *On Sexuality, Vol. 7*, pp. 205–15. Harmondsworth: Penguin.

Freud, S. (1917) On transformations of instinct as exemplified in anal eroticism. In A. Richards (ed.) (1977), *On Sexuality, Vol. 7*, pp. 293–302. Harmondsworth: Penguin.

Freud, S. (1933) *New Introductory Lectures on Psychoanalysis*. Edited by A. Richards, *Vol. 11* (translated by W. J. H. Sprott) Harmondsworth: Penguin.

Friedman, M. (1962) *Capitalism and Freedom*. Chicago: University of Chicago Press.

Friedmann, W. G. (1973) Property. In P. P. Wiener (ed.), *Dictionary of the History of Ideas*, Vol. 3, pp. 650–7. New York: Scribner.

Frisby, D. (1984) *Georg Simmel*. Chichester: Horwood, and London: Tavistock.

Fromm, E. (1978) *To Have or to Be?*. Harmondsworth: Penguin (Originally published in 1976).

Furby, L. (1976) The socialization of possession and ownership among children in three cultural groups: Israeli kibbutz, Israeli city, and American. In S. Modgil and C. Modgil (eds.), *Piagetian Research: Compilation and commentary*, Vol. 8, pp. 95–127. Windsor: NFER Publishing.

Furby, L. (1978a) Possessions: toward a theory of their meaning and function throughout the life cycle. In P. B. Baltes (ed.), *Life Span Development and Behavior*, Vol. 1, pp. 297–336. New York: Academic Press.

Furby, L. (1978b) Possession in humans: an exploratory study of its meaning and motivation. *Social Behavior and Personality*, 6 (1), 49–65.

Furby, L. (1978c) Sharing: decisions and moral judgments about letting others use one's possessions. *Psychological Reports*, 43 (2), 595–609.

Furby, L. (1979) Inequalities in personal possessions: explanations for and judgments about unequal distribution. *Human Development*, 22 (3), 180–202.

Furby, L. (1980a) The origins and early development of possessive behavior. *Political Psychology*, 2 (1), 30–42.

Furby, L. (1980b) Collective possession and ownership: a study of its judged feasibility and desirability. *Social Behavior and Personality*, 8 (2), 165–84.

Furby, L. (1991) Understanding the psychology of possessions and ownership: a personal memoir and an appraisal of our progress. In F. W. Rudmin (ed.), *To Have Possessions: A handbook on ownership and property*. Special issue of *Journal of Social Behavior and Personality*, 6 (6), 457–63.

Furby, L. and Wilke, M. (1982) Some characteristics of infants' preferred toys. *Journal of Genetic Psychology*, 140 (2), 207–19.

Furnham, A. (1982a) The perception of poverty among adolescents. *Journal of Adolescence*, 5 (2), 135–47.

Furnham, A. (1982b) Why are the poor always with us? Explanations for poverty in Britain. *British Journal of Social Psychology*, 21 (4), 311–22.

Furnham, A. (1983) Attributions for affluence. *Personality and Individual Differences*, 4 (1), 31–40.

Furnham, A. (1986) Children's understanding of the economic world. *Australian Journal of Education*, 30 (3), 219–40.

Furnham, A. and Bond, M. (1986) Hong Kong Chinese explanations for wealth. *Journal of Economic Psychology*, 7 (4), 447–60.

Furnham, A. and Jones, S. (1987) Children's views regarding possessions and their theft. *Journal of Moral Education*, 16, (1), 18–30.

Furnham, A. and Lewis, A. (1986) *The Economic Mind: The social psychology of economic behaviour*. Brighton: Wheatsheaf.

Furth, H. G. (1980) *The World of Grown-Ups: Children's Conceptions of Society*. New York: Elsevier.

Geertz, C. (1964) Ideology as cultural system. In D. Apter (ed.), *Ideology and Discontent*. New York: Free Press.

Geertz, C. (1979) From the native's point of view: on the nature of anthropological understanding. In P. Rabinow and W. M. Sullivan (eds.), *Interpretive*

Social Science: A reader, pp. 225–41. Berkeley, CA: University of California Press.

Gergen, K. J. (1973) Social psychology as history. *Journal of Personality and Social Psychology*, 26 (2), 309–20.

Gergen, K. J. (1982) *Toward Transformation in Social Knowledge*. New York: Springer.

Gergen, K. J. (1985) The social constructionist movement in modern psychology. *American Psychologist*, 40 (3), 266–75.

Gergen, K. J. (1986) Elaborating the constructionist thesis. *American Psychologist*, 41, 481–2.

Gergen, K. J. (1989) Social psychology and the wrong revolution. *European Journal of Social Psychology*, 19, 463–84.

Gergen, K. J. and Davis, K. E. (eds.) (1985) *The Social Construction of the Person*. New York: Springer.

Giddens, A. (1990) *The Consequences of Modernity*. Cambridge: Polity Press.

Gilligan, C. (1982) *In a Different Voice: Psychological theory and women's development*. Cambridge, MA: Harvard University Press.

Gilligan, C. and Attanucci, J. (1988) Two moral orientations: gender differences and similarities. *Merrill–Palmer Quarterly*, 34 (3), 223–37.

Ginsburg, H. and Opper, S. (1988) *Piaget's Theory of Intellectual Development, 3rd Edition*. Englewood Cliffs, NJ: Prentice-Hall.

Ginsberg, M. (1935) Symposium on property and possessiveness: II. *Journal of Medical Psychology*, 15, 63–9.

Goff, T. W. (1980) *Marx and Mead: Contributions to a sociology of knowledge*. London: Routledge and Kegan Paul.

Goffman, E. (1951) Symbols of class status. *British Journal of Sociology*, 2, 294–304.

Goffman, E. (1961) *Asylums*. New York: Anchor.

Goffman, E. (1968) The inmate world. In C. Gordon and K. J. Gergen (eds.), *The Self in Social Interaction, Vol. 1: Classic and contemporary perspectives*, pp. 267–74. New York: Wiley.

Golinkoff, R. M. and Markessini, J. (1980) 'Mommy sock': the child's understanding of possession as expressed in two-noun phrases. *Journal of Child Language*, 7 (1), 119–35.

Gonzales, M. H., Davis, J. M., Loney, G. L., Lukens, C. K. and Junghans, C. M. (1983) Interactional approach to interpersonal attraction. *Journal of Personality and Social Psychology*, 44 (6), 1192–7.

Gordon, C. (1968) Self conceptions: configurations of content. In C. Gordon and K. J. Gergen (eds.), *The Self in Social Interaction, Vol. 1: Classic and contemporary perspectives*, pp. 115–36. New York: Wiley.

Gould, S. J. (1978) Biological potential vs. biological determinism. In A. L. Caplan (ed.), The Sociobiology Debate, pp. 343–51. New York: Harper and Row.

Green, P. E., Maheshwari, A. and Rao, V. R. (1969) Self–concept and brand preference: an empirical application of multidimensional scaling. *Journal of the Market Research Society*, 11 (4), 343–60.

Greenacre, M. J. (1984) *Theory and Applications of Correspondence Analysis*. London: Academic Press.

Gribbin, J. R. and Gribbin, M. (1988) *The One Percent Advantage: The sociobiology of being human*. Oxford: Blackwell.

Gronmo, S. (1984) Compensatory consumer behavior: theoretical perspectives, empirical examples and methodological challenges. In P. F. Anderson and M. J. Ryan (eds.), *1984 AMA Winter Educators' Conference: Scientific Method in Marketing*, pp. 184–8. Chicago: American Marketing Association.

Grubb, E. L. and Hupp, G. (1968) Perception of self, generalized stereotypes, and brand selection. *Journal of Marketing Research, 5*, 58–63.

Gulerce, A. (1991) Transitional objects: a reconsideration of the phenomenon. In F. W. Rudmin (ed.), *To Have Possessions: A handbook on ownership and property*. Special issue of *Journal of Social Behavior and Personality, 6* (6), 187–208.

Gurney, C. M. (1989) In search of ontological security: an attempt to operationalise the concept of 'ontological (in)security' in theory and in practice. Unpublished MA dissertation, University of Sussex, England.

Haire, M. (1950) Projective techniques in marketing research. *Journal of Marketing, 14* (5), 649–56.

Hall, G. and Wiltse, S. (1891) Children's collections. *Pedagogical Seminary, 1*, 234–7.

Hall, G. (1898) Some aspects of the early sense of self. *American Journal of Psychology, 9*, 351–95.

Hall, S. (1986) Variants of liberalism. In J. Donald and S. Hall (eds.), *Politics and Ideology*, pp. 34–69. Milton Keynes: Open University Press.

Hallowell, A. I. (1943) The nature and function of property as a social institution. *Journal of Legal and Political Sociology, 1*, 115–38.

Hallowell, A. I. (1955) *Culture and Experience*. London: Oxford University Press.

Hamid, P. N. (1968) Style of dress as a perceptual cue in impression formation. *Perceptual and Motor Skills, 26*, 904–6.

Hamid, P. N. (1969) Changes in person perception as a function of dress. *Perceptual and Motor Skills, 29*, 191–4.

Hamilton, D. L. (1979) A cognitive-attributional analysis of stereotyping. In L. Berkowitz (ed.), *Advances in Experimental Social Psychology, Vol. 12*, pp. 53–84. New York: Academic Press.

Hamilton, D. L. (1981) Stereotyping and intergroup behavior: some thoughts on the cognitive approach. In D. L. Hamilton (ed.), *Cognitive Processes in Stereotyping and Intergroup Relations*, pp. 333–53. Hillsdale, NJ: Erlbaum.

Hamilton, D. L. and Zanna, M. P. (1974) Context effects in impression formation: changes in connotative meaning. *Journal of Personality and Social Psychology, 29* (5), 649–54.

Hamm, B. C. and Cundiff, E. N. (1969) Self-actualization and product perception. *Journal of Marketing Research, 6*, 470–2.

Hampson, S. E. (1988) *The Construction of Personality, 2nd Edition*. London: Routledge.

Hare-Mustin, R. T. and Marécek, J. (1988) The meaning of difference: gender theory, postmodernism, and psychology. *American Psychologist, 43* (6), 455–64.

Harré, R. (1984) Some reflections on the concept of 'social representations'. *Social Research, 51* (4), 927–38.

Harré, R. (1986) *The Social Construction of Emotions*. Oxford: Blackwell.

Harrison, S. (1985) Concepts of the person in Avatip religious thought. *Man, 20*, 115–30.

Hastie, R., Ostrom, T. M., Ebbesen, E. B., Wyer, R. S. Jr., Hamilton, D. L. and Carlston, D. E. (1980) *Person Memory: The cognitive basis of social perception*. Hillsdale, NJ: Erlbaum.

Hebdige, D. (1979) *Subculture: The Meaning of Style*. London: Methuen.

Hebdige, D. (1987) *Cut'N'Mix: Culture, identity and Caribbean music*. London: Commedia.

Heelas, P. and Lock, A. (eds.) (1981) *Indigenous Psychologies: The anthropology of the self*. London: Academic Press.

Heider, F. (1958) *The Psychology of Interpersonal Relations*. New York: Wiley.

Henderson, R., Brosy, G., Lane, S. and Parra, E. (1982) Effects of ethnicity and child's age on maternal judgements of children's transgressions against persons and property. *Journal of Genetic Psychology, 140*, 253–63.

Henley, N. (1977) *Body Politics: Power, sex and non-verbal communication*. New York: Prentice-Hall.

Herskovits, M. J. (1940) *The Economic Life of Primitive Peoples*. New York: Knopf.

Hewitt, J. P. (1979) *Self and Society: A symbolic interactionist social psychology*. Boston: Allyn and Bacon.

Hewstone, M. (1989) *Causal Attribution: From cognitive processes to collective beliefs*. Oxford: Blackwell.

Higgins, E. T. and McCann, C. D. (1984) Social encoding and subsequent attitudes, impressions and memory: 'context-driven' and motivational aspects of processing. *Journal of Personality and Social Psychology, 47* (1), 26–39.

Hindess, B. (1984) Rational choice theory and the analysis of political action. *Economy and Society, 13*, 255–77.

Hirschman, A. O. (1977) *The Passions and the Interests: Political arguments for capitalism before its triumph*. Princeton, NJ: Princeton University Press.

Hirschman, E. C. (1980) Communality and idiosyncracy in popular culture. In J. C. Olson (ed.), *Advances in Consumer Research, Vol. 7*. Ann Arbor, MI: Association for Consumer Research.

Hirschman, E. C. (1981) Comprehending symbolic consumption. in E. C. Hirschman and M. B. Holbrook (eds.), *Symbolic Consumer Behaviour*, pp. 4–6. Ann Arbor, MI: Association for Consumer Research.

Hirschon, R. (ed.) (1984) *Women and Property – Women as Property*. London: Croom Helm.

Hobhouse, L., Wheeler, G. and Ginsberg, M. (1915) *The Material Culture and Social Institutions of the Simpler People: An essay in correlation*. London: Chapman and Hall.

Hochschild, A. R. (1979) Emotion work, feeling rules and social structure. *American Journal of Sociology, 85*, 551–75.

Hochschild, A. R. (1983) *The Managed Heart: Commercialization of human feeling*. Berkeley, CA: University of California Press.

Hoebel, F. A. (1968) *The Law of Primitive Man*. New York: Atheneum.

Hofstede, G. (1980) *Culture's Consequences*. Beverly Hills, CA: Sage.

Hogg, M. A. and Abrams, D. (1988) *Social Identifications: A social psychology of intergroup relations and group processes*. London: Routledge.

Hollowell, P. (1982) Introduction: the nature of property. On the operationalization of property. In P. Hollowell (ed.), *Property and Social Relations*, pp. 1–31. London: Heinemann.

Holman, R. H. (1980) Clothing as communication: an empirical investigation. In J. C. Olson (ed.), *Advances in Consumer Research, Vol. 7*, pp. 372–7. Ann Arbor, MI: Association for Consumer Research.

Holman, R. H. (1981) Product use as communication: a fresh appraisal of a venerable topic. In B. M. Enis and K. J. Roering (eds.), *Review of Marketing 1981*, pp. 106–19. Chicago: American Marketing Association.

Holman, R. (1983) Possessions and property: the semiotics of consumer behavior. In R. P. Bagozzi and A. M. Tybout (eds.), *Advances in Consumer Research, Vol. 10*, pp. 565–8. Ann Arbor, MI: Association for Consumer Research.

Hough, M. and Mayhew, P. (1983) *The British Crime Survey: First report.* Home Office Research Study No. 76. London: Her Majesty's Stationery Office.

Howell, S. (1981) Rules not words. in P. Heelas and A. Lock (eds.), *Indigenous Psychologies: The anthropology of the self*, pp. 133–43. London: Academic Press.

Hudson, L. B. (1984) Modern material culture studies. *American Behavioral Scientist, 28* (1), 31–9.

Hyde, K. R., Kurdek, L. and Larson, P. (1983) Relationships between pet ownership and self-esteem, social sensitivity, and interpersonal trust. *Psychological Reports, 52* (1), 110.

Hyman, H. H. (1970) The value systems of different classes: a social psychological contribution to the analysis of stratification. In R. Bendix and S. M. Lipset (eds.), *Class, Status and Power, 2nd Edition*, pp. 488–99. London: Routledge and Kegan Paul.

Irwin, F., Armitt, F. and Simon, C. (1943) Studies in object preferences: I. The effect of temporal proximity. *Journal of Experimental Psychology, 33*, 64–72.

Irwin, F. and Gebhard, M. E. (1946) Studies in object preferences: II. The effect of ownership and other social influences. *American Journal of Psychology, 59*, 633–51.

Isaacs, S. (1933) *Social Development in Young Children.* London: Routledge and Kegan Paul.

Isaacs, S. (1935) Symposium on property and possessiveness: III. *Journal of Medical Psychology, 15*, 69–78.

Isaacs, S. (1967) Property and posessiveness. In T. Talbot (ed.), *The World of the Child*, pp. 255–65. New York: Doubleday (originally published 1949)

Jackman, M. R. and Senter, M. S. (1980) Images of social groups: categorical or qualified? *Public Opinion Quarterly, 44* (3), 341–61.

Jackson, R. L. (1979) Material good need fulfillment as a correlate of self-esteem. *Journal of Social Psychology, 108* (1), 139–40.

Jaffé-Pearce, M. (1989) No mod cons. *Sunday Times Magazine*, 6 August, 8–10.

Jahoda, G. (1979) The construction of economic reality by some Glaswegian children. *European Journal of Social Psychology, 9* (2), 115–27.

Jahoda, G. (1983) European 'lag' in the development of an economic concept: A study in Zimbabwe. *British Journal of Developmental Psychology, 1* (2), 113–20.

Jahoda, G. (1988) Critical notes and reflections on 'social representations'. *European Journal of Social Psychology, 18*, 195–209.

Jahoda, M. (1981) Work, employment, and unemployment: values, theories, and approaches in social research. *American Psychologist, 36* (2), 184–91.

James, W. (1981/1890) The consciousness of self. In *Principles of Psychology*, *Vol. 1*, pp. 279–379. Cambridge, MA: Harvard University Press.

Joas, H. (1985) *G. H. Mead: A contemporary re-examination of his thought*. Cambridge: Polity Press.

Jones, E. (1919) Anal erotic character traits. *Journal of Abnormal and Social Psychology*, *13*, 261–84.

Jones, R. A. (1977) *Self-Fulfilling Prophecies: Social, psychological and physiological effects of expectancies*. Hillsdale NJ: Erlbaum.

Joy, A. and Dholakia, R. R. (1991) Remembrances of things past: the meaning of home and possessions of Indian professionals in Canada. In F. W. Rudmin (ed.), *To Have Possessions: A handbook on ownership and property*. Special issue of *Journal of Social Behavior and Personality*, *6* (6), 385–402.

Kalymum, M. (1985) The prevalence of factors influencing decisions among elderly women concerning household possessions during relocation. *Journal of Housing for the Elderly*, *3* (3–4), 81–99.

Kaplan, M. F. (1971) Context effects in impression formation: the weighted-average versus the meaning-change formulation. *Journal of Personality and Social Psychology*, *19* (1), 92–9.

Kamptner, N. L. (1989) Personal possessions and their meanings in old age. In S. Spacapan and S. Oskamp (eds.), *The Social Psychology of Aging*, pp. 165–96. London: Sage.

Kamptner, N. L. (1991a) Personal possessions and their meanings in childhood and adolescence. Paper presented at the Joint Conference of the Society for the Advancement of Socio-Economics and the International Association for Research in Economic Psychology on 'Interdisciplinary Approaches to Economic Problems', 16–19 June, Stockholm, Sweden.

Kamptner, N. L. (1991b) Personal possessions and their meanings: a life-span perspective. In F. W. Rudmin (ed.), *To Have Possessions: A handbook on ownership and property*. Special issue of *Journal of Social Behavior and Personality*, *6* (6), 209–28.

Katz, D. and Braly, K. W. (1933) Racial stereotypes of one hundred college students. *Journal of Abnormal and Social Psychology*, *28*, 280–90.

Keller, A., Ford, L. H. and Meacham, J. A. (1978) Dimensions of self-concept in preschool children. *Developmental Psychology*, *14* (5), 483–89.

Kidd, A. H. and Feldmann, B. M. (1981) Pet ownership and self-perceptions of older people. *Psychological Reports*, *48* (3), 867–75.

Kitcher, P. (1985) *Vaulting Ambition: Sociobiology and the quest for human nature*. Cambridge, MA: MIT Press.

Kitcher, P. (1987) Précis of 'Vaulting Ambition: Sociobiology and the quest for human nature'. *Behavioral and Brain Sciences*, *10* (1), 61–100.

Kitzinger, C. (1986) Introducing and developing Q as a feminist methodology: a study of accounts of lesbianism. In S. Wilkinson (ed.), *Feminist Social Psychology: Developing theory and practice*, pp. 151–72. Milton Keynes: Open University Press.

Klausner, S. Z. (1953) Social class and self-concept. *Journal of Social Psychology*, *38*, 201–5.

Kleppe, E. J. (1989) Divine kingdoms in northern Africa: material manifestations of social institutions. In Hodder, I. (ed.), *The Meanings of Things: Material culture and symbolic expression*, pp. 195–201. London: Unwin Hyman.

Kline, L. and France, C. (1899) The psychology of ownership. *Pedagogical Seminary*, *6*, 421–70.

Kline, P. (1981) *Fact and Fantasy in Freudian Theory, 2nd Edition*. London: Methuen.

Klineberg, O. (1940) Acquisitiveness. In *Social Psychology, Revised Edition*, pp. 100–13. New York: Holt.

Kolb, W. L. (1944) A critical evaluation of Mead's 'I' and 'me' concepts. *Social Forces*, *22*, 291–6.

Kon, I. S. (1984) The self as a historical-cultural and ethnopsychological phenomenon. In L. H. Strickland (ed.), *Directions in Soviet Social Psychology*, pp. 29–46. New York: Springer.

Kron, J. (1983) *Home-Psych: The social psychology of home and decoration*. New York: Clarkson N. Potter.

Kuhn, T. (1962) *The Structure of Scientific Revolutions*. Chicago: University of Chicago Press.

Kummer, H. (1991) Evolutionary transformations of possessive behaviour. In F. W. Rudmin (ed.), *To Have Possessions: A handbook on ownership and property*. Special issue of *Journal of Social Behavior and Personality*, *6* (6), 75–83.

Kuper, H. (1973) Costume and identity. *Comparative Studies in Society and History*, *15* (3), 348–67.

LaFargue, P. (1975/1890) *The Evolution of Property from Savagery to Civilization*. London: New Park Publications.

Lakatos, I. (1970) Falsification and the methodology of scientific research programmes. In I. Lakatos and A. Musgrave (eds.), *Criticism and the Growth of Knowledge*, pp. 92–196. Cambridge: Cambridge University Press.

Lalive d'Épinay, C. (1986) Time, space and socio–cultural identity. *International Social Services Journal*, *107*, 89–104.

Lambert, W. E., Hodgson, R. C., Gardner, R. C. and Fillenbaum, S. (1960) Evaluational reactions to spoken languages. *Journal of Abnormal and Social Psychology*, *60* (1), 44–51.

Landon, E. L. (1974) Self concept, ideal self concept, and consumer purchase intentions. *Journal of Consumer Research*, *1* (2), 44–51.

Lasswell, T. E. and Parshall, P. F. (1961) The perception of social class from photographs. *Sociology and Social Research*, *45*, 407–14.

Laumann, E. O. and House, J. S. (1970) Living room styles and social attributes: the patterning of material artefacts in a modern urban community. *Sociology and Social Research*, *54*, 321–42.

Lawton, M. P., Moss, M. and Moles, E. (1984) Pet ownership: a research note. *Gerontologist*, *24* (2), 208–10.

Lea, S. E. G. (1984) *Instinct, Environment and Behaviour*. London: Methuen.

Leahy, R. L. (1981) The development of the conception of economic inequality: I. Descriptions and comparisons of rich and poor people. *Child Development*, *52* (5), 523–32.

Leahy, R. L. (1983a) The development of the conception of social class. In R. L. Leahy (ed.), *The Child's Construction of Social Inequality*, pp. 79–107. New York: Academic Press.

Leahy, R. L. (1983b) The development of the conception of economic inequality. II. Explanations, justifications and concepts of social mobility and change. *Developmental Psychology*, *19*, 111–25.

Lee, D. (1950) Notes on the conception of the self among the Wintu Indians. *Journal of Abnormal and Social Psycholology, 45,* 538–43.

Lefcourt, H. M. (1966) Internal versus external control of reinforcement: a review. *Psychological Bulletin, 65* (4), 206–20.

Lefkowitz, M., Blake, R. R. and Mouton, J. S. (1955) Status factors in pedestrian violations of traffic signals. *Journal of Abnormal and Social Psychology, 51,* 704–6.

Lehman, H. and Witty, P. (1927) The present status of the tendency to hoard. *Psychological Review, 24,* 48–56.

Leigh, T. W. (1981) The effect of non-verbal cues on perception of industrial buyers in the initial sales call. Unpublished doctoral dissertation, Indiana University, USA. As described on p. 114 in Holman, R. H. Product use as communication: a fresh appraisal of a venerable topic. In B. M. Enis and K. J. Roening (eds.), *Review of Marketing 1981,* pp. 106–19. Chicago: American Marketing Association.

Lemaine, G. (1974) Social differentiation and social originality. *European Journal of Social Psychology, 4* (1), 17–52.

LeTourneau, C. (1892) *Property: Its origin and development.* London: Scott.

Leveille, M. and Suppes, P. (1976) Comprehension of the possessive by children. *Enfance, 3,* 309–17.

Levenson, R. (1984) Intimacy, autonomy and gender: developmental differences and their reflection in adult relationships. *Journal of the American Academy of Psychoanalysis, 12* (4), 529–44.

Levine, L. E. (1983) Mine: self-definition in 2-year-old boys. *Developmental Psychology, 19* (4), 544–9.

Levinson, B. M. (1962) The dog as 'co-therapist'. *Mental Hygiene, 46,* 59–65.

Levinson, B. M. (1972) *Pets and Human Development.* Springfield, Illinois: Thomas.

Lévi-Strauss, C. (1965) The principle of reciprocity. In L. A. Coser and B. Rosenberg (eds.), *Sociological Theory.* New York: Macmillan.

Lévi-Strauss, C. (1968) *Structural Anthropology.* London: Allen Lane.

Levy, S. J. (1959) Symbols for sale. *Harvard Business Review, 37,* 117–24.

Lewis, A. (1981) Attributions and politics. *Personality and Individual Differences, 2* (1), 1–4.

Lewis, J. D. (1979) A social behaviourist interpretation of the Meadian 'I'. *American Journal of Sociology, 84,* 261–87.

Lewis, M. (1963) *Language, Thought and Personality in Infancy and Childhood.* London: George Harrap.

Lichtman, R. (1970) Symbolic interactionism and social reality: some Marxist queries. *Berkeley Journal of Sociology, 15,* 75–94.

Lierz, H. (1957) *Psyche und Eigentum.* Doctoral dissertation in medicine, Cologne, Germany.

Litwinski, L. (1942) Is there an instinct of possession? *British Journal of Psychology, 33,* 28–39.

Livingstone, S. M. and Lunt, P. K. (1991) Generational and life cycle differences in experiences of ownership. In F. W. Rudmin (ed.), *To Have Possessions: A handbook on ownership and property.* Special issue of *Journal of Social Behavior and Personality, 6* (6), 229–42.

Lloyd, B. B. and Duveen, G. (1986) The significance of social identities. *British Journal of Social Psychology, 25* (3), 219–30.

Lock, A. (1981) Universals in human conception. In P. Heelas and A. Lock (eds.), *Indigenous Psychologies: The anthropology of the self*, pp. 19–36. London: Academic Press.

Loewental, K. (1976) Property. *European Journal of Social Psychology*, *6* (3), 343–51.

Looft, W. R. (1971) The psychology of more. *American Psychologist*, *26*, 561–5.

Loyd, B. (1975) Woman's place, man's place. *Landscape*, *20* (1), 10–13.

Lowie, R. (1920) *Primitive Society*. New York: Boni and Liveright.

Lukes, S. (1979) *Individualism*. Oxford: Blackwell.

Lukmani, Y. (1979) To have or not to have a 'have': a study in the semantics of have. *Indian Linguistics*, *40*, 253–82.

Lumsden, C. J. and Wilson, E. O. (1981) *Genes, Mind and Culture: The coevolutionary process*. Cambridge, MA: Harvard University Press.

Lumsden, C. J. and Wilson, E. O. (1983) *Promethean Fire: Reflections on the origin of mind*. Cambridge, MA: Harvard University Press.

Lunt, P. K. and Livingstone, S. M. (in press) The meaning of possessions. In *Mass Consumption and Personal Identity*. Milton Keynes: Open University Press.

Lyons, N. P. (1983) Two perspectives: On self, relationships, and morality. *Harvard Educational Review*, *53* (2), 125–45.

MacIntyre, A. C. (1988) *Whose Justice? Which rationality?* London: Duckworth.

Mackie, M. (1973) Arriving at 'truth' by definition: the case of stereotype inaccuracy. *Social Problems*, *20*, 431–47.

MacPherson, C. B. (1962) *The Political Theory of Possessive Individualism*. Oxford: Oxford University Press.

Maguire, M. (1980) The impact of burglary upon victims. *British Journal of Criminology*, *20*, 261–75.

Malinowski, B. (1922) *Argonauts of the Western Pacific*. London: Routledge and Kegan Paul.

Marcuse, H. (1968) *One-Dimensional Man*. Boston: Beacon Press.

Markus, H. R. and Kitayama, S. (1991) Culture and the self: implications for cognition, emotion, and motivation. *Psychological Review*, *98* (2), 224–53.

Marshall, T. H. (1935) Symposium on property and possessiveness: IV. *Journal of Medical Psychology*, *15*, 78–83.

Martin, W. S. (1973) *Personality and Product Symbolism*. Austin, TX: Bureau of Business Research, University of Texas.

Marwick, A. (1980) *Class: Image and Reality*. London: Collins.

Marx, K. (1930/1878) Commodities and Money. In *Capital: A critique of political economy*, *Vol. 1*, pp. 1–128. London: Dent.

Marx, K. (1973/1939) *Grundrisse*. Harmondsworth: Penguin.

Marx, K. and Engels, F. (1965) *The German Ideology*. London: Lawrence and Wishart.

Mauss, M. (1985) A category of the human mind: the notion of person; the notion of self. (Originally published in 1938, translated from the French by W. D. Halls.) In M. Carrithers, S. Collins and S. Lukes (eds.), *The Category of the Person*, pp. 1–25. Cambridge: Cambridge University Press.

McCarthy, E. D. (1984) Toward a sociology of the physical world: George Herbert Mead on physical objects. *Studies in Symbolic Interaction*, *5*, 105–21.

McCauley, C. and Stitt, C. L. (1978) An individual and quantitative measure of stereotypes. *Journal of Personality and Social Psychology*, *36* (9), 929–40.

McCauley, C., Stitt, C. L. and Segal, M. (1980) Stereotyping: from prejudice to prediction. *Psychological Bulletin*, *87* (1), 195–208.

McClelland, D. (1951) *Personality*. New York: Holt, Rinehart and Winston.

McCracken, A. (1987) Emotional impact of possession loss. *Journal of Gerontological Nursing*, *13* (2), 14–19.

McCracken, G. (1985) Clio in the market place: theoretical and methodological issues in the history of consumption. In C. T. Tan and J. N. Sheth (eds.), *Historical Perspective in Consumer Research*, pp. 151–4. National University of Singapore: School of Management.

McCracken, G. (1986) Culture and consumption: a theoretical account of the structure and movement of the cultural meaning of consumer goods. *Journal of Consumer Research*, *13* (1), 71–84.

McCracken, G. (1990) *Culture and Consumption*. Indianapolis: Indiana University Press.

McDonald, R. L. (1968) Effects of sex, race, and class on self, ideal-self, and parental ratings in Southern adolescents. *Perceptual and Motor Skills*, *27*, 15–25.

McDougall, W. (1923/1908) *An Introduction to Social Psychology, 18th Edition*. London: Methuen.

McKeachie, W. J. (1952) Lipstick as a determiner of first impression of personality. *Journal of Social Psychology*, *36*, 241–4.

McKendrick, N., Brewer, J. and Plumb, J. H. (1982) *The Birth of a Consumer Society: The commercialization of eighteenth-century England*. Bloomington: Indiana University Press.

McKinlay, A. and Potter, J. (1987) Social representations: a conceptual critique. *Journal for the Theory of Social Behaviour*, *17* (4), 471–88.

McLeod, B. (1984) In the wake of disaster. *Psychology Today*, *18*, 54–7.

Mead, G. H. (1913) The social self. *Journal of Philosophy*, 374–80.

Mead, G. H. (1924–25) The genesis of the self and social control. *International Journal of Ethics*, *35*, 251–77.

Mead, G. H. (1934) *Mind, Self and Society*. Chicago: University of Chicago Press.

Mead, G. H. (1938) *The Philosophy of the Act*. Chicago: University of Chicago Press.

Mead, G. H. (1968) *On Social Psychology: Selected papers* (ed. A. Strauss) Chicago: Chicago University Press.

Mead, G. H. (1982) *The Individual and the Social Self: Unpublished work of George Herbert Mead* (ed. D. Miller) Chicago: Chicago University Press.

Mervis, C. B. and Rosch, E. (1981) Categorization of natural objects. *Annual Review of Psychology*, *32*, 89–115.

Miller, G. and Johnson-Laird, P. N. (1976) Verbs of possession. In *Language and Perception*, pp. 558–77. Cambridge: MA: Cambridge University Press.

Miller, J. G. (1984) Culture and the development of everyday social explanation. *Journal of Personality and Social Psychology*, *46* (5), 961–78.

Miller, M. and Lago, D. (1990) The well-being of older women: the importance of pet and human relations. *Anthrozoos*, *3* (40), 245–52.

Mitchell, B. R. (1984) *British Historical Statistics*. Cambridge: Cambridge University Press.

Mitscherlich, M. (1984) Die Bedeutung des Übergangsobjektes für die Entfaltung des Kindes. In C. Eggers (ed.), *Bindungen und Besitzdenken beim Kleinkind*, pp. 185–203. Munich: Urban and Schwarzenberg.

Moessinger, P. (1975) Developmental study of fair division and property. *European Journal of Social Psychology*, 5 (3), 385–94.

Montagu, A. (ed.) (1980) *Sociobiology Examined*. New York: Oxford University Press.

Montemayor, R. and Eisen, M. (1977) The development of self-conceptions from childhood to adolescence. *Developmental Psychology*, *13* (4), 314–19.

Morawski, J. G. (1985) The measurement of masculinity and femininity: engendering categorical realities. *Journal of Personality*, *53* (2), 196–223.

Morgan, R. and Cushing, D. (1966) The personal possessions of long-stay patients in mental hospitals. *Social Psychiatry*, *1* (3), 151–7.

Morris, C. (1972) *The Discovery of the Individual 1050–1200*. London: SPCK.

Moschis, G. P. and Smith, R. B. (1985) Consumer socialization: origins, trends and directions for future research. In C. T. Tan and J. N. Sheth (eds.), *Historical Perspective in Consumer Research*, pp. 275–81. National University of Singapore: School of Management.

Moscovici, S. (1981) On social representation. In J. P. Forgas (ed.), *Social Cognition: Perspectives on everyday understanding*, pp. 181–209. London: Academic Press.

Moscovici, S. (1984) The phenomenon of social representations. In R. Farr and S. Moscovici (eds.), *Social Representations*, pp. 3–70. Cambridge: Cambridge University Press.

Moscovici, S. (1988) Notes towards a description of social representations. *European Journal of Social Psychology*, *18* (3), 211–50.

Mukerji, C. (1983) *From Graven Images: Patterns of modern materialism*. New York: Columbia University Press.

Munson, J. M. and Spivey, W. A. (1980) Assessing Self Concept. In J. C. Olson (ed.), *Advances in Consumer Research, Vol. 7*, pp. 598–603. Ann Arbor, MI: Association for Consumer Research.

Myers, E. (1985) Phenomenological analysis of the importance of special possessions. In E. C. Hirschman (ed.), *Advances in Consumer Research, Vol. 12*, pp. 560–5. Provo, UT: Association for Consumer Research.

Myers, G. C. (1915) Grasping, reaching and handling. *American Journal of Psychology*, *26*, 525–39.

Nataraajan, R. and Goff, B. J. (1991) Compulsive buying: toward a reconceptualisation. In F. W. Rudmin (ed.), *To Have Possessions: A handbook on ownership and property*. Special issue of *Journal of Social Behavior and Personality*, *6* (6), 307–28.

Nettler, G. (1986) Construing the world. *American Psychologist*, *41*, 480.

Newson, J. and Newson, E. (1968) *Four Years Old in an Urban Community*. London: Allen and Unwin.

Newson, J. and Newson, E. (1976) *Seven Years Old in the Home Environment*. London: Allen and Unwin.

Ng, S. H. (1982) Power and intergroup discrimination. In H. Tajfel (ed.), *Social Identity and Intergroup Relations*, pp. 179–206. Cambridge: Cambridge University Press.

Ng, S. H. (1983) Children's ideas about the bank and shop profit: developmental stages and the influence of cognitive contrasts and conflict. *Journal of Economic Psychology*, *4* (3), 209–21.

Ng, S. H. (1985) Children's ideas about the bank: a New Zealand replication. *European Journal of Social Psychology*, *15* (1), 121–3.

Nilson, L. B. (1981) Reconsidering ideological lines. *Sociological Quarterly*, 22, 531–48.

Nobles, W. W. (1976) Extended self: rethinking the so-called Negro self-concept. *Journal of Black Psychology*, 2 (2), 15–24.

Oerter, R. (1984) Die Entwicklung des Verständnisses von Besitz und Eigentum im Kindes- und Jugendalter. In C. Eggers (ed.), *Bindungen und Besitzdenken beim Kleinkind*, pp. 96–120. Munich: Urban and Schwarzenberg.

Office of Population Censuses and Surveys (1974) *Census 1971: England and Wales*. London: Her Majesty's Stationery Office.

Office of Population Censuses and Surveys (1980) *Classification of Occupations and Coding Index*. London: Her Majesty's Stationery Office.

O'Guinn, T. C. and Faber. R. J. (1989) Compulsive buying: a phenomenological exploration. *Journal of Consumer Research*, 16, 147–57.

O'Guinn, T. C. and Shrum, L. J. (1991) Mass–mediated social reality: the social cognition and ecology of economic norms. Paper presented at the Joint Conference of the Society for the Advancement of Socio-Economics and the International Association for Research in Economic Psychology on 'Interdisciplinary Approaches to Economic Problems', 16–19 June, Stockholm, Sweden.

Olmsted, A. D. (1991) Collecting: leisure, investment or obsession? In F. W. Rudmin (ed.), *To Have Possessions: A handbook on ownership and property*. Special issue of *Journal of Social Behavior and Personality*, 6 (6), 287–306.

Olson, C. D. (1985) Materialism in the home: the impact of artefacts on dyadic communication. In E. C. Hirschman and M. B. Holbrook (eds.), *Advances in Consumer Research*, Vol. 12, pp. 388–93. Provo, UT: Association for Consumer Research.

Orpen, C. and Low, A. (1973) The influence of image congruence on brand preference: an empirical study. *Psychology*, 10 (3), 4–6.

Paap, W. R. (1981) Being burglarised: an account of victimisation. *Victimology*, 6, 297–305.

Pahl, R. E. and Wallace, C. D. (1988) Neither angels in marble nor rebels in red: privatization and working-class consciousness. In D. Rose (ed), *Social Stratification and Economic Change*, pp. 127–49. London: Hutchinson.

Pandey, J., Sinha, Y., Prakash, A. and Tripathi, R. C. (1982) Right-left political ideologies and attribution of the causes of poverty. *European Journal of Social Psychology*, 12, 327–31.

Papadopoulous, K. (1990) The development of self-reflexive social emotions. Unpublished doctoral thesis, University of Sussex, England.

Parsons, T. and Bales, R. F. (1956) *Family, Socialization and Interaction Process*. London: Routledge and Kegan Paul.

Passman, R. H. (1976) Arousal reducing properties of attachment objects: testing the functional limits of the security blanket relative to the mother. *Developmental Psychology*, 12 (5), 468–9.

Payne, R. Warr, P. and Hartley, J. (1984) Social class and psychological ill-health during unemployment. *Sociology of Health and Illness*, 6 (2), 152–74.

Perec, G. (1965) *Les Choses: Une histoire des annees soixante*. Paris: Julliard.

Potter, J. and Litton, I. (1985) Problems underlying the theory of social representations. *British Journal of Social Psychology*, 24, 81–90.

Potter, J. and Wetherell, M. (1987) *Discourse and Social Psychology*. London: Sage.

Prelinger, E. (1959) Extension and structure of the self. *Journal of Psychology*, 47, 13–23.

Prentice, D. A. (1987) Psychological correspondence of possessions, attitudes, and values. *Journal of Personality and Social Psychology*, 53 (6), 993–1003.

Prentice, D. A. (1991) Personal communication concerning Prentice (1987).

Prown, J. D. (1982) Mind in matter: an introduction to material culture theory and method. *Winterthur Portfolio*, 17, 1–19.

Pryor, J. B., Ostrom, T. M., Dukerich, J. M., Mitchell, M. L. and Herstein, J. A. (1983) Preintegrative categorization of social information: the role of persons as organizing categories. *Journal of Personality and Social Psychology*, 44 (5), 923–32.

Rabbie, J. M. and Horwitz, M. (1988) Categories versus groups as explanatory concepts in intergroup relations. *European Journal of Social Psychology*, 18 (2), 117–23.

Radley, A. (1990) Artefacts, memory and a sense of the past. In D. Middleton and D. Edwards (eds.), *Collective Remembering: Memory in society*, pp. 46–59. London: Sage.

Ramsey, P. G. (1986) Possession disputes in preschool classrooms. *Child Study Journal*, 16 (3), 173–81.

Ramsey, P. G. (1987) Possession episodes in young children's social interactions. *Journal of Genetic Psychology*, 148 (3), 315–24.

Reber, A. S. (1985) *Dictionary of Psychology*. Harmondsworth: Penguin.

Reid, I. (1989) *Social Class Differences in Britain, 3rd Edition*. London: Grant McIntyre.

Reid, L. N. and Buchanan, L. (1979) A shopping list experiment of the impact of advertising on brand images. *Journal of Advertising*, 8, 26–8.

Richins, M. L. (1991) Possessions in the lives of materialists: an analysis of consumption-related affect and expectations. Paper presented at the Joint Conference of the Society for the Advancement of Socio-Economics and the International Association for Research in Economic Psychology on 'Interdisciplinary Approaches to Economic Problems', 16–19 June, Stockholm, Sweden.

Rivers, W. H. R. (1920) The instinct of acquisition. Appendix VIII in *Instinct and the Unconscious*. London: Cambridge University Press.

Robbins, R. H. (1973) Identity, culture and behavior. In J. J. Honigmann (ed.), *Handbook of Social and Cultural Anthropology*, pp. 1199–222. Chicago: Rand McNally.

Rochberg-Halton, E. (1982) Situation, structure, and the context of meaning. *Sociological Quarterly*, 23 (4), 455–76.

Rochberg-Halton, E. (1984) Object relations, role models and cultivation of the self. *Environment and Behavior*, 16 (3), 335–68.

Rochberg-Halton, E. (1985) Life in the treehouse: pet therapy as family metaphor and self-dialogue. *Marriage and Family Review*, 8 (3–4), 175–89.

Rock, P. (1979) *The Making of Symbolic Interactionism*. Totowa, NY: Rocoman and Littlefield.

Rodgon, M. M. and Rashman, S. E. (1976) Expression of owner-owned relationships among holophrastic 14- to 32-month-old children. *Child Development*, 47 (4), 1219–22.

Rodin, J. and Langer, E. (1978) Long-term effects of a control-relevant intervention in the institutionalized aged. *Journal of Personality and Social Psychology*, 35, 897–902.

Rogers, C. R. (1961) *On Becoming a Person*. Boston: Houghton Mifflin.

Rosch, E. *et al*. (1976) Basic objects in natural categories. *Cognitive Psychology*, 8 (3), 382–439.

Ropers, R. (1973) Mead, Marx and social psychology. *Catalyst*, 7, pp. 42–61.

Rosenfeld, L. B. and Plax, T. G. (1977) Clothing as communication. *Journal of Communication*, 27 (2), 24–31.

Rosenkrantz, P., Vogel, S., Bee, H., Broverman, I. and Broverman, D. M. (1968) Sex-role stereotypes and self-concepts in college students. *Journal of Consulting and Clinical Psychology*, 32 (3), 287–95.

Ross, I. (1971) Self-concept and brand preference. *Journal of Business*, 44, 38–50.

Ross, S. A. (1991a) Freedom from possessions: a Tibetan Buddhist view. In F. W. Rudmin (ed.), *To Have Possessions: A handbook on ownership and property*. Special issue of *Journal of Social Behavior and Personality*, 6 (6), 415–26.

Ross, S. A. (1991b) Freedom from possessions: morality, ethics and economics. Paper presented at the Joint Conference of the Society for the Advancement of Socio-Economics and the International Association for Research in Economic Psychology on 'Interdisciplinary Approaches to Economic Problems', 16–19 June, Stockholm, Sweden.

Rudmin, F. W. (1985a) Historical note on the development of possessive pronouns. *Journal of Speech and Hearing Disorders*, 50 (3), 298–9.

Rudmin, F. W. (1985b) Dominance and children's use of possessive case. *Perceptual and Motor Skills*, 61 (2), 566.

Rudmin, F. W. (1986) Psychology of ownership, possession, and property: a selected bibliography since 1890. *Psychological Reports*, 58 (3), 859–69.

Rudmin, F. W. (1988) Dominance, social control, and ownership: a history and a cross-cultural study of motivations for private property. *Behavior Science Research*, 22, 130–60.

Rudmin, F. W. (1990) Cross-cultural correlates of the ownership of private property. Unpublished manuscript, Queen's University, Kingston, Canada.

Rudmin, F. W., Belk, R. W. and Furby, L. (1987) *Social Science Bibliography on Property, Ownership, and Possessions: 1580 citations from psychology, anthropology, sociology, and related disciplines*. Monticello, IL: Vance Bibliographies.

Rudmin, F. W. and Berry, J. W. (1987) Semantics of ownership: a free-recall study of property. *Psychological Record*, 37 (2), 257–68.

Ruke-Dravina, V. (1979) Difficulties in learning personal and possessive pronouns by young children. In K. Pettersson, K. Hyltenstam and M. Linnarud (eds.), *Papers from the Fifth Scandinavian Conference of Linguistics*, pp. 139–49.

Runciman, W. G. (1966) *Relative Deprivation and Social Justice*. London: Routledge.

Ryan, A. (1982) The romantic theory of ownership. In P. Hollowell (ed.), *Property and Social Relations*, pp. 52–68. London: Heinemann.

Ryan, W. (1971) *Blaming the Victim*. New York: Orbach and Chambers.

Sadalla, E. K., Vershure, B. and Burroughs, J. (1987) Identity symbolism in housing. *Environment and Behaviour*, 19 (5), 569–87.

Sahlins, M. (1977) *The Use and Abuse of Biology*. London: Tavistock.

Sampson, E. E. (1977) Psychology and the American ideal. *Journal of Personality and Social Psychology*, 35 (11), 767–82.

Sampson, E. E. (1981) Cognitive psychology as ideology. *American Psychologist, 36* (7), 730–43.

Sampson, E. E. (1983) Deconstructing psychology's subject. *Journal of Mind and Behavior, 4* (2), 135–64.

Sampson, E. E. (1985) The decentralization of identity: toward a revised concept of personal and social order. *American Psychologist, 40* (11), 1203–11.

Sampson, E. E. (1988) The debate on individualism. *American Psychologist, 43* (1), 15–22.

Sampson, E. E. (1989) The challenge of social change for psychology: globalization and psychology's theory of the person. *American Psychologist, 44* (6), 914–21.

Saunders, P. (1990) *A Nation of Home Owners*. London: Unwin Hyman.

Sayers, J. (1986) Sexual identity and difference: psychoanalytic perspectives. In S. Wilkinson (ed.), *Feminist Social Psychology: Developing theory and practice*, pp. 25–38. Milton Keynes: Open University Press.

Schmitt, R. (1973) The desire for private gain: Capitalism and the theory of motives. *Inquiry, 16*, 149–67.

Schudson, M. (1986) The giving of gifts. *Psychology Today, 20* (12), 26–9.

Schütz, A. (1972) *The Phenomenology of the Social World*. London: Heinemann.

Schwartz, B. (1967) The social psychology of the gift. *American Journal of Sociology, 73* (1), 1–11.

Segall, M. H. (1986) Culture and behavior: psychology in global perspective. *Annual Review of Psychology, 37*, 523–64.

Seligman, M. E. P. (1975) *Helplessness*. San Francisco: Freeman.

Semin, G. R. (1986) The individual, the social, and the social individual. *British Journal of Social Psychology, 25* (3), 177–80.

Semin, G. R. (1987) On the relationship between theories in ordinary language and psychology. In W. Doise and S. Moscovici (eds.), *Current Developments in European Social Psychology*, pp. 307–48. Cambridge: Cambridge University Press.

Semin, G. R. (1990) Social constructivist approaches to personality. In G. R. Semin and K. J. Gergen (eds.), *Everyday Understanding: Social and scientific implications*, pp. 151–75. London: Sage.

Semin, G. R. and Gergen, K. J. (1990) *Everyday Understanding: Social and scientific implications*. London: Sage.

Semin, G. R. and Rubini, M. (1990) Unfolding the concept of person by verbal abuse. *European Journal of Social Psychology, 20* (6), 463–74.

Sharp, M. S. (1986) Darwin and sociobiology: a reply to Turke. *American Anthropologist, 88*, 155–6.

Sherman, E. and Newman, E. S. (1977) The meaning of cherished personal possessions for the elderly. *International Journal of Aging and Human Development, 8* (2), 181–92.

Shott, S. (1979) Emotion and social life: A symbolic interactionist analysis. *American Journal of Sociology, 84*, 1317–34.

Shweder, R. A. and Bourne, E. (1982) Does the concept of the person vary cross-culturally? In A. J. Marsella and G. White (eds.), *Cultural Concepts of Mental Health and Therapy*, pp. 97–137. Boston: Reidel.

Shweder, R. A. and Miller, J. G. (1985) The social construction of the person: how is it possible? In K. J. Gergen and K. E. Davis (eds.), *The Social Construction of the Person*, pp. 41–72. New York: Springer.

Siiter, R. and Unger, R. K. (1978) Sex role stereotypes, sex typing, and self typing: some considerations about reference groups. As cited in R. K. Unger (1979), *Female and Male: Psychological perspectives*, pp. 31–3. New York: Harper and Row.

Sirgy, M. J. (1982) Self-concept in consumer behavior: a critical review. *Journal of Consumer Research*, *9* (3), 287–300.

Skevington, S. M. (1980) Intergroup relations and social change within a nursing context. *British Journal of Social and Clinical Psychology*, *19* (3), 201–13.

Skevington, S. M. (1981) Intergroup relations and nursing. *European Journal of Social Psychology*, *11* (1), 43–59.

Skevington, S. and Baker, D. (eds.) (1989) *The Social Identity of Women*. London: Sage.

Smith, A. (1910/1890) *The Wealth of Nations*. London: Dent.

Snare, F. (1972) The concept of property. *American Philosophical Quarterly*, *9*, 200–6.

Snyder, M. and DeBono, K. G. (1985) Appeals to image and claims about quality: understanding the psychology of advertising. *Journal of Personality and Social Psychology*, *49* (3), 586–97.

Snyder, M., Tanke, E. D. and Berscheid, E. (1977) Social perception and interpersonal behavior: on the self-fulfilling nature of social stereotypes. *Journal of Personality and Social Psychology*, *35* (9), 656–66.

Solomon, M. R. (1983) The role of products as social stimuli: a symbolic interactionism perspective. *Journal of Consumer Research*, *10* (3), 319–29.

Solomon, M. R. (1985) *The Psychology of Fashion*. Lexington, MA: Lexington Books.

Solomon, M. R. (1986) Dress for effect. *Psychology Today*, *20* (4), 20–2, 26–8.

Sommers, M. S. (1964) Product symbolism and the perception of social strata. In S. A. Greyser (ed.), *Toward Scientific Marketing*. Chicago: American Marketing Association.

Sommers, M. S. and Bruce, G. D. (1969) Blacks, whites, and products: relative deprivation and reference group behavior. *Social Science Quarterly*, *49*, 631–42.

Sparks, D. L. and Tucker, W. T. (1971) A multivariate analysis of personality and product use. *Journal of Marketing Research*, *8*, 67–70.

Spears, R. (1989) Book review: ideological dilemmas. *British Journal of Social Psychology*, *28* (3), 283–8.

Spence, J. and Helmreich, R. L. (1980) Masculine instrumentality and feminine expressiveness. *Psychology of Women Quarterly*, *5* (2), 147–63.

Stacey, B. G. (1982) Economic socialization in the pre-adult years. *British Journal of Social Psychology*, *21* (2), 159–73.

Stacey, B. G. (1983) Economic socialization. *British Journal of Social Psychology*, *22* (3), 265–6.

Stacey, B. G. and Singer, M. S. (1985) The perception of poverty and wealth among teenagers. *Journal of Adolescence*, *8* (3), 231–41.

Stanjek, K. (1980) *Die Entwicklung des menschlichen Besitzverhaltens: Materialien aus der Bildungsforschung*. Berlin: Max-Planck-Institut.

Staub, E. and Noerenberg, H. (1981) Property rights, deservingness, reciprocity, friendship: the transactional character of children's sharing behavior. *Journal of Personality and Social Psychology, 40* (2), 271–89.

Stenross, B. (1984) Police response to residential burglaries. *Criminology, 22* (3), 389–402.

Stevenson, O. (1954) The first treasured possession. *The Psycho-Analytic Study of the Child, 9*, 199–217.

Stone, G. P. (1962) Appearance and the self. In A. M. Rose (ed.), *Human Behaviour and Social Processes*, pp. 86–118. London: Routledge and Kegan Paul.

Storms, M. D. (1979) Sex role identity and its relationships to sex role attitudes and sex role stereotypes. *Journal of Personality and Social Psychology, 37* (10), 1779–89.

Stroebe, W. and Kruglanski, A. W. (1989) Social psychology at epistemological crossroads: on Gergen's choice. *European Journal of Social Psychology, 19*, 485–9.

Strumpel, B. (1976) Economic life styles, values and subjective welfare. In B. Strumpel (ed.), *Economic Means for Human Needs*, pp. 19–65. Ann Arbor, MI: Institute for Social Research.

Stryker, S. (1980) *Symbolic Interactionism: A social structural view*. London: Benjamin.

Suedfeld, P., Bochner, S. and Mates, C. (1971) Petitioner's attire and petition signing by peace demonstrators: a field experiment. *Journal of Applied Social Psychology, 1*, 278–83.

Suttie, I. D. (1935) Symposium on property and possessiveness: I. *Journal of Medical Psychology, 15*, 51–62.

Swann, W. B. (1984) Quest for accuracy in person perception: a matter of pragmatics. *Psychological Review, 91* (4), 457–77.

Tajfel, H. (1959a) Quantitative judgment in social perception. *British Journal of Psychology, 50*, 16–29.

Tajfel, H. (1959b) A note on Lambert's 'Evaluational reactions to spoken languages'. *Canadian Journal of Psychology, 13* (2), 86–92.

Tajfel, H. (1969) Cognitive aspects of prejudice. *Journal of Social Issues, 25*, 79–97.

Tajfel, H. (ed.) (1978a) *Differentiation between Social Groups*. London: Academic Press.

Tajfel, H. (1978b) *The Social Psychology of Minorities, Report No. 38*. London: Minority Rights Group.

Tajfel, H. (1981a) Social stereotypes and social groups. In J. C. Turner, and H. Giles (eds.), *Intergroup Behaviour*, pp. 144–67. Oxford: Blackwell.

Tajfel, H. (1981b) *Human Groups and Social Categories*. Cambridge: Cambridge University Press.

Tajfel, H. (ed.) (1982) *Social Identity and Intergroup Relations*. Cambridge: Cambridge University Press.

Tajfel, H. (ed.) (1984) *The Social Dimension, Vols. 1 and 2*. Cambridge: Cambridge University Press.

Tajfel, H., Billig, M. G., Bundy, R. P. and Flament, C. (1971) Social categorization and intergroup behaviour. *European Journal of Social Psychology, 1*, 149–78.

Tajfel, H., Sheikh, A. A. and Gardner, R. C. (1964) Content of stereotypes and the inference of similarity between members of stereotyped groups. *Acta Psychologica*, 22, 191–201.

Tajfel, H. and Turner, J. C. (1979) An integrative theory of social conflict. In W. G. Austin and S. Worchel (eds.), *The Social Psychology of Intergroup Relations* pp. 33–47. Monterey, CA: Brooks Cole.

Tajfel, H. and Wilkes, A. L. (1963) Classification and quantitative judgement. *British Journal of Psychology*, 54, 101–14.

Tawney, R. (1922) *The Acquisitive Society*. London: Bell.

Thomas, L. E. (1973) Clothing and counterculture: an empirical study. *Adolescence*, 8, 93–112.

Thompson, E. P. (1968) *The Making of the English Working Class*. Harmondsworth: Penguin.

Thompson, E. P. (1978) *The Poverty of Theory*. London: Merlin Press.

Thompson, K. (1986) *Beliefs and Ideology*. Chichester: Horwood.

Thornton, G. R. (1944) The effect of wearing glasses upon judgments of personality traits of persons seen briefly. *Journal of Applied Psychology*, 28, 203–97.

Tinbergen N. and Perdeck, A. C. (1950) On the stimulus situation releasing the begging response in the newly-hatched herring-gull chick (*Larus argentatus* Pont.) *Behaviour*, 3, 1–39.

Tizard, B. and Hughes, M. (1984) *Young Children Learning*. London: Fontana.

Trasler, G. (1982) The psychology of ownership and possessiveness. In P. Hollowell (ed.), *Property and Social Relations*, pp. 32–51. London: Heinemann.

Triandis, H. C., Bontempo, R., Villareal, M. J., Asai, M. and Lucca, N. (1988) Individualism and collectivism: cross-cultural perspectives on self-ingroup relationships. *Journal of Personality and Social Psychology*, 54 (2), 323–38.

Trivers, R. L. (1971) The evolution of reciprocal altruism. *Quarterly Review of Biology*, 46, 35–9.

Tuan, Y. F. (1982) *Segmented Worlds and Self: Group life and individual consciousness*. Minneapolis: University of Minnesota Press.

Tucker, W. T. and Painter, J. J. (1961) Personality and product use. *Journal of Applied Psychology*, 45 (5), 325–9.

Turner, J. C. (1984) Social identification and psychological group formation. In H. Tajfel (ed.), *The Social Dimension, Vol. 2*, pp. 518–38. Cambridge: Cambridge University Press.

Turner, J. C. (1987) *Rediscovering the Social Group: A self-categorization theory*. Oxford: Blackwell.

Turner, J. C. and Brown, R. J. (1978) Social status, cognitive alternatives and intergroup relations. In H. Tajfel (ed.), *Differentiation between Social Groups*, pp. 201–34. London: Academic Press.

Turner, J. C. and Oakes, P. J. (1986) The significance of the social identity concept for social psychology with reference to individualism, interactionism and social influence. *British Journal of Social Psychology*, 25 (3), 237–52.

Turner, J. H. (1985) *Sociology: The science of human organization*. Chicago: Nelson-Hall.

Tzeng, O. C. S. and Everett, A. V. (1985) A cross-cultural perspective on self-related conceptions in adolescents. *International Journal of Psychology*, 20, 329–48.

Unger, R. K. (1979) *Female and Male: Psychological perspectives*. New York: Harper and Row.

Unruh, D. R. (1983) Death and personal history: strategies of identity preservation. *Social Problems, 30* (3), 340–51.

Van den Bogaard, J. and Wiegman, O. (1991) Property crime victimization: the effectiveness of police services for victims of residential burglary. In F. W. Rudmin (ed.), *To Have Possessions: A handbook on ownership and property*. Special issue of *Journal of Social Behavior and Personality, 6* (6), 329–62.

Van Knippenberg, A. (1978) Status differences, comparative relevance and intergroup differentiation. In H. Tajfel (ed.), *Differentiation between Social Groups*, pp. 171–99. London: Academic Press.

Van Knippenberg, A. (1984) Intergroup differences in group perceptions. In H. Tajfel (ed.), *The Social Dimension, Vol. 2*, pp. 561–78. Cambridge: Cambridge University Press.

Van Knippenberg, A. and Van Oers, H. (1984) Social identity and equity concerns in intergroup perceptions. *British Journal of Social Psychology, 23*, 351–61.

Van Knippenberg, A. and Wilke, H. (1979) Perceptions of collegiens and apprentis re–analyzed. *European Journal of Social Psychology, 9* (4), 427–34.

Veblen, T. (1899) *The Theory of the Leisure Class*. New York: Macmillan.

Vershure, B., Magel, S. and Sadalla, E. K. (1977) House form and social identity. In P. Suedfeld *et al.* (eds.), *The Behavioral Basis of Design, Book 2*, pp. 273–8. Stroudsberg, PA: Dowden, Hutchinson and Ross.

Vidutis, R. and Lowe, V. A. P. (1980) The cemetery as a cultural text. *Kentucky Folklore Record, 26*, 103–13.

Vygotsky, L. S. (1978) *Mind in Society: The development of higher psychological processes*. Cambridge, MA: Harvard University Press.

Walby, S. (1986) Gender, class and stratification. In R. Crompton and M. Mann (eds.), *Gender and Stratification*. Cambridge: Cambridge University Press.

Wallas, G. (1932/1925) *The Great Society: A psychological analysis*. London: Macmillan.

Wallendorf, M. and Arnould, E. J. (1988) My favourite things: a cross-cultural inquiry into object attachment, possessiveness and social linkage. *Journal of Consumer Research, 14*, 531–47.

Ward, L. (1923) Biological basis of property. In J. Wigmore and A. Kocourek (eds.), *Rational Basis of Legal Institutions*, pp. 220–31. New York: Macmillan.

Ward, S. (1974) Consumer socialization. *Journal of Consumer Research, 1* (2), 1–14.

Ward, S., Wackman, D. and Wartella, E. (1977) *How Children Learn To Buy*. London: Sage.

Warr, P. (1983) Work, jobs and unemployment. *Bulletin of the British Psychological Society, 36*, 305–11.

Weber, M. (1958) *The Protestant Ethic and the Spirit of Capitalism*, translated by T. Parsons. New York: Scribner.

Weigart, A. J. (1983) Identity: its emergence within sociological psychology. *Symbolic Interaction, 6* (2), 183–206.

Weigel, R. M. (1984) The application of evolutionary models to the study of decisions made by children during object possession conflicts. *Ethology and Sociobiology*, *5* (4), 229–38.

Weigel, R. M. (1985) Demographic factors affecting assertive and defensive behavior in preschool children: an ethological study. *Aggressive Behavior*, *11* (1), 27–40.

Weintraub, K. J. (1978) *The Value of the Individual: Self and circumstance in autobiography*. Chicago: University of Chicago Press.

Weiss, R. F., Boyer, J. L. , Lombardo, J. P. and Stich, M. H. (1973) Altruistic drive and altruistic reinforcement. *Journal of Personality and Social Psychology*, *25* (3), 390–400.

Wells, W. D., Andriuli, F. J., Goi, F. J. and Seader, S. (1957) An adjective check list for the study of 'product personality'. *Journal of Applied Psychology*, *41*, 317–19.

Wernick, A. (1991) *Promotional Culture: Advertising, Ideology and Symbolic Expression*. London: Sage.

Wertsch, J. V. (ed.) (1985) *Culture, Communication and Cognition: Vygotskian perspectives*. Cambridge: Cambridge University Press.

Wetherell, M. (1982) Cross-cultural studies on minimal groups: implications for the social identity theory of intergroup relations. In H. Tajfel (ed.), *Social Identity and Intergroup Relations*, pp. 207–40. Cambridge: Cambridge University Press.

Whipple, T. W. and Courtney, A. E. (1985) Female role portrayals in advertising and communication effectiveness: a review. *Journal of Advertising*, *14* (3), 4–8, 17.

Whitley, M. (1929) Children's interest in collecting. *Journal of Educational Psychology*, *20*, 249–61.

Wicklund, R. A. and Gollwitzer, P. M. (1980) Der Mensch als Mogelpackung. *Psychologie Heute*, *10*, 56–63.

Wicklund, R. A. and Gollwitzer, P. M. (1982) *Symbolic Self-Completion*. Hillsdale, NJ: Erlbaum.

Wicklund, R. A. and Gollwitzer, P. M. (1985) Symbolische Selbstergänzung. In D. Frey and M. Irle (eds.), *Theorien der Sozialpsychologie, Band III: Motivations- und Informationstheorien*, pp. 31–55. Bern: Huber.

Wikse, J. R. (1977) *About Possession: The self as private property*. Pennsylvania: Pennsylvania State University Press.

Wilder, D. A. (1981) Perceiving persons as a group: categorization and intergroup relations. In D. L. Hamilton (ed.), *Cognitive Processes in Stereotyping and Intergroup Relations*, pp. 213–57. Hillsdale, NJ: Erlbaum.

Wilkins, S. (1981) The study of the comprehension of possessives in children aged between one and a half and five and a half. *Bulletin of the British Psychological Society*, *34*, 102.

Wilkinson, S. (ed.) (1986) *Feminist Social Psychology: Developing theory and practice*. Milton Keynes: Open University Press.

Williams, J. A. (1984) Gender and intergroup behaviour: towards an integration. *British Journal of Social Psychology*, *23* (4), 311–16.

Williams, R. H. (1982) *Dream Worlds: Mass consumption in late nineteenth-century France*. Berkeley, CA: University of California Press.

Willis, P. E. (1978) *Profane Culture*. London: Routledge.

Willis, P. (1990) *Common Culture*. Milton Keynes: Open University Press.

Wilson, E. O. (1975) *Sociobiology: The new synthesis*. Cambridge, MA: Harvard University Press.

Wilson, E. O. (1976) Sociobiology: a new approach to the understanding of human nature. *New Scientist, 71*, 342–5.

Winnicott, D. W. (1953) Transitional objects and transitional phenomena: a study of the first not-me possession. *International Journal of Psycho-Analysis, 24* (2), 89–97.

Winch, P. (1958) *The Idea of a Social Science and its Relation to Philosophy*. London: Routledge and Kegan Paul.

Wirtz, P. W. and Harrell, A. V. (1987) Assaultive versus nonassaultive victimisation: a profile analysis of psychological response. *Journal of Interpersonal Violence, 2* (3), 264–77.

Wittgenstein, L. (1963) *Philosophical Investigations*. Oxford: Blackwell.

Woodside, A. G. (1972) A shopping list experiment of beer brand images. *Journal of Applied Psychology, 56* (6), 512–13.

Woodside, A. G., Bearden, W. O. and Ronkainen, I. (1977) Images on serving marijuana, alcoholic beverages, and soft drinks. *Journal of Psychology, 96* (1), 11–14.

Word, C. O., Zanna, M. P. and Cooper, J. (1974) The nonverbal mediation of self-fulfilling prophecies in interracial interaction. *Journal of Experimental Social Psychology, 10*, 109–20.

Wrightsman, L. S. (1974) *Assumptions About Human Nature: A social-psychological approach*. Monterey, CA: Brooks/Cole.

Wrong, D. H. (1961) The oversocialized conception of man in modern sociology. *American Sociological Review, 26* (2), 183–93.

Author index

Subject index

acquisitive behaviour (*see* possessive
    behaviour)
acquisitive instinct
    and animals, 20, 21, 23, 32–4
    and children, 19–21, 23, 26, 27, 30–2,
        50–1
    and commonsense, 20
    and culture, 21, 24–5, 27, 28–30,
        117–19
    early theories, 23–5
    McDougall on, 23–4
    and politics, 21
    and sociobiology, 23, 25–8, 28–30,
        37–8, 42
adolescence
    and material possessions, 114, 115–17,
        163
    youth subcultures, 8
advertising, 1, 13, 61, 99, 136
altruism, 26–7
anal eroticism, 32, 51–2
animals, 20, 21, 23, 32–4, 107–9
attitude similarity, 169–70, 177–8, 179
attribution (*see* lay explanations)

burglary, 44, 46–7

capitalism, 4, 12, 136
cars, 1–2, 3, 60, 86, 133, 150, 156
child development
    cultural differences, 31, 49, 53, 55, 56
    learning possession-related concepts,
        54–5
    and material possessions, 48–57, 114,
        115–16
    self–identity (*see* self-development)
    socialization, 55–7, 99

chosisme, 7, 166
clothes
    and gender, 135–6
    and identity, 41, 48, 81–2, 157–8,
        159
    and power relations, 70, 80, 81,
        135–6
collections
    in adulthood, 105
    in childhood, 30–1, 32, 51
collectivist culture, 53, 56, 153, 189–90
commodity fetishism, 12, 104, 107
commonsense accounts
    and material possessions, 14, 41, 47,
        114, 130–6, 205
    and psychological theory, 71
    for social inequality, 55, 161–4
communication (*see also* language)
    and material objects, 10, 82–3
    symbolic, 34, 39–40, 76–7, 78–9
    symbolic–communicational model of
        possessions and identity, 85–92,
        119–20, 183, 185, 187, 202
consumer goods (*see also* material
        symbols)
    advertising, 1, 13, 61, 99, 136
    and children, 99
    and gender, 136, 99
    and image
        brand-self congruity, 60–1, 99
        symbolic meanings, 2, 5, 7–8, 14,
            60–1, 87–8, 98–101
    and perceiving others, 156–7
    and social standing, 100
consumer research, 60–1, 87–8, 91,
        98–101, 156–7, 164